Farmer & Chef
Asheville

Farmer & Chef
Asheville

Debby Maugans
Christine Sykes Lowe

ISBN 978-0-9907021-1-5
Copyright 2015
Farmer and Chef, LLC

Editorial services:
markhenrybloom@gmail.com

Book & cover design:
Susan McBride
susanmcbridedesign.com

Photo credits:
Photographs by **Beau Gustafson,**
Big Swede Photography, except:

Erin Adams, Erin Adams Photography,
pages 2 (upper right), 10, 45, 156,
157, 178, 179, 180, 181, 188-193,
221, 225, 263
Ken Shepard, pages 17, 27, 80, 93,
103, 111, 206, 211, 217
Cindy Kunst, CLicKs Photography
pages 138, 139, 148, 186, 187
Lindsay Ayliffe, pages 100, 113, 121, 242
William Dissen, pages 2 (upper left),
153, 184, 246
Christine Sykes Lowe, pages 66, 96 177
Dawn Robertson, pages 32, 11
Michael Rischitelli,
front cover (bottom), page 194
Cynthia Pierce,
back cover, page 116
Casey Toth,
Casey Toth Photography, page 83
Martha Pollay, page 60
Tanya Triber, page 53
Valerie Patton, page 259
Aaron Morrell, Grae Skye Studios, page 168
Jen Altman, Jen Altman Photography, page 231
Omni Grove Park Inn, page 257
Bill Hunt, page 272 (top left)
Chai Pani, page 145

PRINTED IN USA

ABOUT *the* BOOK

What draws people to Asheville? Is it the charm of a smaller city? The gorgeous mountain scenery? The access to a multitude of outdoor activities? The potential of making a difference in our environment, education, or politics? It could be all of the above, but most likely it's the bustling food community that attracts visitors and converts those visitors into transplants.

We who call ourselves Ashevillians see the connection of the land to the food we eat every single day. We appreciate and respect our local growers and producers, from the farmers and purveyors to the chefs and home cooks. We are committed to do our best to sustain them. Quite honestly, we can't imagine any community that can match the support, devotion, and yes, love that we experienced while researching and writing this book. We may have done the work to make this project happen, but in the end, this is a book made by our community of hard-working, creative, and encouraging people.

Farmer and Chef Asheville celebrates that all-inclusive food community, including our burgeoning beverage industry. Meet the farmers, chefs, butchers, producers and growers, and the many others who nourish us on a daily basis. Learn about the people and organizations enriching the lives of all those who stop by for a day, a week, or indefinitely.

Be inspired by The Welcome Table at a city church, where chefs give their time and resources to serve those less fortunate a first-class dining experience.

Explore the WNC Cheese Trail to sample some of the best handmade cheese being made in the South today while soaking in the beauty of rural Western North Carolina. Read about Beer City and learn how our bakers prepare bread with the spent grains from the area breweries.

Of course, we can't forget that this book is about food, and we've included over 200 recipes from our chefs and farmers to more than whet your appetite. The number and quality of the recipes that poured in both astounded and thrilled us. After the testing and editing phase, we found that the mix fit nicely into the arrangement we devised for these pages.

Each section of the book contains mini-chapters that categorize the recipes. For instance, in "Mountain Mornings, 24/7," you'll find B&B Specialties (recipes from our innkeepers), Eggs & Taters (scrambled eggs, tater tots, and more from area restaurants), and Baked To Order (breads and pastries from local bakeries).

To use the book, peruse the Table of Contents to find the section that describes what you're interested in — whether it's a cocktail, breakfast make-ahead dish, game day snacks, meat dish, side dish, pickle or jam, or dessert. Turn to that section and browse through the list of recipes to find the one you want. At the back, the Resources guide tells you where to find some products used in the recipes, as well as information on the local businesses mentioned in the book.

Thank you for choosing this harvest of recipes crafted to give you a taste of Asheville. Enjoy!

Contents

Forward:
Earth to Table • *9*

About the Book •5

Mountain Mornings •10

Our cool mountain mornings arouse healthy appetites, and we have the busy breakfast spots to handle them — no matter what time you want your eggs. Our B&Bs are also known for their incredible morning spreads. Get a taste of what's on the menus.

Sips, Small Plates, & Snacks • 50

You'll find quick-to-make bar snacks, party foods, and appetizers from our favorite haunts…as well as drinks from our craft cocktail culture's mixologists and creative small plates with big, local flavors.

Appalachian Homegrown • 84

Visit one of our farmers markets or come in from the garden to make the herbed lemonade, strawberry smoothie, chilled peach gazpacho, fresh salads, vegetables, pasta and grain sides, and soups.

Market Mains •138

Learn how to make award-winning fried chicken, how to cure corned beef, bacon, and duck confit, and how to prepare perfectly seasoned rainbow trout. Sample meat dishes from farm dinner menus, and take a peek at recipes that local meat producers and chefs prepare at home.

A Little Something Extra •196

The dressings, sauces, jams, chutneys, and pickles here are the lagniappe — the pop of taste that adds layers of complexity and personality. These tasty concoctions complement the dishes throughout this book.

Sweet Cravings •220

Indulge in our sweet life through a variety of unique desserts, hometown favorite cakes and cookies, old-fashioned puddings and pies, and whimsical ice creams.

Resources • 264
Index by Subject • 266
Index by Restaurant • 268
Acknowledgements• 269

Earth & Table

"I. The Universe is nothing without the things that live in it, and everything that lives, eats."

"IV. Tell me what you eat, and I shall tell you what you are."

The Physiology of Taste: Or, *Meditations on Transcendental Gastronomy*
—Jean Anthelme Brillat-Savarin

It is inescapable and undeniable: Food is essential and Food is primary. In our cultural wanderings over the past 60 or 70 years, we have strayed from some immutable truths regarding Food. Driven by the industrial compulsion for efficiency and bottom-line profitability, we have succeeded in robbing ourselves of that truth, which is: Food, first and foremost, is about being nourished and being nurtured.

There are two places where this truth is grounded – Mother Earth and The Table.

Over those same 60 or 70 years, there have been pilgrims, wanderers, growers, thing-makers, hippies, visionaries, and intellects that have either never lost sight of or have rediscovered the truth about Food. Many of them flocked here to the mountainous west of North Carolina — greeted, sometimes reluctantly, by a people already grounded in farm dirt, money-poor and land-rich.

The great Mother Earth spirit also embraced these pilgrims, as this place is a vortex of deeply rooted life energy. All came seeking to renew their relationship with the earth and with themselves.

Through the hands of the grower and the cook, in a humble courtship with the land, another place was created where the Truth of Food was rediscovered — The Table. This is the place where we receive nourishment and where we are nurtured — in the breaking of bread together. It is more than a ritual; it is a daily practice of celebration, sharing, and connecting to one another. It is a healing place, a healthy place.

In a sense, we are experiencing a good old-fashioned revival: A Food Revival. It begins with a love for Mother Earth, passes through the care taking hands of grower and cook, and becomes a gift of shared Food Truth around the Table. It is a loving gift.

Farmer & Chef Asheville celebrates this revival. With an eye to the future, a chapter in the making is the inclusion of all people in this Food Truth.

—Mark Rosenstein, chef and author

Mountain Mornings 24/7

Nest *to* Fork

When you ponder the sounds of the Asheville urban landscape, you might think of barking dogs, fire truck sirens, or the occasional car alarm. But the squawk of a chicken? Proudly and loudly she announces the arrival of her latest egg, or she clucks heartily as she chases a juicy bug that found itself in the wrong place at an inopportune time — for the bug. Urban chicken keeping (or "chicken-tendering", as I affectionately refer to it) here is an upward arcing trend. From the Montford community garden to Villagers homesteading supply store in West Asheville, chickens are just another way in which our mountain town's urban landscape is rapidly changing.

What, then, accounts for our chicken love? The answer is cultural, probably. Asheville recently relaxed restrictions on keeping a variety of urban livestock, including chickens. It's now considerably easier to obtain and successfully keep a flock of hens here than it's been in decades.

Additionally, as the interest in eating real foods and reducing the farm-to-table trek (or, in this instance, "nest-to-fork") grows, keeping a flock of laying hens offers a readily accessible backyard source of protein. You want local? How about from your own backyard?

In WNC, we're all about healthy eating. So part of the sustainable appeal of backyard eggs includes their richer nutrient profiles. Hens are allowed to peck in the dirt, eat grass, and forage for bugs and worms; therefore, they produce more nutrient dense eggs than their caged counterparts.

Lastly, we love our chickens; we consider them treasured members of the family. We give away their eggs with the hen donor's name written on them. We decorate their coops to look like houses and landscape around them.

Whatever the reason, Ashevillians are flocking to keep chickens!

—**Ashley English, author**

Mountain Mornings 24/7

B&B Specialties

Blackberries in Sweet Basil Syrup
with Mascarpone Cream • 14

Peach Vanilla Breakfast Soufflé • 16

Lemon Chess Morning Cake • 17

Roasted Organic Vegetable Frittata • 18

Mountain Quiche • 19

Pumpkin Pudding on Spiced Apple
and Pear Compote with Fried Sage • 20

Roasted Tomato, Smoked
Mozzarella & Basil Frittata • 21

Provençal Starter • 22

Breakfast Pizza • 23

Egg Flowers • 24

Ratatouille Goat Cheese Tart • 25

Pineapple Pecan Sticky Buns
with Sweet Cream • 26

Blueberry Buckle • 27

Peach Vanilla Breakfast Souffle on page 16

Blackberries
in Sweet Basil Syrup
with Mascarpone Cream

—**Susan Murray,** CAROLINA BED & BREAKFAST

Owner Susan Murray shares how she serves the berries: "We usually serve this as a first course at breakfast in an antique champagne glass or a martini glass. It's also great with ice cream or on yogurt."

MAKES 4 TO 6 SERVINGS

FOR THE SYRUP:

1 cup sugar

1/2 cup water

1/2 cup semi-sweet white wine, such as a German Riesling

1/2 vanilla bean, split, or 1/2 teaspoon vanilla extract

1 cup tightly packed basil leaves

Juice of 1 lemon

FOR THE MASCARPONE CREAM:

2 tablespoons mascarpone (at room temperature)

1/4 cup heavy cream

1 teaspoon sugar

1 teaspoon vanilla extract

2 pints fresh blackberries

2 to 3 teaspoons minced candied ginger

Combine the sugar, water, and wine in a small saucepan. Add the vanilla bean, if using. Bring to a boil, stirring constantly until the sugar melts. Remove from the heat and stir in the basil, lemon juice, and vanilla extract, if using; press down on the solids to submerge the leaves. Let the mixture cool to room temperature, about 2 hours.

Strain the mixture through a wire mesh sieve into a medium bowl, pressing down on the solids to extract as much liquid as possible. Add the blackberries; cover the bowl and refrigerate for at least 8 hours and up to 2 days. (The longer they soak, the more basil flavor they will absorb.)

Just before serving, whisk together the mascarpone and the heavy cream in a medium bowl. Stir in the sugar and vanilla extract. Let stand until the cream has thickened slightly, about 5 minutes. You should be able to dollop the cream on the berries; if it is too thick, thin with a little more heavy cream.

To serve, spoon the berries and syrup in stemmed glasses or small bowls; spoon some mascarpone mixture over the berries and top each serving with a little candied ginger.

Peach Vanilla Breakfast Soufflé

—**Susan Murray,** CAROLINA BED & BREAKFAST

"We serve this in summer when perfectly ripe, sweet, juicy peaches are at their best. It can be a soufflé, puffed high when you serve it fresh from the oven. Or if you wish to invert it and show off the peach slices on the bottom, it will sink a little and seem more like bread pudding. Either way it's delicious," says owner Susan Murray.

MAKES 4 SERVINGS

1/2 stick (1/4 cup) unsalted butter

1/2 cup firmly packed brown sugar

1 tablespoon dark corn syrup

About 3 fresh ripe peaches, peeled and thinly sliced

About 4 (1/2-inch-thick) slices white bread, crusts removed, and cubed (need 3 1/2 cups)

4 large eggs

1 cup heavy whipping cream

1 1/2 tablespoons Peach Schnapps

1 teaspoon vanilla extract

Pinch of salt

COOK'S NOTE:
If fresh peaches aren't available, 1 (12-ounce) package frozen sliced peaches works well. Thaw the peaches first.

The night before serving, butter 4 (1-cup) ramekins or ovenproof dishes. Place the ramekins on a rimmed baking sheet for easier handling.

Combine the butter, brown sugar, and corn syrup in a small saucepan; cook over medium-high heat, stirring constantly until the brown sugar is dissolved. Remove from the heat, and spoon the sauce into the prepared ramekins, dividing evenly.

Arrange the peach slices in the bottoms of the prepared ramekins. Fill the ramekins with the bread cubes.

Lightly whisk the eggs in a large bowl; whisk in the cream, liqueur, vanilla, and salt. Pour the mixture evenly over the bread cubes in the ramekins; fill them completely, pressing down lightly on the bread to submerge it in the egg mixture. Cover the baking sheet with the prepared ramekins, and refrigerate overnight.

To bake the soufflés, preheat the oven to 350° F. Place the baking sheet with ramekins in the center of the oven and bake until puffed and the edges of the soufflés are golden brown, 35 to 45 minutes.

Remove the baking sheet from the oven and let stand 5 minutes. Working with one at a time, carefully lift a ramekin from the baking sheet using a flat spatula and place on a thick cloth on the counter. Serve in the ramekins, or invert a serving plate over the ramekin; using the cloth and protecting your free hand with an oven mitt, carefully invert the soufflé onto the plate and remove the ramekin. The hot syrup from the bottom of the ramekin will pour on top of the soufflé.

Lemon Chess Morning Cake

—**Christina Muth,** BEAUFORT HOUSE INN

"Serve them with fresh strawberries and garnish with mint," says owner Christina Muth.

Preheat the oven to 350° F. Butter 8 (1/2-cup) ramekins; place them on a rimmed baking sheet for easier handling.

Combine the sugar, cornmeal, and flour in a large bowl; whisk to blend. Add the eggs, half-and-half, lemon juice, and lemon zest to the mixture; whisk to blend well. Whisk in the butter. Pour into the prepared ramekins, dividing evenly.

Bake until the tops are golden brown and a wooden toothpick inserted in the centers comes out clean, 30 to 40 minutes. Let cool in the dishes on a wire rack for at least 5 minutes; if desired, un-mold onto serving plates. Garnish with fresh strawberries and mint. Serve warm or at room temperature.

COOK'S NOTE:
You can prepare the batter the night before, except for folding in the butter, which you must do in the morning just before baking. Owner Christina Muth sometimes bakes the filling in a partially-baked, 9-inch pie shell. Bake at 350° F. until a knife inserted in center comes out clean, 35 to 40 minutes.

MAKES 8 SERVINGS

1 3/4 cups sugar

2 tablespoons yellow cornmeal

1 1/4 tablespoons all-purpose flour

6 large eggs, beaten until frothy

1/2 cup half-and-half or heavy whipping cream

6 tablespoons fresh lemon juice

1 1/2 tablespoon freshly grated lemon zest

2 tablespoons unsalted butter, melted

Roasted Organic Vegetable Frittata

—Christina Muth, BEAUFORT HOUSE INN

"Fresh farm eggs," says owner Christine Muth, "make the difference in this large, fluffy, healthy baked omelet, loaded with fresh herb-and-lemon-seasoned roasted vegetables.

COOK'S NOTE:
A 10-inch nonstick skillet can be used for baking as long as the handle is heatproof. If it is not, wrap the handle in heavy-duty foil before putting it into the oven.

MAKES 8 SERVINGS

2 tablespoons olive or canola oil

3/4 cup each chopped red bell pepper, zucchini, butternut squash

1/2 teaspoon salt, divided (optional)

10 large or 12 small farm fresh eggs

1/2 cup half-and-half

1/4 teaspoon freshly ground pepper

1 cup shredded Parmesan or Cheddar cheese, divided

1/4 cup chopped fresh basil, parsley, thyme, or other fresh herbs

1/2 stick (4 tablespoons) unsalted butter, melted

1/2 cup plain dry breadcrumbs

Fresh herb sprigs (garnish)

Preheat the oven to 400º F.

Brush the olive oil on the bottom and sides of an ovenproof, 10-inch frittata pan or nonstick skillet. Spread the vegetables into a single layer and sprinkle with 1/4 teaspoon salt, if desired. Roast until the vegetables are softened and slightly caramelized around the edges, 20 to 30 minutes. Reduce the oven temperature to 375º F.

Combine the eggs, half-and-half, and pepper in a blender; process on high speed until frothy.

To assemble the frittata, combine the roasted vegetables, 1/2 cup of the cheese, and the herbs in the prepared pan and toss well to distribute. Gently pour the egg mixture evenly over the vegetables. Bake until eggs are just set, 35 to 45 minutes.

Meanwhile, combine the butter, breadcrumbs, and remaining 1/2 cup cheese in a bowl; mix well. Remove the frittata from the oven; sprinkle with the breadcrumb mixture. Return to the oven and bake until the top is nicely browned, about 10 more minutes. Let cool 5 minutes. Loosen the edges of the frittata with a spatula; invert onto a cutting board. Garnish slices with a fresh herb sprig.

Mountain Quiche

—Patti Strelec, CROOKED OAK MOUNTAIN INN

"This creamy, fluffy quiche can be made ahead in stages," recommends owner Patti Strelec. *The pie crust can be partially baked, and the mushrooms and spinach can be made a day ahead, cooled, covered, and refrigerated; just layer the ingredients before baking.*

Preheat the oven to 350° F. Roll out the pastry and fit into a 9-inch deep-dish glass pie plate. Trim the edges and prick the bottom of crust with a fork. Line the crust with foil; fill to the top with pie weights, dried beans, or rice. Bake 10 minutes. Remove from the oven; lift off the foil, and let the crust cool completely.

Melt the butter in a large nonstick skillet over medium heat; add the mushrooms and sauté until the mushrooms are soft, about 5 minutes. Transfer to a bowl.

Rinse the spinach, shaking off the excess water. Return the skillet to medium heat; add the spinach, a third at a time, stirring until each addition is partially wilted. When all the spinach has been wilted, drain and place the spinach on a cutting board. Coarsely chop.

Combine the eggs, cream, Worcestershire sauce, sugar, onion powder, garlic, and pepper in a large bowl; whisk until well blended. Stir in the chopped spinach, mushrooms, and half of the bacon, if using.

Sprinkle the Parmesan cheese over the bottom of the crust. Pour the egg mixture into the crust and distribute it evenly. Sprinkle with the Parmesan cheese and remaining bacon, if using.

Bake until the quiche is set and a knife inserted in the center comes out clean, about 1 hour in a conventional oven or 25 minutes in a convection oven. Cover the top loosely with a piece of foil if the top is browning too quickly. Let the quiche stand 10 minutes before serving.

MAKES 8 SERVINGS

Pastry for 1 (9-inch) pie crust

1 tablespoon unsalted butter

1 cup chopped fresh mushrooms

1 (9- or 10-ounce) bag fresh spinach

3 large eggs

1 1/2 cups heavy whipping cream

2 teaspoons Worcestershire sauce

1/2 teaspoon sugar

1/2 teaspoon onion powder

1/4 teaspoon finely minced fresh garlic

1/2 teaspoon freshly ground pepper

6 slices bacon, cooked and crumbled (optional)

1 cup (4 ounces) shredded Cheddar cheese

1/3 cup grated Parmesan cheese

COOK'S NOTE:
The quiche can be covered with foil and kept warm in a 180° F. oven for up to 1 hour.

Pumpkin Pudding *on* Spiced Apple *&* Pear Compote *with* Fried Sage

—**Susan Murray,** CAROLINA BED & BREAKFAST

A big fan of winter squash and especially pumpkin, proprietor Susan Murray admits this recipe has been "a while in the making. Pumpkin butter tastes rich, and I have worked on the recipe to find the right amount of pumpkin butter to balance the flavors. I like to serve it with browned sausage."

The night before, butter a 9-inch square baking pan. Cut enough crusty bread into cubes to fill the baking dish quite full. You want some of the bread to remain visible and recognizable.

Place the eggs, milk, pumpkin butter, vanilla, cinnamon, nutmeg, and ginger in a large bowl; whisk to blend well. Pour the egg mixture evenly over the bread cubes. (The mixture will not completely cover the bread cubes.) Cover and refrigerate overnight.

To bake, preheat the oven to 350° F. Sprinkle the pecans and brown sugar evenly on top; bake, uncovered, until puffed, golden, and set in the center.

Cut the pudding into 16 squares. Spoon some warm Spiced Apple and Pear Compote on each serving plate; top with a pudding square. Garnish each pudding square with a Fried Sage Leaf.

COOK'S NOTE:

To fry sage, pat leaves dry. Heat 1/2 inch oil in a small skillet over medium-high heat until hot but not smoking. Fry them, in batches, 2 to 3 seconds. Transfer to paper towels to drain and sprinkle with salt; let cool.

MAKES 16 SERVINGS

Crusty bread

7 large eggs

2 cups milk

1/4 cup pumpkin butter

1 teaspoon vanilla extract

1 teaspoon ground cinnamon

1/2 teaspoon ground nutmeg

Pinch of ground ginger

1/4 cup finely chopped pecans

2 tablespoons brown sugar

Spiced Apple & Pear Compote, heated (page 21)

Fried Sage Leaves (see Cook's Note)

Spiced Apple & Pear Compote

6 firm, ripe pears, peeled and cut into 1-inch pieces

6 tart apples (such as pippin, Macintosh, Granny Smith, or Pink Lady), peeled and cut into 1-inch pieces

1/2 cup dry white wine

2 tablespoons brown sugar

1/2 teaspoon ground cinnamon

1/2 teaspoon ground ginger

1/2 teaspoon ground cardamom

1/2 teaspoon dry mustard

1/2 stick (1/4 cup) unsalted butter

2 teaspoons chopped fresh thyme leaves

Salt and freshly ground pepper to taste

Combine the pears, apples, wine, brown sugar, cinnamon, ginger, cardamom, and dry mustard in a large, heavy saucepan. Bring to a simmer over medium heat; cover, reduce heat, and simmer until the fruit is soft, about 15 minutes.

Remove from the heat and mash coarsely with a potato masher. Return to the heat and cook, uncovered until the mixture is thickened, about 10 minutes. Remove from the heat and stir in butter and thyme until the butter melts. Season to taste with salt and pepper. Store the leftovers in a covered jar in the refrigerator for up to 1 week.

Roasted Tomato, Smoked Mozzarella & Basil Frittata

—**Stacy Shelley,** PINECREST BED & BREAKFAST

"We usually serve this dish during the summer when our garden is abundant," says owner Stacy Shelley. "For best taste, our emphasis is always on local seasonal organic vegetables. The recipe includes a tip on roasting your own tomatoes."

1 tablespoon olive oil

1 1/2 teaspoons unsalted butter

2 shallots, thinly sliced

7 large eggs

3/4 cup milk

1/4 cup fresh basil leaves, chopped

Salt and freshly ground pepper

3/4 cup cubed smoked mozzarella

1/3 cup chopped Roasted Tomatoes in Oil (see Cook's Note, 22)

Sauté shallots in oil and butter in a heavy 9- to 10-inch skillet over medium heat; remove from heat. Whisk eggs, milk, basil, and pinch of salt and pepper until blended; pour over shallots in skillet. Sprinkle cheese and tomatoes over egg mixture. Return to medium heat; cook until sides look set, about 5 minutes. Transfer to oven and bake until firm, about 15 minutes. Let stand 5 minutes before cutting into wedges.

COOK'S NOTE:

To roast tomatoes, drizzle approximately 2 Tbsp of olive oil onto a rimmed baking pan. Then add 3 or 4 sprigs fresh thyme and 1 clove garlic, thinly sliced. Halve a variety of tomatoes and place them on the baking pan in a single layer. Roast in a 325 degree oven for about 2 hours. Place them in mason jars and refrigerate. They will keep this way for about a week and can be frozen.

Provençale Starter

—Claudia Hickl, SWEET BISCUIT INN

This dish is special to the inn proprietors, linking the start of their lives as B&B owners in Provence, France, to the Sweet Biscuit Inn in Asheville. Cavaillon melon is a French variety of muskmelon. You can substitute cantaloupe, crenshaw, or catawba melons in this recipe.

COOK'S NOTE:

To make a basic tomato coulis, sauté a chopped medium onion and 3 minced cloves of garlic in a large skillet until tender, 2 to 3 minutes. Add 1 1/2 pounds peeled, seeded and chopped plum tomatoes; cook until tomatoes are soft and most of liquid is evaporated. Purée and season with salt and white pepper.

MAKES 4 SERVINGS

4 medium eggplants, peeled and sliced

Extra-virgin olive oil

Salt and pepper to taste

Juice of 1 lemon

3 large eggs

4 to 5 tablespoons crème fraîche

Leaves of 1 sprig thyme

4 cups mixed greens

1/2 cup finely diced Cavaillon melon

1/2 cup finely diced cooked red beets

1/2 cup tomato coulis (see Cook's Note)

Vinaigrette of your choice

Preheat the oven to 375° F. Butter 4 (1-cup) ramekins and line the bottoms with rounds of parchment paper. Butter the paper. Sauté the eggplant in a large skillet coated lightly with olive oil over medium heat until browned. Season the eggplant with salt and pepper. Place 1 slice in each ramekin and the remaining slices in a food processor.

Add the next 4 ingredients and process until smooth. Season to taste. Spoon into the ramekins, dividing evenly. Place the ramekins in a baking dish; pour in hot water to come halfway up the sides of the ramekins. Bake until firm, 20 to 25 minutes. Remove them from the water bath and let stand for 5 minutes.

To serve, divide the greens on the upper thirds of 4 serving plates. Invert the eggplant soufflés below the greens. Mound 2 tablespoons of the diced melon to the right of each souffle. Mound 2 tablespoons of the diced beets to the left. Drizzle 2 tablespoons of tomato coulis onto half of each soufflé. Drizzle a little vinaigrette over each salad.

Breakfast Pizza

—**Jim Palmer,** THE LION & THE ROSE BED & BREAKFAST

Proprietor Jim Palmer enjoys preparing breakfast for guests; cooking is his passion. He makes his fresh tomato bruschetta mixture with chopped fresh tomatoes, minced garlic, chopped fresh herbs, a little olive oil, and salt and pepper. You can toss in a drizzle of balsamic vinegar to boost the flavor of tomatoes that aren't perfectly in season.

Preheat the oven to 250º F. Arrange the prosciutto slices in a single layer on a rimmed baking sheet. Bake until crispy, about 45 minutes.

Spoon the tomato bruschetta mixture in a wire-mesh sieve placed over a bowl. Let the mixture stand until it is well drained. Pour the accumulated juices in a small saucepan; add the V-8. Bring to a gentle boil over medium-high heat; cook until reduced by half, 6 to 8 minutes.

Brush each piece of flatbread with olive oil, and crisp in a non-stick skillet over medium-high heat, 1 to 2 minutes per side.

Preheat the oven broiler. To assemble each Breakfast Pizza, place the flatbreads on a baking sheet; spread about 3 tablespoons of ricotta cheese on top of each piece. Spoon the tomato bruschetta mixture over the ricotta layers, dividing evenly. Scatter the mozzarella over the tomato mixture; broil briefly to melt the cheese. Top each with 2 eggs, and sprinkle with 2 tablespoons of Parmesan. Sprinkle with pepper to taste. Top with slices of crisped prosciutto. Spoon the reduced V-8 mixture on the plate around the pizzas, dividing evenly.

MAKES 4 SERVINGS

1/2 pound thinly sliced prosciutto

1 cup fresh tomato bruschetta mixture

1/2 cup V-8

2 flatbreads, halved

Extra-virgin olive oil

About 3/4 cup ricotta cheese

2 cups cubed fresh mozzarella

8 large eggs, cooked over easy

1/2 cup freshly grated Parmesan cheese

Freshly ground pepper

Egg Flowers

—Kristen Dusenbery, DRY RIDGE INN

MAKES 6 SERVINGS

About 3 tablespoons unsalted butter for greasing the muffin cups

6 sheets thawed, frozen phyllo pastry

3 tablespoons unsalted butter, melted

2 tablespoons freshly grated Parmesan cheese

6 large eggs

About 2 tablespoons minced fresh chives

Salt and freshly ground pepper

Owner Kristen Dusenbery describes this dish: layers of buttered phyllo squares form crispy nests for farm-fresh eggs that are seasoned and baked to perfection.

Preheat the oven to 350° F. Generously butter 6 regular-size muffin cups.

Stack the phyllo sheets on a work surface; cover with a piece of plastic wrap. Place one phyllo sheet on the work surface. Brush to the edges with about 1/2 tablespoon melted butter. Top with another sheet and brush it with butter. Cut the stack of 2 sheets into 6 (4-inch) squares. Stack 3 of the 2-layer squares together like a pinwheel, rotating them so the corners do not overlap. Press this 6–layer pinwheel into one of the buttered muffin cups. Repeat this stacking, brushing, and cutting process to make 5 more pinwheels, pressing each into a buttered muffin cup.

Sprinkle 1 teaspoon Parmesan cheese into each phyllo-lined cup. Break 1 egg into each cup. Sprinkle the chives over the eggs, about 1 teaspoon each. Season with salt and pepper. Bake until the pastry is golden and the eggs are set, 15 to 20 minutes. Use a thin metal spatula to help lift the egg-filled pastry shells out of the muffin cups. Place on serving plates.

Ratatouille
Goat Cheese Tart

—**Emily Flynn McIntosh,** A BED OF ROSES VICTORIAN BED & BREAKFAST

This tart shows off the lovely Ratatouille that proprietor Emily McIntosh makes. The herbed cooked vegetables are delicious in a quiche-like custard topped with melted goat cheese. Serve for breakfast or as a first course or main dish.

Roll the Our Favorite Quiche & Tart Crust dough into a 10 1/2 - to 11-inch circle; fit into a 9-inch pie plate. Trim the edges of the dough 1/2- to 1-inch larger than the pie plate edges; tuck the extra under and crimp the edges of the crust. Wrap the pie plate and crust with plastic wrap and refrigerate overnight.

Preheat the oven to 400° F. Coat a large piece of foil with cooking spray in a 10- to 11-inch circle and set aside.

Remove the pie plate from the refrigerator and prick holes in the bottom and sides of the crust; place in the freezer for 10 minutes.

Line the foil, coated side down, on top of the crust, with coated area in contact with the crust. Fill with pie weights, rice, or dried beans. Bake 10 minutes. Remove from oven; carefully lift off the pie weights and foil. Let the crust cool on a wire rack.

Whisk the eggs and salt in a large bowl until frothy. Add the cream and whisk to blend. Place the pie plate with crust on a rimmed baking sheet for easier handling. Spoon the ratatouille into the prepare crust, spreading in an even layer. Crumble the goat cheese over the filling. Gently pour the egg mixture evenly over the vegetable mixture. Sprinkle with pepper.

Bake until the tart filling is puffed and set, about 40 minutes. Let cool 10 minutes before slicing.

MAKES 6 TO 8 SERVINGS

1 Our Favorite Quiche & Tart Crust (page 247)

4 large eggs

Pinch of salt

1/2 cup heavy whipping cream

3/4 cup prepared Ratatouille (page 111)

4 ounces goat cheese

Freshly ground pepper to taste

Pineapple Pecan Sticky Buns
with Sweet Cream

—Christina Muth, BEAUFORT HOUSE INN

The upside-down cake-like buns are soft and sweet with caramelized pineapple. Serve them warm with dollops of sweetened sour cream.

To prepare the sweet cream, combine the sour cream and brown sugar in a bowl and whisk until the sugar is dissolved. Cover and chill until you are ready to serve.

To prepare the buns, combine the eggs and sugar in a large mixing bowl; beat at medium speed with an electric mixer until well blended.

Place the flour, baking powder, and salt in a medium bowl; whisk the dry ingredients to distribute. Add the flour mixture to the egg mixture, a little at a time, and beat until the mixture is well blended. (The mixture will be thick.)

Combine the half-and-half and 1/4 cup of the butter in a small saucepan. Cook over medium-high heat, stirring constantly until the butter melts. Do not boil. Remove from the heat and gradually add to egg mixture, beating until the mixture is well blended. Rinse and dry the saucepan.

To bake, preheat the oven to 350° F. Butter 12 muffin cups.

Combine the remaining 1/2 cup butter, brown sugar, and corn syrup in the small saucepan; cook over medium heat until the butter melts, stirring constantly until the sugar is dissolved. Spoon into the prepared muffin cups, dividing evenly. Top with 1 tablespoon pecans, then 4 to 6 slivers of fresh pineapple. Spoon the batter into the muffin cups, filling to within 1/4 inch from the tops.

Bake until the tops of the buns are lightly browned and the buns spring back when lightly touched in the centers, 20 to 25 minutes. Meanwhile, grate a little nutmeg on the top of the sweet cream mixture.

Remove the muffin pan from the oven and let it cool on a wire rack, 5 minutes. Invert the muffin pan onto a cutting board or large platter. Transfer the sticky buns to serving plates; dust with confectioners' sugar and garnish with mint sprigs. Pass the sweet cream when serving.

MAKES 12 SERVINGS

**FOR THE
SWEET CREAM:**

2 cups sour cream

1/2 cup firmly packed light brown sugar

FOR THE BUNS:

2 large eggs

1 cup sugar

1 cup all-purpose flour

1 teaspoon baking powder

Pinch of salt

1/2 cup half-and-half

1 1/2 sticks (3/4 cup) unsalted butter, divided

1/2 teaspoon vanilla extract

3/4 cup firmly packed light brown sugar

1 1/2 tablespoons dark corn syrup

3/4 cup chopped pecans

1/4 cored, peeled fresh pineapple, cut into paper thin slices

Confectioners' sugar and mint sprigs (garnish)

Blueberry Buckle

—Patti Strelec, CROOKED OAK MOUNTAIN INN

MAKES 9 SERVINGS

FOR THE TOPPING:
1/2 stick (1/4 cup) unsalted butter, softened

1/2 cup sugar

1/2 cup all-purpose flour

1 teaspoon ground cinnamon

FOR THE CAKE:
2 cups all-purpose flour

2 1/2 teaspoons baking powder

1/4 teaspoon salt

1 stick (1/2 cup) unsalted butter, softened

3/4 cup sugar

1 large egg

3/4 cup whole milk

2 cups fresh blueberries

"Blueberry Buckle is a dense, old-fashioned cake, named for the way the streusel topping "buckles" as the cake batter sinks a little during baking," explains owner Patti Strelec about her morning coffee cake. *"It's a perfect treat baked with local wild-picked or Farmers Market berries."*

Preheat the oven to 375° F. Butter an 8- or 9-inch square baking pan. Cut 2 (14 x 8-inch or 14 x 9-inch) strips of parchment paper and lay them in the pan, crisscrossed and overlapping, so that the sides are lined and there is overhang on each side. (You'll use the overhang to lift the cool cake out of the pan.)

To prepare the topping, stir together the flour, sugar, and cinnamon in a small mixing bowl. Add the butter and mix in with a fork until the topping is crumbly.

To prepare the cake, combine the flour, baking powder, and salt in a small bowl; whisk to blend. Combine the butter and sugar in a large mixing bowl; beat at medium speed until fluffy. Add the egg and beat well. Add the flour mixture alternately with the milk, beginning and ending with the dry ingredients and beating just until blended after each addition. Fold in the blueberries.

Scrape the batter into the prepared pan. Sprinkle the topping evenly over the cake batter. Bake until the topping is golden and a toothpick inserted in the center comes out clean. Let the cake cool to lukewarm with the pan on a wire rack. Carefully lift the cake from the pan using the parchment overhanging edges and place it on the wire rack to cool further. Cut and serve warm.

Mountain Mornings 24/7

Eggs & Taters

Scrambled Eggs with Ramps & Asparagus • 30

Tater Tots • 31

Breakfast Veggie Strata • 32

Sausage & Sweet Potato Scramble • 33

Sausage & Sweet Potato Scramble on page 33

Scrambled Eggs *with* Ramps *&* Asparagus

—**Denny Trantham**, FORMERLY OF GROVE PARK INN

MAKES 2 SERVINGS

About 4 large ramps

4 medium
asparagus spears

1 tablespoon
unsalted butter

1/4 cup sliced morels

4 large eggs,
beaten just to blend

Salt and freshly
ground pepper

This recipe is a spring celebration, according to chef Denny Trantham. It is as delicious for lunch or supper as it is for breakfast. This simple farm dish is worthy of kings; the delicate flavor of farm eggs and earthy fresh asparagus butter up the prized morels.

Trim and thinly slice the ramp bulbs and slender stems; thinly slice the green tops to measure 1 cup. Trim and cut asparagus diagonally into 1/2-inch pieces. (You'll need about 1/2 cup.)

Melt the butter in a medium nonstick skillet over medium heat. Add the ramp bulbs and stems; sauté 3 minutes. Add the green tops, asparagus, and morels; sauté until asparagus is crisp-tender, about 4 to 5 minutes. Pour in the eggs; sprinkle lightly with salt and pepper. Cook, stirring gently and frequently, until eggs are softly set, about 2 minutes.

Ramp Obsession

Chef Denny Trantham's ramp love began at an early age. "I can remember digging ramps with my grandfather in the early spring. Grandma would pick branch lettuce from the creek banks and place them in a metal dishpan with cut-up ramps, salt, pepper and a little bit of cider vinegar. She would then heat up some fatback grease and 'kilt' the lettuce (a.k.a., kilt branch lettuce).

"We would also put ramps into everything from fried potatoes to scrambled eggs. Kids would get sent home for putting ramps in the pencil sharpener at school! You have to know where to look and what to look for in the early spring. Ramp digging is an art and a skill set — part of our Appalachian heritage."

Tater Tots

—**Eric Kang,** THE ADMIRAL

While these sound perfect for breakfast, you can enjoy them with steak or sandwiches. Sous chef Eric Kang tells us these are so popular he can't take them off the menu. Russet potatoes have more starch in them than others; the starch helps bind the bites together.

Place the potatoes in a large pot; fill with cold water to cover. Bring the water to a boil; when the water comes to a boil, set a timer for 5 minutes. Remove from the heat and check a few of the potatoes with a fork; they should be al dente, just tender but still firm.

Meanwhile, prepare a large bowl of ice and water. Drain the potatoes immediately and plunge into a bowl of ice water to stop the cooking process. Drain and let the potatoes cool completely. (Cooling is very important.)

When the potatoes are completely cool, peel them. Grate the potatoes using the grater attachment of a food processor or with the large holes of a box grater. The grated potatoes should be sticky. Place the sticky potatoes in a large bowl and add the egg; toss well. Add the cornstarch, garlic powder, onion powder, salt, and pepper; mix well.

Form, by tablespoons, into tater-tot shape. Heat about 4 inches of oil in a large saucepan to 350° F. Working in batches, drop Tater Tots into hot oil and fry until browned and hot, about 4 minutes. Drain on paper towels; serve hot.

Note: Tater Tots may be frozen in an airtight container.

COOK'S NOTE:
Don't skip the cooling step for the potatoes; Chef Kang says, "The only tricky part of the recipe is the proper cooking (to proper firmness) and cooling of the potatoes."

MAKES 6 DOZEN

6 (10- to 12-ounce) russet potatoes (1 3/4 pounds total), unpeeled

1 large egg

1/2 cup cornstarch

1 tablespoon garlic powder

1 tablespoon onion powder

1 1/2 teaspoons kosher salt

1 1/2 teaspoons freshly ground pepper

Vegetable oil for deep-frying

Breakfast Veggie Strata

—Cathy Cleary, WEST END BAKERY

Cathy Cleary, co-owner of West End Bakery, shares her popular fresh vegetable, cheese, bread, and egg casserole. They use what's fresh in the market in this strata; according to Cleary, "Blanched broccoli florets, greens, and diced peppers work well, as do cooked cubed potatoes and diced meaty tomatoes. Any cheese you have — Cheddar, mozzarella, crumbled goat cheese — will do."

The night before, butter a 13 x 9-inch baking dish and set it aside. Butter a large piece of aluminum foil in an area the size of the casserole. You will cover the casserole with the foil; the buttered area will prevent it from sticking to the ingredients.

Sauté the onion in oil in a large, heavy skillet over medium-high heat until tender, about 3 minutes. Transfer to a large bowl.

Add the French bread cubes, vegetables, cheese, and garlic to the bowl; toss well and spread in the prepared baking dish.

Using the same large bowl, whisk the eggs until blended; whisk in the milk, basil, salt, and pepper. Pour evenly over the layers. Cover with the foil, buttered side down; refrigerate overnight.

In the morning, remove the strata from the refrigerator 1 hour before baking. Preheat the oven to 350º F.

Bake 1 hour; carefully remove the foil and continue baking until the center is set, 25 to 30 minutes additional minutes.

MAKES 16 SERVINGS

1 large onion, diced

1/4 cup vegetable oil

10 cups cubed French bread

4 cups vegetables

2 3/4 cups (11 ounces) shredded cheese

3 cloves garlic, crushed

12 large eggs

2 cups milk

1 teaspoon dried basil

2 teaspoons salt

1 teaspoon freshly ground pepper

Sausage *&* Sweet Potato Scramble

— **John and Julie Stehling,** EARLY GIRL EATERY

The Stehlings have enjoyed much acclaim for their hip combinations of local ingredients in breakfasts all day. Chef John comes from a family of deep Southern cooking roots; Julie is all about healthy eating. So when their influences intersect on their menus, you get a creative mix of grits, bacon, eggs, and other regional favorites without the greasy diner element. Whether you are a carnivore or a vegetarian, you're at home here.

From the beginning, Julie and John have depended on local farmers to supply their food. That's one reason why their food is delicious — their commitment to supporting our community shows in every bite. Says Julie Stehling: "The farmers we have come to know through this business have been a great part of why we do what we do."

Cook the bacon in a heavy, medium skillet over medium-high heat until it starts to brown. Add the sausage and fry, breaking up the sausage, until both are browned. (Do not drain.) Reduce the heat to medium-low; add the mushrooms and sauté until tender, about 2 minutes. Add the Candied Yams; cook and stir until the mixture is hot, about 3 minutes.

Add the eggs, green onions, salt, and pepper; cook, stirring frequently and gently, to prevent burning but to not break up the eggs too much as they set. Spoon onto a serving plate.

MAKES 1 SERVING

FOR EACH PLATE:

2 slices thick-cut bacon, chopped

1/2 cup cooked Candied Yams (recipe page 115)

2 ounces local bulk sausage

1/4 cup sliced shiitake mushrooms

3 large eggs

1 tablespoon chopped green onions

1/4 to 1/2 teaspoon salt

Freshly ground pepper to taste

Mountain Mornings 24/7

Baked to Order

Jammin' Pop Tarts • 37

Fresh Fig and Walnut Muffins • 38

Apple Pecan Streusel Muffins • 39

Gluten-Free Banana Muffins • 41

Cornbread • 42

Gluten-Free Buttermilk Biscuits • 43

No Knead Bread • 44

Spent Grain Baguette • 46

Granola • 49

Jammin' Pop Tarts

—**Walter Harrill,** IMLADRIS FARM

MAKES 6 TO 9 SERVINGS

2 cups all-purpose flour

1 teaspoon salt

1 stick (1/2 cup) cold unsalted butter, cut into small pieces

1/4 to 1/2 cup ice water

1/2 cup jam

1 large egg white beaten with 1 teaspoon water

Imladris Farm has been in Walter Harrill's family since his ancestors immigrated here from Ireland in the early 1800s. When the Harrills moved to the abandoned family farm, they found prosperous fruit trees and berry bushes as well as other fruits still thriving. They now tend to those blackberries, blueberries, and raspberries and make incredible jams and preserves with the berries.

Combine the flour and salt in a large bowl; whisk to blend the dry ingredients. Cut in the butter pieces with a pastry blender or your fingers until the butter pieces are the size of small peas. Sprinkle 3 to 4 tablespoons ice water over the mixture and toss until the dough starts to clump together; add more water, by tablespoons, until the dough holds together.

Form the dough into a rough ball; divide it into 2 equal pieces. Flatten each piece into a disc on pieces of plastic wrap; wrap the discs and refrigerate 30 minutes.

Preheat the oven to 375° F. Line a large baking sheet with parchment paper.

Roll each disc of dough into a 14-inch square shape on pieces of parchment paper; trim edges of each disc with a knife to form an even 12-inch square. Spoon the jam on one square of dough, spreading to within 1/4 inch from the edges. Lay the other square of dough on top of the jam, fitting edges together; if one is larger than the other, use it on top.

Use a rolling pin to press down and seal the edges of both squares. To make individual pop tarts out of the large sheet, lay the rolling pin down the length and width of the surface, patterned like a tic-tac-toe board, and press down firmly to seal pastry into 6 to 9 pieces. Use a long sharp knife to cut down the center of the seals made by the rolling pin. Carefully transfer the dough on the parchment paper to a baking sheet and refrigerate until it is firm, about 30 minutes.

Remove the baking sheet from the refrigerator and separate the pop tarts. Use a fork to seal decorate the edges of the pop tarts; use a fork to poke 6 steam holes in the tops of them. Brush the edges with the egg white mixture.

Bake until the pop tarts are browned, 20 to 25 minutes.

Fresh Fig *and* Walnut Muffins

—**Cathy Cleary,** WEST END BAKERY

MAKES 1 DOZEN

2 cups unbleached all-purpose flour

1 1/2 teaspoons baking powder

1/2 teaspoon salt

1 teaspoon ground cinnamon

1 large egg

3/4 cup milk

1/2 cup sour cream or plain Greek yogurt

1/3 cup oil

1/2 teaspoon vanilla extract

3/4 cup sugar

1 1/4 cup chopped fresh figs

1/2 cup chopped walnuts, toasted

Additional chopped walnuts for sprinkling on tops

COOK'S NOTE:
If you can't find fresh figs, substitute 1 cup chopped dried figs, but soak the figs in milk for 1 hour to soften them before adding them to the batter.

"I developed this recipe when a neighbor shared figs from his tree; all he wanted was for friends to eat them and not birds or ants," says owner Cathy Cleary. *"Of course we rewarded him with muffins for his sweet gesture."*

Preheat the oven to 350° F. Butter and flour a 12-cup muffin tin.

Sift together the flour, baking powder, salt, and cinnamon in a fine-mesh sieve placed over a large bowl.

Whisk the egg in a medium bowl until blended; whisk in the sour cream, oil, and vanilla. Whisk in the sugar. Add the mixture to the dry ingredients and stir until just combined. Gently stir in the figs and toasted walnuts. Spoon the batter into prepared muffin cups, dividing evenly. Sprinkle tops with about a teaspoon of chopped walnuts.

Bake until a wooden toothpick inserted in the centers comes out clean, about 15 minutes.

Cathy Cleary, owner of the West End Bakery, is the creator of FEAST (Fresh, Easy, Affordable, Sustainable, Tasty) — a program that teaches children about healthy eating. To Cleary, "It's about choice. We are much more likely to choose healthy food if we prepare it."

Through in-school and camp cooking classes, volunteers for FEAST encourage children and their families to make good food choices. By teaching skills needed to make fresh, wholesome, tasty food, the organization empowers people of all income levels to cook and eat healthy meals.

The hands-on classes teach students how to follow recipes, look for seasonal, local foods, and choose moderate portions. They practice kitchen safety; and perhaps more importantly, the experiences teach students that healthy cooking can be fun. Read more at feast.slowfoodasheville.org.

Apple Pecan Streusel Muffins

—Cathy Cleary, WEST END BAKERY

"This muffin is the perfect way to start off a crisp fall morning," says bakery owner Cathy Cleary. "It works with any kind of apple, but in my opinion, an apple like Granny Smith is the best. A local apple called Mutzu (that is similar to Granny Smith) can be cooked all the way through, but not get mushy in your muffin! You can add any kind of nuts or dried fruit to these muffins to make them even sassier; try fresh cranberries instead of the pecans."

MAKES 1 DOZEN

FOR THE STREUSEL TOPPING:

1/2 cup unbleached all-purpose flour

1/2 cup firmly packed light brown sugar

1/2 stick (1/4 cup) cold butter, cut into small pieces

1/4 cup finely chopped pecans

1 teaspoon ground cinnamon

FOR THE BATTER:

2 cups unbleached all-purpose flour

1 1/2 teaspoons baking powder

1/2 teaspoon salt

1/2 teaspoon ground cinnamon

1/2 teaspoon ground ginger

1 cup plain or vanilla yogurt

1/3 cup oil

1 large egg

2/3 cup sugar

2 medium-size local apples, peeled and thinly sliced

1/2 cup chopped pecans, toasted

Preheat the oven to 350° F. Butter and flour a 12-cup muffin tin.

To prepare the streusel, combine the flour and brown sugar in a medium bowl; sprinkle with the butter pieces and rub together with your fingers until the crumb mixture has butter pieces no larger than small peas. Mix in pecans and cinnamon.

To prepare the batter, sift together the flour, baking powder, salt, cinnamon, and ginger in a fine mesh sieve placed over a bowl.

In a separate bowl, whisk together the yogurt, oil, egg, and sugar. Add the yogurt mixture to the dry ingredients; stir just until combined. Gently fold in apples and pecans. Spoon the batter evenly into the muffin cups; sprinkle with the streusel mixture. Bake until a wooden toothpick inserted into the centers comes out clean, 25 to 30 minutes.

Gluten-Free Banana Nut Muffins

Anthony Cerrato, STRADA

This Italian neighborhood trattoria is also home to an in-house artisan bakery, and they bake wonderfully moist muffins as well as a variety of homemade breads. According to chef/owner Anthony Cerrato, "We use a several hundred-year-old process with a slow-fermentation method that takes, on average, three days to carry out." See www.stradaasheville.com/bakehouse/ for information on their bread varieties, such as Peasant Batard, Sourdough, Challah, Chocolate Cherry Bread, and more.

Preheat the oven to 375° F. Lightly butter and flour a muffin tin.

Combine the flour, cinnamon, nutmeg, soda, baking powder, and salt in a medium bowl; whisk the dry ingredients to blend them.

Add the brown sugar to the mashed bananas in a large bowl and whisk the mixture until no lumps of sugar remain. Whisk in the eggs until they are blended; whisk in the oil and vinegar. Add the dry ingredients and stir with a wooden spoon just until the dry ingredients are moistened. Stir in the milk to thin the batter; fold in the pecans.

Spoon the batter into the muffin tin, dividing it evenly among the cups. Bake until a toothpick inserted in the centers comes out clean, 20 to 25 minutes.

MAKES 1 DOZEN

1 1/2 cups gluten-free all-purpose flour

1 teaspoon ground cinnamon

1/4 teaspoon ground nutmeg

1 teaspoon baking soda

1 teaspoon baking powder

1/4 teaspoon salt

2 medium bananas, mashed (need 1 cup)

1 cup firmly packed light brown sugar

2 large eggs

1/4 cup canola oil

1/4 cup distilled white vinegar

1/4 cup milk

1/2 cup chopped pecans

Cornbread

—William Dissen, THE MARKET PLACE RESTAURANT

MAKES ONE 13 x 9-INCH PAN, OR 12 TO 15 SERVINGS

1 stick (1/2 cup) unsalted butter, melted and divided

1 1/2 cups yellow cornmeal

1 1/2 cups all-purpose flour

1/4 cup sugar

2 teaspoons baking soda

2 teaspoons salt

3 large eggs

2 1/2 cups buttermilk

This is chef/owner William Dissen's go-to cornbread recipe; like a good Southerner, he uses buttermilk for tangy flavor and a tender crumb. Try toasting cubes and using them as croutons in salads.

Preheat the oven to 425° F. Brush a 13 x 9-inch baking pan with 2 tablespoons of the melted butter.

Combine the cornmeal, flour, baking soda, sugar, and salt in a medium bowl; whisk to blend the dry ingredients.

Whisk the eggs in a large bowl; whisk in the buttermilk and the remaining 6 tablespoons of butter. Add the cornmeal mixture to the buttermilk mixture; stir with a wooden spoon just until the dry ingredients are moistened; do not over-mix.

Pour the batter into the buttered pan and bake until golden brown and a wooden pick inserted in the center comes out clean, about 15 minutes. Let it cool for 15 minutes on a wire rack before cutting.

Farmer to Miller to Baker

Here we return to the old ways of baking bread: farmers grow premium-quality, organic grain varieties; local millers stone-grind the grains, and bakers bake bread with a distinctly local flavor. With freshly milled grains — wheat, rye, corn, and more, grown by farmers we trust — our bakers produce breads and pastries with superior flavor and texture.

Carolina Ground, a mill devoted to stone-grinding locally grown, organic grains, links the farmer, miller, and baker. Offering a distinctly local Carolina flour blend for a loaf of bread or pastry improves the quality of the product, offering a tangible level of security and sustainability to the bakery, farms, and mill. Read more at carolinaground.com.

Gluten-Free Buttermilk Biscuits

—Rebekah Abrams, EAT MORE BAKERY

We met owner Rebekah Abrams at the farmers market, where she sells her Eat More Bakery gluten-free cakes, breads, cookies and more. She combines just the right flour blends for each recipe, not stopping until she finds the blend that yields the best results. Look for Eat More Bakery at local farmers markets; or visit the website eatmorebakery. com for ordering information.

Preheat the oven to 400° F.

Whisk the eggs and buttermilk in a small bowl.

Combine the tapioca starch, sorghum flour, potato starch, millet flour, xanthem gum, baking powder, and salt in the large bowl of a stand mixer fitted with the paddle attachment. Mix a few seconds to blend the dry ingredients. Add the cold butter pieces; mix on low speed until the butter is rubbed into the dry ingredients and the butter pieces are no larger than small peas. Add the egg mixture and stir just until combined.

Turn the dough out on a floured surface (any of the flours); gently roll out to 1 inch. Cut out biscuits with a biscuit cutter and place on a baking sheet. Bake until golden brown, about 25 minutes. Brush hot biscuits with melted butter, if desired.

MAKES 8 TO 10 BISCUITS

2 large eggs

1/2 cup buttermilk

1 1/4 cups tapioca starch

3/4 cup sorghum flour

3/4 cup potato starch

1/4 cup millet flour

2 teaspoons xantham gum

1 1/2 teaspoons baking powder, sifted

1 1/2 teaspoons salt

1 1/2 sticks (3/4 cup) cold unsalted butter, cubed

No Knead Bread

—**Steve Bardwell and Gail Lunsford,** WAKE ROBIN FARM BREADS

Wake Robin Farm is a century-old farm run by the owner's family since the early 1800s. Originally, the farm supported tobacco, corn, and cattle; now it's under a forest management plan dedicated to the reintroduction of the American chestnut. To support the farm, the husband-wife team bake European-style and whole-grain artisan breads in a wood-fired oven. The flour is grown and ground here in WNC. Look for their breads at the Montford and UNCA tailgate markets and in many local restaurants.

Steve Bardwell explains that they make this bread during the off-season, when they are not baking many loaves. However, they still have to keep the starter going by removing some and then feeding it with flour and water. When the removed starter isn't needed for baking bread, they make this recipe for themselves.

MAKES 2 (1 3/4-POUND) LOAVES

2 pounds bread flour

1 tablespoon salt

1/2 teaspoon instant dry yeast

1 pound 11 ounces warm water

8 ounces leftover firm starter (levain)

COOK'S NOTE:
Bakers measure flour and liquid in weight for recipe accuracy.

Combine the flour, salt, yeast, water, and starter in a large bowl. Use just one hand to mix together until all dry ingredients are incorporated. (The dough will be lumpy.) Cover the bowl and let it stand in a warm place.

Every 20 minutes for the next 2 hours (6 times total), fold and stretch the dough several times. It helps to moisten one hand, push it under the dough, then pull the dough over itself. After the first folding, you will see it start turning into bread dough.

After the final folding and stretching, cover the bowl and let the dough rest for 5 to 6 hours in a warm place or until it has tripled in size. Place the bowl in the refrigerator overnight.

The next day, turn the cold dough out onto a lightly floured suface. Gently divide the dough into 2 equal pieces, taking care not to disturb the bubbles. Carefully pull each piece into a ball: stretch the bottom of the dough (where the flour is) up and over the piece, pulling and shaping into a ball. (This step takes practice!)

Generously dust 2 wooden bowls with flour; place each dough ball, smooth sides down, in a bowl. The bowl will help the dough retain its shape while it proofs. Cover each bowl with a tea towel and let them stand in a warm place for 3 hours.

After 2 hours, put two covered casserole dishes, Dutch ovens, or bread cloches in the oven and turn on the oven to 450° F. Let them heat for 1 hour.

Sprinkle the top of each ball of dough with semolina flour or cornmeal. Using oven mitts, remove the casseroles from the hot oven and remove the tops. Gently lift each dough ball from its bowl and carefully turn it over and place, smooth-side-up, in a hot casserole. Cover casseroles with the tops and return the casserole dishes to the oven.

Bake 45 minutes. Using oven mitts, remove the casseroles from the oven and remove the tops. Return the casseroles to the oven and reduce the oven temperature to 425° F; bake uncovered for 30 minutes or until browned to desired color. Carefully remove the breads and let them cool about 1 hour.

Asheville Artisan Bread Baker's Festival

In 2004, Steve Bardwell and Gale Lunsford, owners of Wake Robin Farm Breads invited local bakers to a potluck dinner at The Market Place to share their craft and ideas. And the Asheville Artisan Bread Baker's Festival took root.

Since the next year, area bakers have shared loaves and knowledge at this annual festival. Offering samples and hands-on workshops, guest instructors include esteemed figures in the artisan bread-baking world, such as Peter Reinhart — a James Beard Award-winning author, teacher, and consultant — and Lionel Vatinet — French master baker, author, and owner of La Farm Bakery in Cary, NC.

Says Reinhart, "Asheville and its surrounding area, with a very small population, supports more artisan bakeries than most states. The bakeries are all small, but truly artisan in the purest sense of the word."

Read more at:
ashevillebreadfestival.com.

Spent Grain Baguette

—**Brian Dennehy**, CITY BAKERY

General manager Brian Dennehy shared this recipe for using spent grains from local brewers to add a grain texture and a slightly nutty and malty flavor to the bread. Spent grains are the cracked, malted grains and husks leftover from the brewing process; they are often given back to farms for livestock feed.

To prepare the *pâté fermentée*, combine the flours, salt, yeast, and water in a large mixing bowl. Using the paddle attachment, mix on low for 1 minute. Switch the attachment to the dough hook; mix 4 minutes on medium speed. Scrape the starter dough into a well-oiled 4-quart bowl and cover with plastic wrap. Let the dough stand in a warm place until it has doubled in size, about 2 hours. Punch the dough down and knead lightly on a floured board to remove the gasses. Place the dough back in the bowl, cover with plastic wrap, and refrigerate overnight.

To prepate the bread, remove the *pâté fermentée* from the refrigerator and cut into 3 equal pieces; let them rest at room temperature for 1 hour.

Mix the flours and salt in a large mixing bowl with the paddle attachment on low speed to blend. Add the three pieces of *pâté fermentée*, water, and beer grains to the dry ingredients and mix 1 minute. Switch the attachment to the dough hook; mix on medium speed until dough is smooth, 6 minutes. Place in an oiled 4-quart bowl and cover with plastic wrap.

Let the dough stand in a warm place until it has doubled in size, about 2 hours. Shape the dough into baguettes on a floured board; cover loosely and let proof for at least 45 minutes.

Preheat the oven to 450º F. Gently lift the baguettes onto a pizza peel; place in the oven on the pizza stone. Bake until golden brown, about 30 minutes.

Note: If you don't have a pizza peel and stone, line a heavy, rimmed baking sheet with parchment.

COOK'S NOTE:
Pate fermentee is the French term for a "pre-ferment" or starter dough that has been made a day ahead. Bakers that make quantities of bread use scraps of bread dough from the loaves they bake that day, refrigerating it overnight to ferment and develop flavors. This type of starter significantly boosts the flavor of the baked bread.

FOR THE PÂTÉ FERMENTÉE:

1 1/8 cups unbleached all-purpose flour

1 1/8 cups unbleached bread flour

3/4 teaspoon sea salt

1/2 teaspoon instant dry yeast

3/4 cup water

FOR THE DOUGH:

3 cups *pâté fermentée*

1 1/4 cups unbleached all-purpose flour

1 1/4 cups unbleached bread flour

3/4 teaspoon sea salt

1/2 teaspoon instant dry yeast

3/4 cup water

1/2 cup dried and coarsely ground spent beer grains

From Spent Grains to Breads

What's a brewery—or homebrew aficionado—to do with the leftover malted grain? Large breweries are giving it to farms for feed. If you're brewing smaller batches, you can rely on composting.

Or you can add the chewy, earthy grains to breads.

Get spent grains from your brew-enthusiast neighbor or your favorite brewpub hangout. It comes in a wet mass; you can add the wet grains to dough — like they do at City Bakery in their Spent Grain Baguette — or you can dry and grind them. Follow the instructions below:

Turn your oven to the lowest setting, 200° F.

Spread the wet spent grain in an even layer — no thicker than 1/2 inch — on a large, rimmed baking sheet. Bake it in the oven, stirring 2 or 3 times each hour, until the grains are very dry and not sticking together. This can take 4 to 7 hours, depending on how wet the grains were.

Once the grains are cool, you can process them, in batches of about 1 to 1 1/2 cups, in a food processor or blender until they are ground. Store them in an airtight container in the freezer.

Granola

—**Brian Dennehy,** CITY BAKERY

General Manager Brian Dennehy shared their wildly popular granola that's served layered in yogurt and fresh fruit parfaits. It's full of nuts and seeds, and not one bit of oil is used to bind it — just apple juice and local, Haw Creek honey.

Preheat the oven to 325° F. Combine the apple juice and honey in a small saucepan; bring to a boil. Remove from heat and stir in vanilla.

Combine the oats, wheat bran, pumpkin seeds, sunflower seeds, almonds, salt, and cinnamon in a large bowl. Pour the hot apple juice mixture over the oat mixture and mix just until it begins to hold together in clumps.

Spread the mixture in thin, even layers on 2 rimmed baking sheets. Bake until the granola is golden brown and dry, 30 to 40 minutes; stir the mixture and rotate the baking sheets in the oven every 15 minutes. Let the granola cool completely before stirring in raisins. Store in an airtight container.

MAKES 16 CUPS

COOK'S NOTE:
For gluten-free granola, substitute oat bran for wheat bran.

1 1/2 cups apple juice

3 tablespoons local honey

2 teaspoons vanilla extract

7 1/2 cups (1lb 14 oz) rolled oats

1 1/3 cups (6 ounces) wheat bran

1 1/4 cups (6 ounces) pumpkin seeds

1 1/4 cups (6 ounces) sunflower seeds

1 2/3 cups (6 ounces) sliced almonds

1 3/4 teaspoons (1/2 ounce) kosher or sea salt

2 1/4 teaspoons ground cinnamon

2 cups raisins

Sips, Small Plates
& Snacks

Spirit Savvy Cocktail Culture

In my former life, I worked happily in the Napa Valley wine business for 10 years. When I moved to Asheville, I became enamored with the vitality and enthusiasm of the bar community here. While a lot of attention is paid — and deservedly so — to the food we eat, where it comes from, and the science and artistry that goes into creating it, I found that same spirit has carried over into our cocktail culture.

I chose to anchor my work in this revitalized pre-Prohibition beverage industry. Spirit Savvy is an event production company highlighting talented bartenders and beautiful spirits who celebrate the well-made cocktail.

The Asheville cocktail scene is surely one to watch. Just like our food scene, our "spirit-savvy" scene is on par with that of much larger metropolitan cities. What makes our cocktail culture top-notch is the camaraderie fostered in our community of Asheville bartenders. Theirs is a tight group; they share new information and techniques with each other and really believe that "a rising tide lifts all ships."

My job allows me to witness the growth and development of Asheville's cocktail culture, and it's been incredibly rewarding to me personally as well as professionally. I am very proud to shine a light on our truly creative team of liquid chefs! Spirit Savvy, indeed.

—Mary Rich Hill

Sips, Small Plates & Snacks

Cocktails

End of the Tunnel • 53

Aardvark Gin Sing • 54

Nebulous • 55

Erato • 55

Hopped Scotchem • 56

Spiced Sorghum Syrup • 57

Sorghum Old Fashioned • 58

Knickerbocker • 58

Pocket Square for a Nehru Jacket• 59

FOR EACH COCKTAIL:

6 fresh sweet cherries, pitted

1/2 ounce (1 tablespoon) Luxardo liqueur (maraschino cherry liqueur)

1/2 ounce (1 tablespoon) agave nectar

1/4 ounce (1 1/2 teaspoons) tart balsamic vinegar reduction

3 pepper mill twists

1 3/4 ounce (3 tablespoons plus 1 1/2 teaspoons) Lunazul Blanco Tequila

Dash of chilled club soda

1/2 ounce (1 tablespoon) fresh lemon juice

Lemon zest

End *of the* Tunnel

—**Jason Crosby,** THE JUNCTION

When Tanya and Charles Triber opened their first Asheville restaurant, The Junction, they put together a food and beverage team they could consider family, with voices on establishing the vitality of the place. Jason Crosby was named bar manager; he charmed guests with confident hospitality, extensive knowledge of mixology, and creative drink interpretations, such as this cocktail.

Put the cherries, liqueur, agave nectar, balsamic reduction, and pepper in an old fashioned glass, and muddle. Add ice to come three-fourths of the way up the glass; add tequila and lemon juice; top with soda. Tumble the drink with a shaker and serve on the rocks with a lemon zest.

Jason Crosby, A Tribute
—**Tanya and Charles Triber,** OWNERS OF THE JUNCTION

Jason Crosby came to The Junction with an impressive résumé, with extensive experience in bartending and management, as well as time spent as a liquor purveyor.

But it was his personality and passion that got him the Bar Manager job and subsequently captured the attention of not only our guests and regulars, but also the Asheville and WNC communities as a whole. He was charismatic, he was funny, he was handsome, and he could make one hell of a drink. Jason used to say, "A cocktail has three key components: it should be beautiful, it should deliver on the nose, and of course be balanced on the palate",

A trained sommelier and dedicated craft beer connoisseur, Jason could just as easily chat beer and wine as the history of bourbon or the nuances of mescal. And he won over guests with his unforgettable smile and sense of humor.

After months of dealing with undetermined health problems, Jason was diagnosed with stage 4 pancreatic cancer on Valentine's day, 2013. He passed away in late October of the same year, leaving behind a wife and two young daughters. Though his times with us was far too brief, he left us with a wealth of memories and an incredible collection of cocktail recipes, one of which we are honored to share in his memory.

Fresh baby ginger

COOK'S NOTE:
Fresh baby ginger is less woody and the flesh is tender with a strong ginger flavor. When it's available at markets in early summer, grab it up. It freezes well, and can be sliced or grated without scraping off the woody peel.

FOR EACH COCKTAIL:

2 ounces gin

2 to 3 thin slices
fresh ginger

2 to 3 drops bitters

2 to 3 large ice cubes

Cold ginger beer

1 thin wedge lime

1 sprig mint

1 stalk lemon grass

Aardvark Gin Sing

—Rett Murphy, AARDVARK FARM

Owners Rett Murphy and Kathryn Skelley-Watts grow all-natural, high-quality fruits, herbs, and vegetables along the Cane River in Yancy County. Murphy offered this refreshing gin drink that combines the ginger, mint, and lemongrass they grow on the farm. It must taste even better when the ingredients are fresh and you are drinking your favorite gin; theirs is Hendrick's.

Muddle the gin and ginger together in a sturdy highball glass. Add bitters and ice cubes; fill with ginger beer. Squeeze in the lime and garnish with the mint. Soften the lemongrass stalk with the back of a knife and use as a stirrer.

Nebulous

—**Courteney Foster,** THE JUNCTION

Bar manager Courteney Foster is engaging and not afraid to flex her creativity muscles. Which she does, enlightening and entertaining patrons while she works her mixology magic. Is this cocktail "confused" as the name suggests? Not with this savvy person doing the mixing. It's masterful.

Salt half of the rim of a chilled coupe glass. Combine the cantaloupe juice, rum, lavender simple syrup, and lime juice in a shaker; shake well with ice and strain into the glass. Garnish with the mint.

FOR EACH COCKTAIL:

2 ounces (1/4 cup) fresh cantaloupe juice

1 1/2 ounces (3 tablespoons) light rum

1/2 ounce (1 tablespoon) lavender simple syrup

1/4 ounce (1 1/2 teaspoons) fresh lime juice

Sea salt

1 sprig fresh mint (as garnish)

Erato

—**Anthony Cerrato,** SOCIAL LOUNGE

Chef/owner Anthony Cerrato named this cocktail for the Greek muse Erato. Toasting to the goddess of music, dance, and song, the drink is also lovely and desirable…especially on the rooftop during our cool, breezy Asheville evenings.

Combine the main ingredients in a shaker. Shake and strain into a chilled juice glass. Garnish with an orange twist.

FOR EACH COCKTAIL:

2 ounces vodka

1 ounce cold pomegranate juice

3/4 ounce fresh lime juice

1/2 ounce cinnamon syrup

2 drops orange flower water

Orange twist (as garnish)

Hopped Scotchem

FOR EACH COCKTAIL:

1 1/2 ounces Hochstädter's Rock and Rye

3 dashes Bittermans Hopped Grapefruit Bitters

3 ounces Spiced Sorghum Syrup (page 57), heated

Clove-spiced grapefruit peel strip (as garnish)

—**Hank Fuseler,** RHUBARB

The beverage manager at Rhubarb shared the secret to this drink: a Spiced Sorghum Syrup using Noble Cider's semi-dry hard cider. Cheers to Hank Fuseler and John Fleer, chef/owner of Rhubarb, for the creative blend of tastes.

This cocktail closely resembles the Old Fashioned. The blend of straight rye whiskey, citrus, rock candy, and horehound flavors became an American saloon staple that survived prohibition and is still bottled today.

Combine the liquor, bitters, and sorghum syrup in a mug; float the garnish on the top. Serve warm.

Noble Cider: WNC's First Hard Cider

What does Noble Cider have in common with Appalachian settlers of the late 18th century? Both plant Newtown Pippins and other heirloom varieties for cider-making. Both are orchardists. Both introduce their native land to the delicious cider that is made from handpicked, local apple varieties. And if you walked through the entry of each homestead and establishment, you'd likely be offered a cold glass of crisp, homemade cider.

In early America, drinking cider was woven into the fabric of everyday life. From farmers to citizens, homesteads grew cider apple trees and fermented the fruit's juices into hard cider. Prohibition eliminated that tradition.

With our rich local history of apple farming, the team at Noble Cider has started the hard cider renaissance in Western North Carolina. They are planting and sourcing heritage and heirloom varieties for fermenting and crafting into semi-dry cider. Allowing the crisp apple aromas to dominate, the cider does not rely on sweetness for taste, but rather they depend on perfect quality apples to determine the drink...a windfall for Asheville mixologists.

For more info, go to noblecider.com.

Spiced Sorghum Syrup

MAKES ABOUT 2 CUPS

—**Hank Fuseler,** RHUBARB

1/2 cup mustard seeds

2 tablespoons cardamom pods

2 tablespoons coriander seeds

2 tablespoons whole cloves

4 cinnamon sticks, broken

Zest of 3 grapefruits, shaved off with vegetable peeler into strips

4 cups sorghum

2 cups water

4 cups Noble Cider

Beverage manager Hank Fuseler recommends using "the darker the better" sorghum for this recipe.

Combine the spices in a large, heavy saucepan; crush with a pestle until most of them are cracked. Place over medium heat and cook, shaking the pan occasionally, until the spices are slightly toasted and fragrant, about 2 minutes. Add the zest, sorghum and water; bring to a low boil. Reduce heat and simmer until thickened into a sugar syrup consistency, adjusting heat as necessary, 2 to 3 hours.

Strain the syrup through a wire mesh sieve into a bowl. Clean the saucepan. Return the syrup to the saucepan and stir in the cider; cook until hot. If you're using it right away for more than one cocktail, you can keep it warm over low heat. Otherwise, store it in a covered jar in the refrigerator for up to a month.

Sweet Sorghum

In the Appalachian Mountains, sorghum is known for its long-sweetnin' complex finish. In Southern backcountry sorghum-making tradition, you can often see it being pressed at festivals from local, hand-harvested cane in mule-drawn cane mills in late August through October.

Some folks refer to the rich-as-honey syrup as sorghum molasses, but it's not molasses. Though the consistencies and amber colors can be similar, molasses is a by-product of the sugar industry, whereas sorghum is the syrup produced when the extracted juice from the plant is boiled down. The sorghum plant is a member of the grass family and native to Africa. Introduced in America in the mid 1800s, it soon became the primary sweetener in the rural South before granulated sugar became cheap and plentiful. National sorghum production peaked at 24 million gallons in the 1880s. In 1975, just 2,400 acres produced less than 400,000 gallons of the syrup.

Today the number of farms who grow the grain, press the tender stalks, and boil down the juices into syrup has been on the rise. According to an article in the *Mountain Xpress* in Western North Carolina, "Sorghum syrup once flowed like creek water in the Southern Appalachians, and there are signs that this ultimate "slow food" may be flowing again. Local farmers have revved up production of the rich, old-fashioned syrup."

Sorghum is made in cool weather before freezing takes place, after the hot days of summer in which the plant grows and thrives. Look for local, small-batch jars of sorghum at farmers markets beginning in the fall.

Sorghum Old Fashioned

—**Clint Thorman,** KING DADDY'S

FOR EACH COCKTAIL:

2 ounces bourbon, such as Evan Williams

1 bar spoon sorghum

2 dashes Angostura bitters

Lemon twist (as garnish)

King Daddy's Chicken and Waffles in West Asheville is the newest restaurant of Chef John and Julie Stehling. If you love Early Girl, you must try the fried chicken and homemade waffles they dish up at King Daddy's — as decadent or as gluten-free as you want. Like Early Girl, it, too, is a gathering place; only this time, there is a bar — with a smart list of cocktails, sake and wine, and beer.

Here's a Southern twist on the classic Old Fashioned, lightly sweetened with sorghum instead of a sugar cube.

Stir the bourbon, sorghum, and bitters in a glass; add a few cubes of ice and garnish with a lemon twist.

Knickerbocker

—**Clint Thorman,** KING DADDY'S

Manager Clint Thorman says, "This recipe goes back to the mid-1800s. It is possibly the first punch-style cocktail on record."

Combine the rum, liqueur, lime juice, and raspberry syrup in a cocktail shaker. Shake well and strain over ice in a double old-fashioned glass. Garnish with a slice of lime.

FOR EACH COCKTAIL:

1 1/2 ounces (3 tablespoons) Mount Gay rum

1/2 ounce (1 tablespoon) Grand Marnier

3/4 ounce (1 1/2 tablespoons) fresh lime juice

1/4 ounce (1 1/2 teaspoons) raspberry syrup

Lime slice (as garnish)

Pocket Square *for a* Nehru Jacket

—Chall Gray, Thirsty Monk Pub & Brewery

Chall Gray, Vice President of Thirsty Monk, developed this cocktail especially for the book. He uses Amaro Ramazzotti, an Italian digestif of the bitters category: 33 herbs, roots, flowers, bark, and citrus peels are macerated in alcohol, mixed with sugar syrup, and aged. And the blood orange liqueur made exclusively on the island of Sicily, well....divine. (See what you think of a Margarita made with it!)

Muddle the cardamon pods, ginger, and bourbon in a cocktail shaker. Add the liquers. Add ice; shake, and strain into a chilled cocktail glass. Garnish with a twist of orange zest.

FOR EACH COCKTAIL:

3 cardamon pods

2 quarter-size slices peeled fresh ginger

1 1/2 ounces high proof bourbon, such as Baker's or Henry MeKenna 10-year

1/2 ounce Amaro Ramazzotti

1/2 ounce Solerno Blood Orange Liquer

Strip of orange zest

The Craft Beverage Institute of the Southeast: Training Grounds for a Local Industry

Witnessing the explosion of the craft beverage industry in Western North Carolina and throughout the Southeast, AB Technical Community College recognized a demand for topnotch quality training. If the market was growing at a rapid-fire pace, employment opportunities for a well-trained workforce would follow suit. AB Tech created The Craft Beverage Institute of the Southeast, offering curriculum and non-credit courses in brewing, distilling, fermentation, and related business practices.

Through accredited degrees and workforce development, the Institute prepares individuals for positions in brewery, distillery, or micro-winery operations and management, distribution, sales and marketing, customer service, as well as entrepreneurial ownership of new ventures.

For more info, visit abtech.edu.

BREW-Ed

—Cliff Mori, FOUNDER OF BREW-ED

In the late 1970s, a rebellion against the nation's one-flavor-fits-all model for beer production started in Northern California. The reawakening American palate demanded more than the corporate breweries could provide. Ramshackle startups began producing flavorful ales and lagers unlike anything most American beer drinkers had ever tasted before. As the industry grew, the desire for a more authentic beverage spread east.

In 1994, Highland Brewing Company initiated Asheville's brewing industry. The facts defy logic: a Jamaican-raised retired nuclear engineer of Chinese descent started a Scottish-themed brewery in the basement of a pizzeria. At the time, North Carolina had fewer than a dozen breweries; the mountain region had none. Yet the community's artistic vibe and support for local business helped this tiny brewery spark the beginning of a local industry that is expected to draw one million visitors a year to the area by 2016.

Since then, Western North Carolina has become home to over twenty-five breweries, and new ones seem to open nearly every season. The brewers work together within Asheville's Brewers Alliance to grow the industry and inspire each other to produce the best beers possible. That commitment has spurred many Asheville breweries on to earn medals at national competitions. The same community support that kept Highland Brewing in operation when no one in WNC knew what a craft beer was has led Asheville to win the title "Beer City USA" four times. Then, to seal the city's reputation, two of the biggest craft breweries in the country named Asheville as the home of their East Coast expansions.

Today, Asheville's beer scene remains unrivaled in the Southeast. You can find an enthusiastic community in the local breweries' tasting rooms or at one of the many annual beer festivals, such as Brewgrass or the Beer City Festival that wraps up Asheville's Beer Week each May. With the abundance and variety of the local beer scene, a one-flavor-fits-all mentality seems laughable.

Cliff Mori, BREW-ed's founder, was WNC's first Certified Cicerone®, recognized as an expert in matters pertaining to beer. Cliff's goal is to share his expertise with others. To that end, BREW-ed offers walking tours of several Asheville breweries, beer-themed private events, and beer education, as well as consulting for bars and restaurants.

Find out more at www.brew-ed.com.

Sips, Small Plates *&* Snacks

Small Plates

Deviled Eggs with Smoked Paprika Aioli,
Bacon Jam & Fried Sage • 64

Gravlax • 64

Jumbo Lump Crab Cakes • 65

Chicken Liver Pâté • 66

Venison Pâté • 67

Fried Green Tomato Napoleon • 68

Bruschetta with Fresh Ricotta &
Minted Lima & Green Pea Mash • 70

Crostini with Goat Cheese &
Lemon Chutney • 72

Deviled Eggs with
Smoked Paprika Aioli,
Bacon Jam, and Fried Sage
page 64

MAKES 2 DOZEN
OR 8 TO 12 SERVINGS

12 large eggs

Aioli and Smoked Paprika Aioli (page 203)

Salt and freshly ground pepper

About 3/4 cup Bacon Jam (page 207)

12 Fried Sage leaves (page 21)

COOK'S NOTE:
You may find it difficult to peel really fresh eggs; the albumen (egg white) tends to adhere to the inner shell membrane and make it tough to pull off larger pieces of the shell. Running the egg under cold water as you peel may help loosen the membrane from the cooked egg. Older eggs peel more easily.

Deviled Eggs *with* Smoked Paprika Aioli, Bacon Jam, *and* Fried Sage

—Sam Etheridge, AMBROZIA

Chef/owner Sam Etheridge's menu at Ambrozia is Southern-based, but also brings in Southwestern, Caribbean, Asian, and European influences. These deviled eggs are a popular first course.

Place the eggs in a large saucepan; cover with cold water. Bring to a boil over medium-high heat, gently turning eggs occasionally with a wooden spoon to keep the egg yolk in the center of the egg as it cooks. Remove from the heat; cover and let stand for 18 minutes. Drain the eggs and plunge into a bowl of ice water to cool.

Peel the eggs and cut them in half lengthwise. Scoop out the yolks and mix with 1/2 cup of the Aioli. Season to taste with salt and pepper.

Pipe or spoon the egg yolk mixture into the egg white cavities. Top each with a scant 1 1/2 teaspoons of the Bacon Jam and a Fried Sage leaf. Arrange the egg halves on serving plates and drizzle some Smoked Paprika Aioli onto the plates.

Gravlax

—Heidi Dunlap, THE WILD SALMON CO.

Owner Heidi Dunlap feels she has the best of both worlds: a life in Asheville tending her business when the salmon aren't running and when they are, life on her salmon-fishing boat in Alaska. Heidi explains, "We love what we do. We are blessed to take part in a natural cycle literally thousands of years in the making."

Heidi makes Gravlax during the Christmas holidays for family and friends. Here she shares her own recipe.

MAKES 8 APPETIZER SERVINGS

1 pound center-cut Wild Salmon Co. sockeye salmon fillet, thawed

1 1/2 tablespoons sea salt

1 heaping tablespoon sugar

1 teaspoon freshly ground pepper

1 tablespoon dry gin or tequila, optional

Fresh dill sprigs

Crostini, softened cream cheese, and fresh dill (as accompaniments)

Place the fillet, flesh side up, in the center of a large piece of plastic wrap.

Mix the salt, sugar, and pepper in a small bowl; add the liquor and mix well. Rub evenly on the salmon flesh. Arrange dill sprigs on the salmon. Fold the plastic wrap edges over the salmon to wrap it tightly. Wrap the package of salmon in a second piece of plastic wrap.

Place the wrapped and seasoned fillet on a plate. Place another plate, bottom side down, on the salmon; place two full 15- or 16-ounce cans of beans on the top plate to weight down the salmon. Place in the refrigerator. Flip the salmon package every 12 hours; let it cure in the refrigerator for 2 to 3 days.

Remove the salmon from the plastic wrapping; discard the dill and rinse the fillet well. Pat dry with paper towels. Cut the gravlax into paper-thin slices with a very sharp knife with the grain of the belly, pulling the slices away from the skin. Serve on crostini with cream cheese and fresh dill.

MAKES 4 TO 8 SERVINGS

1 large egg

1 cup mayonnaise

1 teaspoon dry mustard

1 teaspoon seafood seasoning, such as Old Bay

Juice of 1 lemon

3 1/2 cups diced (1/2-inch) tender white bread, crusts removed

2 pounds jumbo lump crabmeat

Remoulade (page 208)

Lemon slices (as garnish)

Jumbo Lump Crab Cakes

—**Denny Trantham,** FORMERLY OF GROVE PARK INN

"The trick in making succulent crab cakes is not to overmix them," explains chef Denny Trantham. *"After paying the price for jumbo lump crabmeat, the last thing you want to do is break up those massive chunks of sweetness."*

Whisk the egg in a large bowl; whisk in the mayonnaise, dry mustard, seafood seasoning, and the lemon juice. Stir in the bread, breaking up the large pieces. Fold in the crabmeat gently, taking care not to break up the lumps. Cover and refrigerate up to 6 hours or until you are ready to cook the patties.

Preheat the oven to 350° F. Form the crab mixture into 8 patties, and arrange them on a parchment-lined, rimmed baking sheet. Bake until cooked through, 10 to 15 minutes. Serve with Remoulade and lemon slices.

Chicken Liver Pâté

—**Steven Goff,** FORMERLY OF KING JAMES PUBLIC HOUSE

Chef Goff packs the pâté into 2-ounce canning jars — they make handy serving containers. Or spoon the pâté into bowls or half-pint jars for storing in the refrigerator, sealed with a layer of clarified butter.

MAKES ABOUT 12 SERVINGS

1 tablespoon canola oil

3 shallots, minced

1/2 cup bourbon

2 cups (about 1 pound) chicken livers

2 1/2 sticks (1 1/4 cups) unsalted butter, divided

1 cup cream

1 tablespoon Lusty Monk mustard

5 fresh thyme sprigs, leaves picked and stems discarded

Natural Pickles (page 211)

Heat a large, heavy skillet over medium heat; add the oil and heat until hot but not smoking. Add the shallots; cook, stirring frequently, until they are caramelized, about 8 minutes. Add the bourbon and stir to deglaze the skillet. Cook until almost all the bourbon has evaporated, 4 to 5 minutes. Add the chicken livers and cook halfway through; they should still be pink inside. Add the cream, mustard, and thyme, and simmer gently until the liver is fully cooked, about 10 minutes.

Meanwhile, melt 1 stick of the butter in a small saucepan. Remove from the heat and let it stand 3 minutes. Skim the froth from the butter and carefully pour the clarified butter into a small dish, leaving the milky solids in the bottom of the saucepan.

Melt the remaining 1 1/2 sticks of butter in another saucepan. Purée the chicken liver mixture and melted butter in a blender together; if necessary, purée in two batches. Pass through a chinoise or very fine mesh strainer. Spoon or pipe into small, 2-ounce jars while still hot.

Spoon enough of the clarified butter over the pâté in each jar just to cover in a thin layer. Seal the jars and refrigerate at least 4 hours or overnight. Serve with toasted French bread or crusty artisan grain bread slices and Natural Pickles.

66   Farmer & Chef Asheville

Venison Pâté

—**Brian Knickrehm,** RED STAG GRILL

Chef Brian Knickrehm serves this house-made pâté for the first course platter of prosciutto, San Giuseppe salamis, Brie cheese, Lusty Monk mustard, olives, pickled vegetables, and lavash crisps.

MAKES ABOUT 20 FIRST
COURSE SERVINGS

2 pounds venison shoulder

8 ounces pork
fatback, unsalted

1 1/2 tablespoons
kosher salt

1/2 teaspoon freshly
ground black pepper

2 large eggs

1/2 cup heavy
whipping cream

2 tablespoons brandy

2 tablespoons flour

1 small clove
garlic, minced

1 1/2 tablespoons
minced shallots

1 teaspoon minced
fresh thyme

1/4 teaspoon freshly
grated nutmeg

Using a food grinder with large die, grind the venison and pork; add the salt and pepper. Alternately use a food processor to chop the meat very finely. Cover and refrigerate.

Whisk the eggs, cream, brandy, and flour in a bowl. Combine the egg mixture, meats, garlic, shallots, thyme, and nutmeg in the bowl of a stand mixer fitted with the paddle attachment. Mix on low speed until well combined, about 2 minutes. Alternately, mix well with a wooden spoon.

Preheat the oven to 350° F. Line a 9-inch loaf pan with plastic wrap, allowing it to extend over the sides by 2 inches — spraying the pan first with cooking spray makes this task easier. Pack the meat mixture in the prepared loaf pan; fold the overhanging plastic wrap over the mixture. Cover tightly with aluminum foil.

Place the terrine in a baking pan. Add enough hot water to come about 1 to 2 inches up the sides of the terrine.

Bake until an instant-read thermometer placed in the center of the terrine reads 155° F., about 1 hour. Remove the terrine from the oven and allow it to cool for 1 hour. Then place another 9-inch loaf pan on top of the wrapped terrine, bottom side down; fill that loaf pan with cans to weight it down, pressing the terrine as it cools. Refrigerate overnight.

To serve, unwrap the terrine and invert it onto a platter, removing the foil and plastic wrap. Slice and serve with crusty bread and your favorite mustard.

Fried Green Tomato Napoleon

—John and Julie Stehling, EARLY GIRL EATERY

At Early Girl, chef/owner John Stehling serves this stack of crispy fried green tomatoes with goat cheese, basil, and salsa on a bed of their infamous stone-ground grits with a drizzle of vinaigrette. FGTs don't get any better.

To prepare the fried green tomatoes, remove the cores from the tomatoes; trim the ends, and slice them about 1/2 inch thick. Arrange them on a rack and let them stand for 15 to 20 minutes.

Combine the flour, salt, and pepper in a shallow dish. Whisk the eggs and milk in another shallow dish. Combine the breadcrumbs, Parmesan, parsley, and orange zest in a third shallow dish.

Heat about 1/2 inch of oil in a large, heavy skillet over medium heat until hot but not smoking. Meanwhile, dredge the tomato slices first in the flour mixture, then in the egg wash, then in the bread crumbs.

Fry in small batches (if you crowd the slices, they will not crisp), turning once, until they are golden brown on both sides. Return them to the rack and let them drain.

To serve, spoon the hot grits onto 6 serving plates, dividing evenly. Center one fried tomato slice on each plate. Sprinkle one-third of the goat cheese and one-third of the chopped basil on the slices, dividing evenly. Repeat the stacking with the remaining fried green tomato slices, cheese, and basil. Top each stack with 2 tablespoons salsa and drizzle with 1 or 2 tablespoons of the Balsamic Vinaigrette.

MAKES 6 SERVINGS

FOR FRIED GREEN TOMATOES:

5 green tomatoes

2 cups flour

1 tablespoon salt

1 teaspoon freshly ground black pepper

2 eggs

1/4 cup milk

3 cups breadcrumbs

1/4 cup freshly grated Parmesan

2 tablespoons fresh parsley, minced

Grated zest of 1 orange

Vegetable oil for frying

FOR SERVING:

2 ounces goat cheese

1/4 cup chopped fresh basil leaves

3/4 cup salsa

1/4 cup plus 2 tablespoons Balsamic Vinaigrette (page 201)

About 2 cups hot, cooked stone-ground grits

Bruschetta *with* Fresh Ricotta *&* Minted Lima *&* Green Pea Mash

—Debby Maugans, FOR THE SEASONAL SCHOOL OF CULINARY ARTS

MAKES ABOUT
2 DOZEN APPETIZERS

FOR THE BRUSCHETTA:

1/2 narrow loaf French or Italian bread, sliced diagonally 3/4-inch thick

2 to 3 tablespoons extra-virgin olive oil

1/2 teaspoon coarse sea salt, or to taste

FOR THE RICOTTA:

1 quart whole milk

1/2 cup heavy cream

1/2 teaspoon salt

1 1/2 tablespoons lemon juice

This summery bruschetta was the first course during one wine tasting. A soft pillow of homemade ricotta was spread on toast, topped with a lightly minted lima bean and garden pea pesto; the dish was paired with a refreshing Portugese Vinho Verde.

To prepare the bruschetta, preheat the oven to 400° F. Arrange the bread slices on a foil-lined baking sheet. Brush the bread slices liberally with olive oil and sprinkle lightly with salt. Bake until they are toasty, 8 to 10 minutes. Let them cool.

To prepare the ricotta, line a colander with 2 layers of cheesecloth and place it over a large bowl. Combine the milk, cream, and salt in a heavy saucepan; bring to a boil over medium heat, stirring to prevent scorching. Reduce the heat to low and stir in the lemon juice; simmer, stirring gently and constantly, until the mixture curdles. Let the mixture stand 10 minutes; pour it gently through the lined colander. Let it drain 30 to 45 minutes, pouring off the liquid as it collects. Transfer the cheese to a bowl; cover and refrigerate until well chilled and up to 2 days.

Gently pour the mixture through the cheesecloth-lined strainer. Let it drain for 1 minute. (The curds will still be wet.) Transfer the curds to a bowl; cover and refrigerate until well chilled, about 2 hours and up to 2 days.

FOR THE MINTED PEA MASH:

1 cup fresh or frozen, thawed baby lima beans

1 cup fresh or frozen green peas

1 clove garlic

3 tablespoons fresh mint leaves

3 tablespoons fresh cilantro leaves

2 tablespoons freshly grated Parmesan cheese

1 tablespoon extra-virgin olive oil

2 teaspoons freshly grated lemon rind

1/4 teaspoon salt, or to taste

FOR SERVING:

Freshly ground pepper

Extra-virgin olive oil

Microgreens, optional (as garnish)

To prepare the lima and pea mash, cook the lima beans in boiling, salted water until tender, about 20 minutes. In the meantime, add the peas to the cooking water after 15 minutes of cooking time. Drain well and let them cool completely.

With the food processor running, drop the garlic through the food chute and process until the garlic is minced. Add the mint, cilantro, Parmesan, and olive oil; pulse until the herbs are minced. Add the lima beans, peas, lemon rind, and salt; pulse until the mixture is coarsely mashed.

To serve, spread about 2 teaspoons of the ricotta on each piece of toast; then spread about 2 teaspoons of the lima and pea mash on top of the ricotta. Sprinkle lightly with pepper; if desired, drizzle each bruschetta with about 1/4 teaspoon of olive oil. Garnish with the microgreens or pea tendrils, if desired.

Crostini *with* Goat Cheese *&* Lemon Chutney

—Traci Taylor, FIG

According to chef Traci Taylor, the sweet-tart lemony chutney recipe makes enough for leftovers. We just had to taste it with goat cheese and found it's a perfect marriage for a quick appetizer on toasts or crackers.

MAKES 1 DOZEN SERVINGS

12 diagonally-cut (3/4-inch thick) slices French bread

2 to 3 tablespoons extra-virgin olive oil

3 to 4 ounces goat cheese, softened

About 1/2 cup Lemon Chutney (page 205)

Preheat the oven to 400° F. Arrange the bread slices on a foil-lined baking sheet. Brush the bread slices liberally with olive oil. Bake until toasty, 8 to 10 minutes. Let them cool.

To serve, spread about 2 teaspoons of goat cheese on each piece of toast. Top each with about 2 teaspoons of Lemon Chutney.

Sips, Small Plates & Snacks

Snacks

Fig & Pig Pizza • 76

Chocolate Covered Bacon • 77

Asiago Truffled Popcorn • 77

White Tire Dip & Pretzel Bites • 78

Pimento Cheese • 78

Baked Pack Square with Peach Chutney • 79

Simple Salsa • 80

Salsa Verde • 80

Cold Smoked Trout Wrap with Goat Cheese
& Hudson's Smoked Tomato Jam• 81

Candied Marcona Almonds • 81

Baba Ghanoush • 82

Fig and Pig Pizza
on page 76

Fig & Pig Pizza

—Laura & Ben Mixson, PIZZA PURA

COOK'S NOTE:
Leftover fig purée can be stored, refrigerated, in an airtight container for up to a week.

MAKES 1 LARGE PIZZA

1 pound dried black mission figs

1/2 teaspoon salt, or to taste

1/4 teaspoon freshly ground pepper, or to taste

1 ounce pancetta, cooked and drained

1 (9 1/2-ounce) dough ball

1 clove garlic, very thinly sliced

About 2 tablespoons extra-virgin olive oil

Handful of fresh baby arugula

1/2 to 2/3 cup (about 2 1/2 ounces) gorgonzola cheese, crumbled

1/4 cup (about 2 ounces) fresh Kadota or Calimyrna figs, quartered

What you see first when you enter Pizza Pura is the mighty indoor wood-burning oven that fire-cooks the pizza — it's artistically covered in a mosaic of glass beads. Chef/owner Laura Mixson showed up one day with craft supplies and freehanded the work of art on the oven. With that much pizza-oven love, you know what comes out of it has to be impressive.

To make the fig paste, soak the black mission figs overnight in warm water to just cover them (about 4 cups); drain and reserve the soaking liquid. Using a food processor, purée the drained figs until smooth, adding enough of the soaking liquid to make a thick paste that is almost pourable. Season with 1/2 teaspoon salt and 1/4 teaspoon pepper, or to taste.

Cut the pancetta into strips. Heat a heavy skillet over medium heat; add the pancetta strips and sauté until they are browned and fat is rendered out. Transfer to a paper towel-lined plate to drain.

To make the pizza, place a pizza stone on the lowest rack in the oven and preheat the oven to 450°F. If you don't have a pizza stone, stack 2 heavy baking sheets together and line the top one with a piece of parchment paper.

Sprinkle a pizza peel or the parchment on the prepared baking sheet lightly with the cornmeal. Roll the pizza dough ball to a 12-inch round; lift and place it on the pizza peel, directly on the cornmeal. Carefully spread 3 to 4 tablespoons of the fig paste over the dough to within 1/2 inch from the edge. Top with sliced garlic and drizzle with the olive oil. Scatter the baby arugula, gorgonzola, pancetta, and fresh figs over the top.

Slide the pizza onto the preheated stone or place the baking sheet stack in the oven. Bake until the crust is golden brown, 15 to 20 minutes. Transfer to a cutting board, slice and serve.

Chocolate Covered Bacon

—**Anthony Cerrato,** SOCIAL LOUNGE

Sweet meets salty in a perfect combination of delicious chocolate and smoky bacon: perfect bar food from chef/owner Anthony Cerrato.

Preheat the oven to 350º F. Place bacon on a rimmed baking sheet.

Mix the brown sugar, coriander, and 1/4 teaspoon red pepper; sprinkle on bacon. Bake until crispy, about 14 minutes. Place bacon on paper towels to drain and cool.

Place the chocolate in the top a double boiler. Set it over barely simmering water in the sauce pan. Cook until the chocolate melts, stirrring it frequently with a rubber spatula once the outer edges start to melt. Remove from the waterbath.

Dip each piece of bacon into the warm chocolate mixture, coating it well. Place the coated pieces on a parchment-lined baking sheet. If desired, sprinkle with the coconut, sea salt, chopped nuts, or dried fruit. Let the bacon stand until the chocolate is set before serving.

MAKES 4 TO 6 SERVINGS

1/2 cup brown sugar

1/4 teaspoon ground coriander

3/4 teaspoon ground red pepper, divided

1 pound thick-cut bacon (about 16 pieces)

4 cups (about 1 1/2 pounds) chopped bittersweet dark chocolate (60% cacao)

1 teaspoon salt

1/2 teaspoon ground cinnamon

Flaked coconut, coarse sea salt, finely chopped nuts, or dried fruit (as garnish)

Asiago Truffle Popcorn

—**Anthony Cerrato,** SOCIAL LOUNGE

MAKES 3 SERVINGS

1 (3-ounce) bag of microwave popcorn or 1/4 cup of popcorn kernels, popped in a saucepan with 1 tablespoon vegetable oil

1 teaspoon truffle oil

2 ounces Asiago cheese, grated

1 scallion, finely chopped

Chef/owner Anthony Cerrato opened the wall between Strada and an adjacent bar space, forming the Social Lounge. This is one of the popular snacks served on the breezy rooftop — a lovely spot to enjoy tapas and cocktails, with a birds' eye view of Asheville's nightlife.

In a bowl, drizzle the truffle oil over the hot, freshly-popped popcorn in a large bowl; toss gently to mix. Add the cheese and green onion, and toss again.

White Tire Dip *&* Pretzel Bites

—**Leisa Payne,** THIRSTY MONK

This warm cheese dip showcases Fat Tire beer from New Belgium — one of the latest breweries to take root in Asheville. According to chef Leisa Payne, it's a menu favorite at the downtown pub.

Preheat the oven to 400° F. Slightly thaw the pretzels; cut them into bite-size pieces. Place them on a rimmed baking sheet, spacing them 1 1/2 inches apart; mist the pieces with water and sprinkle with the salt. Bake until hot, 4 to 5 minutes.

Toss the cheese and flour, mixing well. Bring the cream and beer to a simmer in a medium saucepan over medium heat; simmer 3 minutes. Add the cheese mixture and cook, stirring constantly, until the cheese is melted. Season to taste with the salt and pepper. Serve in a glass with the pretzel pieces.

MAKES 2 TO 3 SERVINGS

1 or 2 packages frozen soft pretzels, such as Super Pretzels

1 cup (4 ounces) shredded sharp white Cheddar cheese

1 tablespoon plus 1 teaspoon all-purpose flour

1/2 cup plus 2 tablespoons heavy whipping cream

1/4 cup New Belgium Fat Tire Amber Ale

1/4 teaspoon salt, or to taste

1/4 teaspoon ground white pepper, or to taste

Pimento Cheese

MAKES ABOUT 4 3/4 CUPS

4 cups (1 pound) shredded Cheddar cheese

4 ounces cream cheese, softened

1/4 cup mayonnaise

1/2 cup diced roasted red bell pepper or drained, canned pimiento

2 teaspoons Texas Pete® hot sauce

1 tablespoon dill pickle juice

1 teaspoon Worcestershire sauce

1/2 teaspoon garlic powder

1/4 teaspoon salt, or to taste

1/2 teaspoon freshly ground pepper, or to taste

—**Mark Demarco,** CEDRIC'S TAVERN

To roast the red peppers, char on all sides over an open flame. Place in a bowl and cover with plastic wrap until they cool; the peppers will sweat and the skin will loosen. Peel off the skin. Chef Demarco warns not to rinse them because you'll wash away the flavor.

Combine the Cheddar cheese and cream cheese in a large bowl; mix well. Stir in the mayonnaise, roasted pepper, hot sauce, pickle juice, Worcestershire sauce, garlic powder, salt, and pepper. Store in an airtight container in the refrigerator.

Baked Pack Square
with Peach Chutney

—**Jennifer Perkins,** LOOKING GLASS CREAMERY

Owner Jen Perkins shared this delicious appetizer using the distinctive Pack Square, an award-winning cheese from Looking Glass Creamery, made brie-style in a square format. The milk comes from the Pack Family Dairy, which — along with Pack Square Park in downtown Asheville — inspired the name. The cheese has a buttery flavor, drawing from the rich taste of grass-fed Jersey cow milk. Visit the Cheese Shop or order it online at www.ashevillecheese.com.

MAKES 8 SERVINGS

1/2 (17-ounce) package frozen puff pastry, thawed according to package directions

1 Looking Glass Creamery Pack Square cheese

1 large egg, lightly beaten with 1 tablespoon water

Peach Chutney (page 207)

Fresh mint (as garnish)

Crackers

Preheat the oven to 400° F. Unfold the puff pastry on a lightly floured work surface. Place the Pack Square cheese in the center; fold the pastry edges up and over the cheese to enclose it. Trim off the excess pastry and pinch the edges together to seal the pastry edges.

Brush the seams with the beaten egg and place it, seam side down, on a rimmed baking sheet or in a baking dish. Brush the top with the egg mixture, if desired, to give it a golden hue.

Bake until the pastry is puffed and golden and the cheese is soft, 20 to 25 minutes. Let it stand for 15 to 20 minutes before serving. Serve warm with Peach Chutney; garnish with mint and serve with crackers.

WNC Cheese Trail

Hard, soft, fresh, aged, goat's milk, cow's milk: Western North Carolina's talented farmstead and artisan cheese makers do it all. And there's perhaps no better way to sample their award-winning creations than by heading out on the WNC Cheese Trail!

In 2012, the region's cheese makers banded together to form a nonprofit cheese making cooperative to support each other and promote our region's thriving cheese culture. Now, along with a group of local food-loving sponsors and supportive businesses, they're putting WNC cheese on the map — literally. Pick up their guide from members, at the ASAP office (Appalachian Sustainable Agriculture Project, page 105), or at the Asheville Convention and Visitors Bureau, then set out to see their operations firsthand.

And don't forget a cooler! Because after you taste it, you'll want to take some home.

Simple Salsa

—Brian Sonoskus, TUPELO HONEY CAFÉ

MAKES 1 CUP

When vine-ripe tomatoes aren't in season, use Roma tomatoes for best flavor.

Combine three fourths of the chopped tomatoes, the jalapeño pepper, cilantro, lemon juice, salt, and pepper in a bowl. Garnish with the remaining chopped tomatoes and cilantro sprigs. Keep in an airtight container in the refrigerator for up to 7 days.

From *Tupelo Honey Café: New Southern Flavors from the Blue Ridge Mountains* by Elizabeth Sims and chef Brian Sonoskus, Andrews McMeel Publishing, 2014. Used with permission.

4 large ripe Roma tomatoes, seeded and chopped

1/3 jalapeño pepper, seeded and minced

2 tablespoons minced fresh cilantro

1 teaspoon freshly squeezed lemon juice

1/8 teaspoon salt

1/8 teaspoon freshly ground black pepper

Fresh cilantro sprigs

Salsa Verde

—Jennifer Perkins, LOOKING GLASS CREAMERY

MAKES ABOUT 10 CUPS

2 poblano peppers

2 1/2 pounds tomatillos

1 small onion, halved crosswise

1 head garlic, cut in half crosswise

3 cups fresh cilantro leaves, chopped

Juice and grated zest of 1 lime

1/2 teaspoon salt, or to taste

Green salsas, made from tomatillos instead of tomatoes, almost always have mild heat. The tangy, smoky flavor comes from roasting the vegetables first.

Position the oven rack so that the vegetables will be positioned 4 to 6 inches from the heat source. Preheat the oven broiler. Lightly oil a rimmed baking sheet.

Arrange the peppers, tomatillos, onion, and garlic, cut sides up, on the baking sheet. Broil until the vegetables are soft and charred, turning them as necessary, 8 to 10 minutes. As the vegetables are cooked to desired doneness, remove them with tongs and place them on a plate; cover with plastic wrap and let them cool.

Remove the skins from the tomatillos. Peel the skins from the poblanos, remove the stems and seeds, and pop the garlic cloves out of their skins. Place them all in a blender; add the cilantro, lime juice and zest, and salt. Process until the mixture is the desired consistency, scraping the blender as necessary.

Cold Smoked Trout Wrap *with* Goat Cheese *and* Hudson's Smoked Tomato Jam

—**Charles Hudson,** SUNBURST TROUT FARMS

MAKES 4 SERVINGS

8 ounces soft goat cheese or cream cheese

1/2 cup Hudson's Smoked Tomato Jam

4 flour tortillas

4 (4-ounce) Sunburst cold smoked trout fillets

4 lettuce leaves or 1 cup fresh sprouts

Here's a tip from Research and Develpopment Chef, Charles Hudson of Sunburst Trout Farms, turn the wraps into hors d'oeuvres by layering thin cucumber slices on the trout instead of the lettuce. Roll tightly, wrap, and chill; then slice to serve.

Stir together the cheese and Smoked Tomato Jam. Briefly warm each tortilla in a skillet over medium-low heat, about 20 seconds: spread one-fourth of the cheese mixture over each. Top with trout and lettuce, and roll up. Diagonally slice the wraps to serve.

Candied Marcona Almonds

—**Jake Schmidt,** EDISON CRAFT ALES + KITCHEN

Popular in Mediterranean countries and more recently in the U.S., the prized almonds are sweeter and softer than our native variety. The flavor is reminiscent of almond essence that is used in baked goods.

Preheat the oven to 250° F. Line a large, rimmed baking sheet with parchment paper.

Stir the brown sugar, salt, and cayenne pepper together in a large bowl; add the almonds. Sprinkle with the water and toss until the almonds are evenly coated. Place the nuts on the lined baking sheet and spread them in a single layer.

Roast the almonds until the sugar has caramelized and turned a rich brown, stirring every 10 minutes. Let them cool. Store in an airtight container at room temperature for 1 week.

MAKES 1 POUND

1 tablespoon light brown sugar

1 teaspoon salt

1/2 teaspoon cayenne pepper

1 pound raw Marcona almonds

1 tablespoon water

Baba Ghanoush

—Suzy Phillips, GYPSY QUEEN FOOD TRUCK

The garlic-y eggplant spread that Suzy Phillips makes is simple and outstanding because she knows how to pick out quality eggplant. Look for unblemished, firm eggplant that does not feel spongy. Phillips chars the whole eggplant on a charcoal grill and saves some of the peel to add to the mixture. "It adds a beautiful smokiness to the dip — a typical Lebanese flavor."

Preheat a grill for medium-high heat. Prick the eggplants with a fork and grill them, turning to char all sides, until charred and tender, 25 to 30 minutes. Alternately, you can preheat the oven to 350° F. and roast the eggplants for 45 minutes.

MAKES ABOUT 2 CUPS

2 (1-pound) eggplants

3 tablespoons tahini

1 to 3 cloves garlic, peeled and finely crushed, to taste

1 tablespoon fresh lemon juice

1/2 teaspoon kosher salt, or to taste

Chopped parsley, olive oil, paprika, pine nuts, or pomegranate seeds (as garnish)

Suzy Philllips **in her Gypsy Queen food truck**

Asheville's food truck business is booming, setting up shop in The Lot (a downtown parking lot on Coxe Avenue reserved just for food truck and customer parking) and in front of area restaurants who open their lots during non-business hours. They travel from farmer's markets to festivals, breweries, weddings, fundraisers, and private parties.

Customers can choose their meals by location or cuisine. Search for Asheville Food Trucks on Facebook, or keep track of them at .www.asheville-foodtrucks.com. From Lebanese to Portuguese, fitness fuel to BBQ, tacos to grilled cheese sandwiches and more, Asheville just keeps on truckin'.

Fried Cauliflower from Gypsy Queen Food Truck.

Let the eggplants stand for about 5 minutes; use a thin, sharp knife to help you remove the peel while handling carefully. (They are best peeled while they are still hot.) Save about a quarter of the charred peel and discard the rest.

Place the eggplant in a colander; let stand 15 to 20 minutes to remove some of the liquid. Then place the eggplant in a large bowl and mash with a fork or a pastry blender along the grain of the pulp. Stir in the tahini, lemon juice, salt, and 1 or 2 cloves of the garlic; taste and add more garlic and salt, if desired.

Spoon into a shallow bowl; if desired, garnish with parsley, drizzled olive oil, paprika, pine nuts, or pomegranate seeds.

The BLTP from Nate Kelly, Lowdown Food Truck

Appalachian Homegrown

These Mountains Speak

ESSAY

The Appalachian Mountains are the oldest and most bio-diverse on earth. Home to a lush and verdant temperate rain forest, they roll into a smoky blue horizon. These mountains harbor ancient secrets and teach earth's rhythms.

Farming in Appalachia requires following the sun, hunting shadows, and hoarding daylight. Farming families understand that coaxing food from mountain soil requires a reverence for the challenging terrain. It takes ingenuity to survive the early spring frosts, vigilance to overcome the heavy rains, and prayer to endure the lingering seasonal drought. Mountain farming means watching the signs, planting by the moon, and studying the almanac.

Come harvest time, the farmers gather sweet potatoes, apples, blueberries, ramps, pumpkins, cresses, cabbages, corn and squash and beans and tomatoes. With deep gratitude, they set tables laden with bright oranges, deep greens, succulent reds, and golden yellows. Year after year, they prepare family recipes with their bounty. Then it's time for canning, pickling, curing, and drying. Time to make jam, chow chow, jelly, kraut, and butter — all for meals shared around a blazing wood stove when the mountains have fallen under winter's reign.

We stay here because our mountains speak to our hearts. They whisper in our ears to marvel at their beauty and majesty. They challenge us to climb and explore and discover their secrets. They inspire us to place seeds in the ground. They feed our spirit, our minds, and our bodies with their magnificent glory and generous mineral-rich yield. They call on us to be watchful sentinels of our shared air and land and water. They speak to us, and we vow to listen, to honor, and to protect..

—**Elizabeth Sims, author**

Appalachian Homegrown

Chillin'

Rosemary Lemonade with Sage Honey • 88

Chilled Peach Gazpacho with Crisp Country
Ham & Toasted Apricot Kernal Granola • 90

Strawberry Basil Smoothie • 93

Bloody Mary Gazpacho • 93

Rosemary Lemonade with
Sage Honey on page 88

Rosemary Lemonade
with Sage Honey

—**Laurey Masterton,** LAUREY'S

MAKES ABOUT 11 CUPS

1/2 cup honey, preferably sage honey

4 fresh rosemary sprigs

12 lemons, or enough to make about 2 cups juice

Additional rosemary sprigs for garnish

We excerpt this refreshing lemonade recipe from chef Laurey Masterton's book, The Fresh Honey Cookbook. *In her words,"This recipe started with my friend Chris, who shared many of her favorite recipes from her travels in Mexico. This is one of my favorites, though her version was made with sugar. The honey here adds a layer of complexity that makes the flavor so much more interesting. We now serve her not-too-sweet rosemary lemonade in my cafe on a regular basis, varying the type of honey according to availability."*

To make a simple syrup, combine the honey and 1/2 cup water in a small saucepan and bring to a boil over high heat.

Remove from the heat and add 4 of the rosemary sprigs; let them steep in the syrup until it has cooled to room temperature. Remove the rosemary and discard.

Squeeze the lemons and combine with the rosemary honey syrup in a large pitcher or container; stir in 8 cups water. Pour into ice-filled glasses and garnish with rosemary sprigs.

Laurey Masterton, A Tribute
by Emily and Adam Thome

If you ever met Laurey Masterton, you'd surely not forget her. "She was a force of nature," to quote a friend. Some people knew Laurey for the community projects she got behind or for her work with children in our city schools to develop healthy eating habits. Others knew her because she fed them — and fed them well.

When Laurey touched your life, you were never the same afterward. It was impossible not to look at life differently after a conversation with Laurey. It's hard to say exactly what it was about her that shifted you inside. It may have been her openness and willingness to try anything and everything that presented itself to her. It may have been the quiet fight in her that led her to never give up and the grace she had when she knew she'd been beaten (the unicycle comes to mind here). She truly lived by the words: "Don't Postpone Joy." As should we all.

Chilled Peach Gazpacho *with* Crispy Country Ham *&* Toasted Apricot Kernel Granola

—**Jake Schmidt,** EDISON CRAFT ALES + KITCHEN

Chef Jake Schmidt adds an additional layer of taste and texture to the purée with a spoonful of granola in the bottom of the bowl and, occasionally, a sprinkling of crispy country ham.

Preheat the oven to 300° F. Line a rimmed baking sheet and a square baking pan with heavy-duty foil.

Cut the peaches in half; remove the pits. Place them, skin sides down, on the prepared baking sheet. Brush the cut sides with 3 to 4 tablespoons of olive oil and sprinkle them lightly with 1/2 teaspoon salt.

At the same time, toss the onions with 2 tablespoons of olive oil, smoked paprika, and 1/4 teaspoon salt in the prepared baking pan; bring the edges of the foil over the onions and crimp to seal the package.

Roast the peaches and onions until they are very tender, about 45 minutes. Remove from the oven and let them cool completely. Remove the peels from the peaches.

Working in batches, place the peaches, onions, and accumulated juices of both in a blender; process until the mixture is smooth and transfer to a pitcher or large bowl. Add the cucumber juice, vinegar, lime juice, white soy sauce, and ground red pepper, stirring well to blend. Cover and refrigerate until chilled.

To serve, spoon about 2 tablespoons of the granola into each bowl; pour 2/3 cup of the gazpacho over it. Sprinkle with the crispy ham bits or garnish with an edible flower.

MAKES 6 TO 8 SERVINGS

10 large fresh peaches, unpeeled

About 1/3 cup extra-virgin olive oil, divided

Salt

1 medium onion, cubed

1/4 teaspoon smoked paprika

Juice from 2 medium cucumbers

1 cup rice vinegar

Grated zest and juice of 3 limes

1/4 teaspoon ground red pepper, or to taste

3 slices good quality country ham, finely diced and cooked until crispy

Toasted Apricot Kernel Granola (page 92)

INGREDIENTS NOTE:
White soy sauce is brewed from lighter wheat, which gives this soup soy flavor without throwing off the colors of the peaches. Look for it in specialty markets or order it online.

COOK'S NOTE:
To render cucumber juices, grate the cucumbers over a bowl, then push the mixture through a fine mesh sieve to extract as much juice as possible; discard the solids.

1 cup rolled oats

1 cup toasted
 apricot kernels

1/4 cup plus 2 tablespoons
firmly packed
dark brown sugar

1/4 cup plus
2 tablespoons maple syrup

1/4 cup vegetable oil

3/4 teaspoon salt

1 cup finely diced dried
apricots

INGREDIENTS NOTE:
Toasted apricot kernels can
be found in some health
food stores and online.

Toasted Apricot Kernel Granola

—**Jake Schmidt,** EDISON CRAFT ALES + KITCHEN

Preheat the oven to 250 degrees F. Combine the oats, apricot kernels, and brown sugar in a large bowl.

Combine the syrup, oil, and salt in another bowl, stirring well. Pour over the oats mixture and toss until well mixed. Pour onto 2 rimmed baking sheets.

Bake until golden brown, about 1 hour and 15 minutes, stirring every 15 minutes. Let the oat mixture cool; then transfer to a large bowl and mix in the apricots. Store in an airtight covered container.

The Evolution of a "Foodtopian Community"

Nestled in the highest peaks in the East, Asheville boasts a culinary culture that is unique to the Southern Appalachians. We believe our Southern roots, independent mountain spirit, and "locavore" sensibilities have created a food community that transcends the farm-to-table movement, culminating in an all-out way of life.

The Asheville community boasts over 250 independent restaurants that work in a collaborative nature with the local farmers, artisans, and foragers. They express themselves through epicurean innovation, resulting in cuisine that has a distinctive Southern fusion with a broad worldview.

Recognizing this exceptional distinction, the term Foodtopia® was coined by the Asheville Convention & Visitors Bureau in order to capture and express the distinctive spirit of this vibrant culinary community. The underlying concept of Foodtopia® goes beyond singular chefs, growers, and artisans; instead, it encompasses all of them.

Read more at exploreasheville.com/foodtopia/

Strawberry Basil Smoothie

—**Randy Talley,** GREEN SAGE COFFEEHOUSE AND CAFÉ

MAKES 2 SERVINGS

1 cup unsweetened almond milk

1 cup fresh or frozen strawberries

1 cup fresh baby spinach

3 fresh basil leaves

1 medium banana, sliced and frozen

Juice of 1/4 lemon or lime

Creative dishes with a mix of natural, local, organic ingredients go into all the meals served at Green Sage, living up to their motto: "Eat healthy, live healthy." All of the ingredients for this nourishing smoothie go into the blender — no need for special equipment. Serve it for breakfast all day or as a pick-me-up, just like they do at the café.

Combine all the ingredients in a blender; process until smooth.

Bloody Mary Gazpacho

—**Debby Maugans, author**

This is just what you need to start off a tailgate party or brunch. Serve in bowls, old-fashioned glasses, or even oversized martini glasses.

Process the tomatoes and 1/2 cup tomato juice in a food processor until coarsely puréed. Add the cucumber, peppers, and onion; pulse until they are finely chopped. Pour into a large pitcher; stir in the remaining tomato juice, lime juice, Worcestershire sauce, and celery salt. Stir in vodka; season with salt and hot sauce to taste. Cover and refrigerate at least 4 hours or until chilled.

To serve, peel, pit and dice the avocado; toss with remaining 1 tablespoon lime juice. Ladle gazpacho into glasses and sprinkle avocado on top. Garnish as desired.

MAKES 12 CUPS

3 cups coarsely chopped tomatoes

6 cups tomato juice, divided

1 1/2 cups chopped peeled and seeded cucumber

2 large roasted red bell peppers, chopped

1/4 cup chopped onion

5 tablespoons fresh lime juice, divided

1 tablespoon Worcestershire sauce

1 teaspoon celery salt

3/4 cup vodka or tequila

Sea salt and hot sauce to taste

2 avocados

Garnishes: lime wedges, celery stalks, cucumber sticks

Appalachian Homegrown

Fresh Picked Salads

Black-Eyed Peas Relish with
Heirloom Tomatoes • 96

Marinated Tomato Salad with
Kalamata Olives & Cheese • 97

Spring Pea & Mushroom Salad
with Beef Bacon • 97

Celery & Gorgonzola Salad • 98

Hendersonville County Mutsu Apple Salad with
Candied Marcona Almonds • 99

Bacon Dijon Vinaigrette • 99

Grilled Romaine Salad with Grilled Chicken, Curry
Viniagrette & Lemon Chutney • 100

Raw Citrus Kale Salad • 102

Fried Green Tomatoes with Watercress,
Pepper Jelly, & Blue Cheese Dressing • 103

Grilled Stuffed Avocado • 102

Tabouleh • 105

Pantry Salad • 106

From top to bottom:
Raw Citrus Kale Salad,
Spring Pea &
Mushroom Salad,
Marinated Tomato Salad
with Kalamata Olives
& Cheese

FOR THE DRESSING:

1/4 cup plus 2 tablespoons extra-virgin olive oil

1/4 cup fresh lemon juice

1/4 cup white wine vinegar

3 tablespoons minced garlic, rinsed in cold water and drained

1 tablespoon minced fresh oregano

1/4 teaspoon crushed red pepper, optional

1/2 teaspoon kosher salt, or to taste

1 teaspoon freshly ground pepper, or to taste

FOR THE SALAD:

5 cups cooked black-eyed peas

2 cups peeled, seeded, and diced cucumber

1/4 cup sliced green onion

1/4 cup diced celery

1/4 cup diced red or yellow bell pepper

2 1/2 cups seeded, diced heirloom tomatoes or halved cherry tomatoes

COOK'S NOTE:
Fresh black-eyed peas have an earthier flavor than canned. Grab them when you can find them in the summer and freeze them, shelled, for a treat later on. Also, tomatoes do not taste as sweet — and they lose their meaty texture — if you refrigerate them. To preserve their flavor, add them up to an hour before serving.

Black-Eyed Pea Relish *with* Heirloom Tomatoes

—**Jeff Miller,** LUELLA'S BAR-B-QUE

"I enjoy serving this dish in the summer; it makes a great complement to the rich, smokey flavor of barbecue and grilled meat," says chef/owner Jeff Miller. *"It is a bright, crisp, and fresh burst of garden flavors coupled with the earthy taste of black-eyed peas. Dice the cucumber, celery, and pepper the size of the peas. Toss the tomatoes, including the juices, into the salad an hour before serving; the sweet tomato juices will marry with the relish but preserve the texture of a perfectly ripe tomato."*

To prepare the dressing, combine the olive oil, lemon juice, vinegar, garlic, oregano, crushed red pepper, salt, and pepper in a jar; cover and shake to blend.

To prepare the salad, combine the black-eyed peas, cucumber, green onion, celery, and bell pepper in a large bowl; pour about two-thirds of the dressing over the ingredients and toss well. Cover and refrigerate 6 hours or overnight, stirring occasionally.

Up to an hour before serving, add the tomatoes and additional dressing, if desired.

Marinated Tomato Salad *with* Kalamata Olives *&* Cheese

—**Charles Hudson,** SUNBURST TROUT FARMS

Serve as a side dish with pan-seared Sunburst Trout and thick grilled slices of artisan bread.

Combine the tomatoes, olives, vinegar, olive oil, salt, and pepper in a bowl; toss lightly. Add the cheese and gently mix in.

MAKES 4 SERVINGS

3 medium tomatoes (about 2 pounds), cut into wedges or coarsely chopped

3/4 cup halved, pitted kalamata olives

2 tablespoons balsamic vinegar

1 tablespoon extra-virgin olive oil

1/2 teaspoon sea salt, or to taste

1/2 teaspoon freshly ground pepper, or to taste

2 ounces Parmesan, Romano, Asiago, or Manchego cheese, shaved

Spring Pea *&* Mushroom Salad *with* Beef Bacon

—**Meredith and Casey McKissick,** FOOTHILLS DELI & BUTCHERY

MAKES 4 TO 6 SERVINGS

1 pound fresh snow peas, sugar snap peas, or shelled garden peas

1/2 pound fresh morels or oyster mushrooms, stems removed and halved

3 tablespoons extra-virgin olive oil

2 tablespoons white wine vinegar

2 tablespoons minced fresh thyme

1 tablespoon minced shallots

1/4 teaspoon salt, or more to taste

1/4 cup heavy whipping cream

3 strips Beef Bacon (page 150), cooked and crumbled

Use the freshest-picked peas available: snow peas, garden green peas, or sugar snaps. You'll have to forage for the morels — and only in early spring, when the ground is warming up and you can see the fern fronds poking up in the woods. You can substitute oyster or cremini mushrooms in lieu of morels. The cured Beef Bacon is a nice contrast of flavors to the crisp peas and earthy mushrooms.

Blanch the peas in boiling water until they are bright green, about 1 minute. Drain and place in a large bowl of ice water to stop the cooking. Drain and pat dry; place in a large bowl and add the mushrooms.

Whisk together the olive oil, vinegar, thyme, shallots, salt, and pepper. Pour over the peas and mushrooms, and toss to combine. Add the cream and toss gently; taste and season with additional salt and pepper, if desired. Sprinkle the Beef Bacon pieces over the salad and toss gently.

Celery & Gorgonzola Salad

—Traci Taylor, FIG

When fresh organic celery is in season at the market, this is the recipe to make!

To prepare the dressing, combine the shallots, oil, vinegar, thyme, salt, and pepper in a small bowl.

To prepare the gorgonzola cream, combine the gorgonzola and vinegar in a food processor; process until smooth, adding cream by tablespoons, to make a silky texture. Mix in pepper.

To assemble the salads, smear the gorgonzola cream on salad plates. Whisk the dressing mixture again, and pour over the lettuces and celery in a large bowl; toss well. Divide the salads on the salad plates; sprinkle with chives. Refrigerate any leftover dressing.

FOR THE DRESSING:

1 shallot, minced

1/4 cup plus 2 tablespoons canola oil

2 tablespoons sherry vinegar

1 tablespoon minced fresh thyme

1/4 teaspoon salt, or to taste

1/2 teaspoon freshly ground pepper, or to taste

FOR THE GORGONZOLA CREAM:

1/2 cup soft gorgonzola cheese

1 teaspoon sherry vinegar

1 tablespoon heavy whipping cream, plus additional for thinning the sauce

FOR THE SALAD:

3 cups torn romaine

3 cups torn frisee

2 stalks celery, diagonally sliced

1/4 cup snipped chives

Blue Ridge Food Ventures

Blue Ridge Food Ventures is a shared-use food and natural products manufacturing facility in Asheville, North Carolina. Artisan food entrepreneurs, farmers, chefs, bakers, caterers, mobile and food cart operators, and natural products manufacturers can find the equipment and resources they need there to make and market their products.

The first facility of its kind in North Carolina and the largest in the Southeast, Blue Ridge Food Ventures is a job-creation initiative of AdvantageWest, a nonprofit regional economic development organization serving Western North Carolina. Since its start in 2005, Blue Ridge Food Ventures has helped launch more than 235 small businesses.

BRFV also offers co-packing services and operates a community supported agriculture program (CSA) that distributes locally grown produce during the winter months, processed and frozen at the facility.

Read more at advantagewest.com/food-and-natural-products.

Hendersonville County Mutsu Apple Salad *with* Candied Marcona Almonds

—**Jake Schmidt,** EDISON CRAFT ALES + KITCHEN

MAKES 4 SERVINGS

3 local apples

3 stalks celery, diagonally sliced 1/4-inch thick

1/4 cup tender celery leaves

About 1/2 cup Bacon-Dijon Vinaigrette (recipe follows)

About 1/2 cup Apple Butter (page 206)

About 1/2 cup Candied Marcona Almonds (page 81)

Thin slices of French bread, toasted

Chef Schmidt recommends freezing the bacon for 15 minutes for easier dicing. Mutsu apples are also known as Crispin apples.

Core the apples and cut into 1/4 x 1/4-inch strips. Toss with the celery, celery leaves, and 1/4 cup of the Bacon-Dijon Vinaigrette, adding more vinaigrette if needed.

On each plate, spoon 2 tablespoons of the Apple Butter in the center and smear with the back of a spoon. Using tongs, place 1/4 of the apple mixture on the Apple Butter; garnish with about 2 tablespoons of the Candied Marcona Almonds and 2 to 3 slices of toast.

Bacon-Dijon Vinaigrette

—**Jake Schmidt,** EDISON CRAFT ALES + KTCHEN

MAKES ABOUT 2 CUPS

1/4 pound applewood smoked bacon, finely diced

1/2 cup apple cider vinegar

1 tablespoon dry mustard

1 shallot, sliced

1 cup canola oil

1/4 teaspoon salt, or to taste

1/4 teaspoon freshly ground pepper, or to taste

This apple cider vinaigrette adds a bite of smoky flavor to the Henderson County Mutsu Apple Salad.

Cook the bacon in a large, heavy skillet over medium heat until crisp. Using tongs, transfer the bacon to paper towels and let drain. Pour the drippings into a small bowl and reserve.

Cook the shallots in the skillet until they are transparent, about 1 minute. Add the garlic and sauté until both are browned, 1 to 2 minutes. Add the vinegar to the skillet; bring it to a simmer, stirring to loosen the clinging particles. Remove from the heat and pour the vinegar mixture into a blender container. Let it cool.

Add the mustard, salt, and pepper to the vinegar mixture. With the blender running, slowly add the bacon drippings and the oil, processing until the dressing is emulsified. Scrape into a bowl and stir in the reserved bacon; season with additional salt and pepper. If you are not using the vinaigrette within the hour, store it in a covered container in the refrigerator, but serve at room temperature.

Grilled Romaine Salad *with* Grilled Chicken, Curry Vinaigrette, *&* Lemon Chutney

—Traci Taylor, FIG

Lightly sear small, fresh romaine halves for a pretty presentation and lovely summer grilled chicken salad. You can easily double or triple the recipe to serve guests and larger families. If your chicken breast halves are large, use only one: pound it to even thickness, and halve it crosswise before grilling and serving.

MAKES 2 SERVINGS

2 (4-ounce) skinless, boneless chicken breast halves

Kosher salt

Freshly ground pepper

Curry Dijon Vinaigrette (page 202), divided

About 1/2 cup Lemon Chutney (page 205)

About 1 tablespoon olive oil

1 small head romaine lettuce, halved lengthwise

Lightly pound the chicken between pieces of wax paper to even thickness. Sprinkle lightly with salt and pepper, if desired, and brush with 2 tablespoons of the Curry Dijon Vinaigrette. Let the chicken stand while you preheat the grill.

Prepare the grill for medium-high heat; oil the rack. Grill the chicken until just cooked through, about 3 minutes on each side, brushing with 1 tablespoon of the Lemon Chutney during the last minute of cooking.

Coat the cut sides of the lettuce halves with cooking spray or brush with a little olive oil (using a clean brush); grill, with the cut sides down, until lightly charred, about 2 minutes.

To serve, place the romaine halves, cut sides up, on serving plates and lean the chicken on the lettuce. Drizzle the remaining Curry Dijon Vinaigrette on the salads and serve with the Lemon Chutney.

ABCs of CSAs

The basics of Community Supported Agriculture: a farmer offers "shares" to the public, consisting of a box (or bag or basket) of vegetables, meats, and/or other farm products. Consumers pay a "membership" fee at the beginning of the farming season; in return, they receive this package of seasonal produce each week.

With a CSA, you can: enjoy ultra-fresh food with maximum nutrition, get exposed to new foods and ways of cooking, develop relationships with the people who grow your food, and support our local farmers. To sign up for a CSA, visit: asapconnections.org/events/csa-fair/.

**Casara Logan and her fiancé Matthew Coffay own
Second Spring Market Garden,**

"one of Asheville's first four-season farms," says Logan. "We are a
small farm modeled on the market gardens of 19th-century France.
We aim to produce the highest quality, freshest, healthiest local
food throughout all four seasons — even in the middle of winter —
using minimal fossil fuel inputs. We do intensive gardening, meaning we optimize our yields using a minimal amount of land."

Sign up for their CSA at secondspringfarm.com, follow them on
Facebook, and look for them at the Asheville City Market.

Raw Citrus Kale Salad

3 cups torn kale

3 cups thinly sliced cabbage

1/2 cup shredded carrot

1/2 cup shredded beet

1/4 cup raisins

2 tablespoons raw pumpkin seeds

1/2 cup Citrus Dressing (page 199)

1 orange, sectioned

1 avocado, peeled and sliced

—**Randy Talley,** THE GREEN SAGE COFFEEHOUSE AND CAFÉ

This popular salad embodies the lifestyle and nourishment doctrines of owner Randy Talley. "To soften the kale," says Talley, "dress the greens early and let it marinate." And don't skimp on the dressing for best flavor.

Combine the kale, cabbage, carrot, beet, raisins, and pumpkin seeds in a large bowl. Pour the dressing over the salad and toss very well to coat. Let the salad stand for 5 minutes before serving.

To serve, divide the salad among 2 to 3 serving bowls; arrange the orange sections and avocado slices on the salads.

Fried Green Tomato Salad
with Watercress, Pepper Jelly, *&* Blue Cheese Dressing

—**Jake Schmidt,** EDISON CRAFT ALES + KITCHEN

Chef Jake Schmidt makes his own pepper jelly with banana peppers; it needs to be prepared ahead of time. The dressing can be prepared up to a week before you need it and stored in the refrigerator. With those two made, just fry the tomatoes and assemble the salads quickly.

MAKES 8 SERVINGS

1 cup all-purpose flour

1 teaspoon salt

1 teaspoon freshly ground pepper

1 large egg

1/2 cup buttermilk

1 cup panko (Japanese-style breadcrumbs)

1 cup stone-ground cornmeal

8 (3/4-inch-thick) slices green tomatoes

Oil for frying

About 1/2 cup Pepper Jelly (page 206) or store-bought pepper jelly (warmed slightly)

8 handfuls of watercress

Blue Cheese Dressing (page 201)

Whisk the flour, salt, and pepper to blend in a shallow dish. Whisk the egg and buttermilk in a shallow dish. Process the panko and cornmeal together until panko is finely ground; place in a shallow dish.

Heat about 1/2 inch oil in a large, heavy skillet over medium-high heat until hot but not smoking. Working with a few at a time, dredge tomato slices in flour mixture, then egg wash, then panko mixture, coating well. Slip them into the oil and fry (do not crowd the pan), turning once, until golden brown on both sides. Transfer to a rack to drain while you fry the remaining tomatoes.

To serve, toss the watercress with a little of the Blue Cheese Dressing to just coat the greens. Place a tomato on each serving plate; top with 2 to 3 teaspoons of Pepper Jelly and then another tomato. Place the salad on top.

103

Grilled Stuffed Avocado

—**Ann Marie Bolin,** THE CANTINA

MAKES 6 TO 8 SERVINGS

When we asked owner Sherrye Coggiola if we could publish this salad, she enthusiastically told us that the General Manager, Ann Marie Bolin, created it. With pleasure, we credit Bolin for her clever combination of flavors and presentation. It's a winner for summer entertaining.

FOR THE BLACK BEAN AND CORN SALAD:

1/4 cup red wine vinegar

2 tablespoons sugar

1/2 teaspoon ground cumin

1 teaspoon chili powder

1/2 teaspoon salt

1 teaspoon freshly ground black pepper

1 cup cooked black beans, rinsed and drained

1 cup fresh cooked cut corn

1/4 cup chopped cilantro

1 tablespoon minced garlic

4 green onions, chopped

1/2 medium red onion, finely diced

FOR THE AVOCADO:

6 ripe Haas avocados

Seasoned Salt

Olive oil

1/2 cup (2 ounces) shredded Monterey Jack cheese

1/2 cup queso fresco, crumbled

Sour cream

FOR THE SEASONED SALT

1 tablespoon kosher salt

1 1/2 teaspoons garlic powder

1 1/2 teaspoons black pepper

1 1/2 teaspoons chili powder

Combine the red wine vinegar, sugar, cumin, chili powder, salt, and pepper in a large bowl; whisk to blend. Add the black beans, corn, cilantro, garlic, green onions, and red onion; stir well.

To make the seasoned salt, combine all the spices in a jar; cover tightly and shake to blend them well.

Prepare the grill for medium-high heat. Slice the avocados in half; remove the pits. Score the cut sides and brush them with olive oil; sprinkle with seasoned salt to taste. (Reserve remaining seasoned salt for other uses.)

Place the avocados, oiled sides down, on the hot grill and grill until they are well marked, 3 to 5 minutes. Remove from the grill and place, grilled sides up, on serving plates. Spoon the black bean mixture on the avocados; sprinkle with cheeses and top with sour cream.

Tabouleh

—**Suzy Phillips,** GYPSY QUEEN FOOD TRUCK

Western versions use water-soaked bulgur for the bulk of the salad instead of herbs. Suzy Phillips's version is authentic down to her Lebanese roots, but she adds quinoa instead of bulgur in this raw salad when she makes it for sale at Katuah Market and on her Gypsy Queen Cuisine food truck. For the best flavor, look for young flat-leaf parsley and and fresh summer tomatoes.

Place the bulgur in the bottom of a large bowl. Finely dice the tomatoes, collecting their juices; pour the juices, olive oil, lemon juice, and 1/2 teaspoon salt over the bulgur and mix well.

Stir in the parsley, mint, and green onions. Taste and add additional salt, if desired. Refrigerate for at least 2 hours, stirring occasionally, so the grains will soften.

MAKES ABOUT 2 CUPS

1/3 cup bulgur, quinoa, or millet

1 1/2 pounds firm, ripe tomatoes

1/2 cup extra-virgin olive oil

1/4 cup fresh lemon juice

1/2 teaspoon kosher salt, or to taste

2 bunches flat leaf parsley, stems removed and very finely chopped

1/2 bunch of fresh mint, stems removed and very finely chopped

1/2 bunch green onions, very thinly sliced

Romaine lettuce leaves for serving

ASAP: The Ringmaster of Asheville's Farms & Food Producers

Asheville's strong network of farmers, food producers, and supporting restaurants and businesses didn't happen randomly. The local nonprofit ASAP (Appalachian Sustainable Agriculture Project) has been orchestrating this synergy since the 1990s, when they formed to help area tobacco growers transition to other crops after the crippling end of the federal tobacco program.

Since that time, ASAP has enabled farmers with education, networking opportunities, and one-to-one business planning and marketing strategy training. By building the demand for local food through sales promotions, Western North Carolina has bucked the national trend of farmland loss. Instead, the region has added acres and now serves as a place where farmers and local food businesses can prosper.

Each year, ASAP certifies upwards of 700 farms and 400 businesses — and those numbers are climbing — as Appalachian Grown™. These farms and producers use and display the Appalachian Grown logo, which helps consumers vote with their dollars by purchasing authentically local food. Look for many of them at the ASAP-run Asheville City Market (in downtown and South Asheville).

To learn more, visit asapconnections.org.

Pantry Salad

—**Devon Quick,** AVENUE M

Chef Devon Quick serves this healthy and colorful salad with a choice of dressings from the menu. We suggest dressing with one from this book or use your own favorite.

Place the greens in a shallow bowl; layer the carrots, almonds, pumpkin seeds, tomato, cranberries, and bean sprouts on top of the greens. Fan the avocado slices on top. Serve with desired dressing.

The healthy and colorful salad is served with your choice of dressings from the menu. We suggest dressing with one from this book, such as your choice of these:

Chipotle Citrus Vinaigrette, page 200

Balsamic Vinaigrette, page 201

Bacon Dijon Vinaigrette, page 99

Blue Cheese Dressing, page 201

MAKES 1 SERVING

3 cups mixed spring greens, arugula, and baby spinach

1/3 cup shredded carrots

1/4 cup slivered or sliced almonds, toasted

1/4 cup toasted pumpkin seeds

1/4 cup crumbled gorgonzola cheese

1/4 cup diced fresh tomato

1/4 cup dried cranberries

1 large pinch of bean sprouts

1/4 avocado, peeled and sliced

Appalachian Homegrown

Just Veggies

Summer Corn Skillet Cakes • 110

Roasted Corn on the Cob • 110

Ratatouille • 111

Collard Greens in Coconut Milk • 112

Shiitake Mushroom Chips • 113

Fennel Hushpuppies • 114

Pop Pop's Potato Pancakes • 114

Candied Yams • 115

Tomato & Gruyere Quiche • 116

Roasted Brussels Sprouts • 118

Steamed Broccolini with Dried Cherry
Vinaigrette & Walnuts • 119

Sesame Kale • 119

Rattlesnake Beans with Thyme-Infused
Honey Drizzle • 120

Summer Corn
Skillet Cakes
on page 110

Summer Corn
Skillet Cakes

—**Brian Sonoskus,** TUPELO HONEY CAFÉ

MAKES 14 CAKES

1 egg

2 tablespoons buttermilk

1/8 teaspoon
Cholula Hot Sauce

2 cups corn kernels, cut
from Roasted Corn on the
Cob (recipe follows)

3 tablespoons
all-purpose flour

1/8 teaspoon baking soda

1/8 teaspoon salt

1/8 teaspoon freshly
ground black pepper

Butter or bacon grease

Simple Salsa (page 80)

Serve these sweet little pancakes loaded with fresh roasted corn with summer fresh tomato Simple Salsa and a dollop of sour cream as a side dish. Or make them smaller and reheat them to serve as appetizers.

Whisk the egg, buttermilk, and hot sauce in a medium bowl. Add the corn and stir well. Add the flour, baking soda, salt, and pepper, stirring until the ingredients are well mixed.

Heat a skillet over medium heat. Add 1 tablespoon butter or bacon grease and allow it to melt. Working in batches, drop the batter by rounded tablespoons into the skillet and cook for 2 minutes per side or until the cakes are browned. Add additional butter or grease to the skillet as necessary between the batches. Serve with Simple Salsa.

From *Tupelo Honey Cafe: New Southern Flavors from the Blue Ridge Mountains* by Elizabeth Sims and chef Brian Sonoskus, Andrews McMeel Publishing 2014, used with permission.

Roasted Corn *on the* Cob

—**Brian Sonoskus,** TUPELO HONEY CAFÉ

MAKES 2 TO 2 1/4 CUPS

3 ears yellow corn

1/8 teaspoon salt

1/8 teaspoon freshly
ground black pepper

3 tablespoons olive oil

Preheat the oven to 400° F. Sprinkle the corn with the salt and pepper. Heat the oil in a large, heavy ovenproof skillet over medium-high heat; add the corn. Cook for 3 to 4 minutes, turning frequently in the oil, until lightly browned.

Transfer the skillet to the oven and cook the corn for 7 to 10 minutes, just until tender. Any leftover corn is delicious in salsas or hotcakes.

From *Tupelo Honey Cafe: New Southern Flavors from the Blue Ridge Mountains* by Elizabeth Sims and chef Brian Sonoskus, Andrews McMeel Publishing 2014, used with permission.

MAKES ABOUT 6 CUPS,
OR 6 TO 8 SERVINGS

2 tablespoons olive oil

4 scallions, chopped

3 cloves garlic, crushed

2 leeks, white parts only,
thinly sliced

1 green bell pepper,
roughly chopped

1/2 medium red onion,
thinly sliced

1/4 cup chopped
fresh chives

2 tablespoons chopped
fresh rosemary

1 teaspoon dried oregano
or Italian herb blend

1/2 teaspoon crushed
red pepper

4 cups coarsely chopped
tomatoes

2 medium zucchini,
quartered lengthwise
and sliced

1 Japanese eggplant,
unpeeled and cubed

3 tablespoons chopped
fresh parsley

1/2 teaspoon salt,
or to taste

1/2 teaspoon freshly
ground pepper, or to taste

Ratatouille

—**Emily Flynn McIntosh,** A BED OF ROSES VICTORIAN BED & BREAKFAST

*In the summer, proprietor Emily McIntosh heads to
the market for just-picked, small-to-medium zucchini,
young Japanese eggplant, and fresh tomatoes to make
the ratatouille. She bakes the Ratatouille Goat Cheese
Tart (page 25) for a savory breakfast, saving leftovers
for filling omelets or topping pasta — with a sprinkle
of freshly grated Parmesan cheese.*

Heat the oil in a large, deep skillet or saucepan over medium heat;
add the scallions, garlic, leeks, green pepper, and red onion. Cook
until the vegetables are just tender, stirring often, about 10 minutes. Stir in the chives, rosemary, oregano and crushed red pepper
and cook for 1 minute. Add the tomatoes; simmer uncovered for
10 minutes, stirring often. Add the zucchini and eggplant; simmer
uncovered until the vegetables are tender, about 15 minutes.

Remove from the heat and stir in the parsley, salt, and pepper.

MAKES 4 TO 6 SERVINGS

1 (14-ounce) can
coconut milk

1 medium onion,
peeled and chopped

6 cloves garlic, minced

2 tablespoons peeled,
minced fresh ginger

1/2 teaspoon crushed
red pepper

2 bunches collard greens,
washed, stems removed,
and torn

1/2 teaspoon salt,
or to taste

1/2 teaspoon freshly
ground pepper, or to taste

Collard Greens
in Coconut Milk

—**Annie Louise Perkinson,** FLYING CLOUD FARM

Farmer Annie Louise Perkinson says, "We make this all the time. I adapted the recipe from the Edible Schoolyard *— Alice Waters's school garden project." Serve it with brown basmati rice.*

Pour 1/4 cup of the coconut milk in the bottom of a large, heavy skillet; place over medium heat until the coconut milk simmers. Add the onion, garlic, ginger, and crushed red pepper; sauté for 3 minutes. Add the greens and pour in the remaining coconut milk, stirring to coat the greens. Cover and simmer until the greens are tender, about 10 minutes. Stir in the salt and pepper to taste. Serve with basmati rice, if desired.

The Local "Mushroom Man"

Alan Muskat, self-described Grand Poopah, has forged the first "forage-to-table" program in the US, educating people from all over the country as they join him on foraging tours. "We are located in the richest temperate ecosystem on earth," says Muskat. And though you may not have run into him on his treks through our local field and forest, both his extensive knowledge—of wild foods and cooking, natural medicine, ecology, folklore, and more — and his easy, spirited and comedic banter make a culinary scavenger hunt sound seductive.

Muskat has been featured on Bizarre Foods and other nationally syndicated cable networks, and his tours have been ranked as one of the five best travel experiences by Southern Living Magazine. By the time this writing has published, he will have conducted a private forage-to-table tour and dinner for the visiting James Beard Celebrity Chef Tour hosted by Chef William Dissen at The Market Place, and lectured at a speaking engagement at the US Botanical Garden in DC.

Tours focus on safely identifying and cooking with mushrooms and other wild plants. You may end up gathering chicken of the woods or wild persimmons, fishing for trout, brewing sassafras root beer, or feasting on ramps and morels. Whatever's out there in our Western North Carolina backyard is fair game. For more information, go to: notastelikehome.org.

Shiitake Mushroom Chips

—**Susan and Alan Fox,** THE MUSHROOM HUT @ FOX FARMS

Mark your calendar for the annual ASAP (Appalachian Sustainable Agriculture Project) Farm Tour. Don't miss Fox Farms in Burnsville. They'll take you up the hill to see the mushroom crib: a Lincoln-log-type structure they've stacked so they can grow shiitake mushrooms. Their hospitality makes this a must-stop on the tour; each time we return, we come away with another tidbit of deliciousness. Find out more about them at: www.localharvest.org/the-mushroom-hut-fox-farms-M27083.

Preheat the oven to 400° F.

Meanwhile, place the mushrooms in a deep bowl; drizzle with the oil and quickly toss until the mushrooms are coated. Sprinkle with the salt and pepper, tossing until coated. Spread the mushroom in a single layer on a rimmed baking sheet.

Roast until the mushrooms are crispy, about 15 minutes.

MAKES 2 SERVINGS

3 ounces shiitake mushrooms, stems trimmed and very thinly sliced

2 teaspoons extra-virgin olive oil or melted bacon fat

1/8 teaspoon coarse salt, or to taste

1/8 teaspoon freshly ground pepper, or to taste

Fennel Hushpuppies

—**Chad Kelly,** THE JUNCTION

A convenient way to measure out the hushpuppy batter is to use a small, 1- to 2-tablespoon ice cream scoop to scoop out the batter and drop them into the hot oil, advises chef Chad Kelly. In addition to serving these hushpuppies on the side with fried fresh fish, we think they make tasty bites with cocktails.

Combine the cornmeal, flour, sugar, baking powder, fennel seeds, and salt in a large bowl; whisk to blend the dry ingredients.

Combine the buttermilk, water, melted butter, onion, roasted fennel, and hot sauce; stir well. Add to the cornmeal mixture and stir just to blend. Let stand for 10 minutes.

Meanwhile, fill a large saucepan or deep-fryer halfway with oil; heat to 350° F. Working in batches, drop the batter, by spoonfuls, into the oil and fry until golden brown, about 2 minutes. Drain on paper towels; keep warm in a low oven until all are fried and ready to serve.

MAKES 2 DOZEN

1 cup stone-ground cornmeal

1/2 cup all-purpose flour

2 1/2 tablespoons sugar

2 teaspoons baking powder

1 1/2 teaspoon fennel seeds, toasted and slightly crushed

1 teaspoon kosher salt

1/2 cup buttermilk

1/2 cup water

1/4 stick (2 tablespoons) unsalted butter, melted and cooled

1/2 small onion, minced

1/2 cup roasted fennel bulb, finely diced

1/2 teaspoon hot sauce

Oil for frying

Pop Pop's Potato Pancakes

—**Brian Sonoskus,** TUPELO HONEY CAFÉ

MAKES 14 TO 16 PANCAKES

3 large (2 1/4 pounds) baking potatoes, peeled and finely chopped

1/2 cup all-purpose flour

1/2 cup chopped onion

1 teaspoon kosher salt

1 teaspoon freshly ground pepper

1 large egg

1 tablespoon bacon fat or vegetable shortening

Use russet potatoes, which have a high starch content with dry, snowy white flesh. They make tender pancakes that are never gummy. Fry them in bacon drippings for delicious homespun flavor. Serve with sour cream or Apple Butter (page 206).

Combine the potatoes, flour, onion, salt, pepper, and egg in a food processor. Cover and process until very smooth, scraping sides of bowl as needed.

Heat a large heavy skillet or griddle over medium heat. Add the shortening and melt. Working in batches, add batter, by 2-tablespoon increments, to the skillet without overcrowding; cook until browned on each side and cooked through, about 2 minutes per side. If necessary, add an additional shortening to skillet. Drain on paper towels and serve hot.

Candied Yams

—**John and Julie Stehling,** EARLY GIRL EATERY

We Southerners do love our sweet potatoes, and these are a classic recipe for roasting them in a spiced sweet and lemony syrup. For us, they are not just for laden holiday buffets. Chef/owner John Stehling roasts sweet potatoes from local farmers to sweet perfection.

Preheat the oven to 350° F.

Meanwhile, peel the sweet potatoes and cut them into 1-inch cubes; place them in a large bowl. Add the brown sugar, lemon juice, oil, nutmeg, sea salt, pepper, and Tabasco sauce; mix thoroughly.

Scrape the sweet potato mixture into a 13 x 9-inch baking pan and spread in an even layer. Cover tightly with foil; bake 25 minutes. Uncover, stir, and bake until top is caramelized, 25 to 40 minutes.

MAKES 8 TO 10 SERVINGS

4 pounds sweet potatoes

1 cup firmly packed brown sugar

1/2 cup fresh lemon juice

1/4 cup oil or melted butter

1 teaspoon freshly grated nutmeg

1 tablespoon sea salt

1 teaspoon freshly ground pepper

2 to 3 dashes Tabasco sauce, or to taste

Tomato & Gruyere Quiche

—**Cynthia Pierce,** YUZU PATISSERIE

Pastry Chef Cynthia Pierce owns a small bake shop in Gallery Mugen, in Cotton Mills Studios in the River Arts District. She shares the space with her husband, ceramic artist Akira Satake. Cynthia bakes pastries in the style of European bakeshops and coffeehouses — much like these individual tarts. Staying true to the season when planning the savories and sweets to bake each day, she often enhances the pastries with Japanese ingredients like matcha, ginger, satsumaimo, and yuzu — the aromatic citrus fruit for which her shop is named.

Having frequented her booth at the Asheville City Market — before Yuzu Patisserie — and enjoyed her tomato tarts, we asked if she would share the recipe. Here is the formula for a whole tart.

Pastry for single-crust,
9 or 10-inch tart crust

2 tablespoons butter

2 tablespoons
extra-virgin olive oil

2 medium onions,
thinly sliced

2 cloves garlic, minced

3/4 teaspoon salt,
or to taste

2 cups (8 ounces)
shredded Gruyere cheese

2 tablespoons chopped
fresh basil or thyme

1/2 teaspoon freshly
ground pepper

1 pint cherry
tomatoes, halved

2 large eggs

3/4 cup heavy whipping
cream or half-and-half

Lightly oil the pie plate. Roll out the dough and fit it into the pie plate; crimp the edges. Refrigerate for at least 1 hour. Position the oven rack in lower third of oven. Preheat the oven to 400° F.

Place the butter and olive oil in a large, heavy skillet over medium heat; when the butter melts, add the onions. Cook, turning and separating with tongs, until they are soft and beginning to brown. Add the garlic and sauté for 1 minute. Remove from the heat and season with 1/2 teaspoon salt. Whisk together the eggs and cream with 1/4 teaspoon salt. Remove the pie crust from the refrigerator; sprinkle about one-third of the cheese on the bottom. Cover with the onions and garlic, then sprinkle with another one-third of the cheese. Sprinkle with the herbs and pepper. Arrange the tomatoes on top and sprinkle with the remaining cheese. Carefully pour the egg mixture over the layered ingredients. Place the quiche in the oven and immediately reduce the oven temperature to 375° F. Bake until the top is nicely puffed and browned, 35 to 45 minutes. If you are using a glass pie plate, make sure the bottom of the crust has baked. If it looks raw, cover the top of the quiche loosely with foil and bake for 5 additional minutes.

AIR is an Association of more than 120 Local, Independent Restaurants

dedicated to keeping Asheville's food scene eclectic, authentic, interesting, fresh and flavorful. In this vibrant mountain city, flavors from around the world complement those of the Southern Appalachian Mountains. Since its founding in 2004, AIR has been a moving force behind Asheville's emergence as a culinary destination and the growth of the region's farm-to-table movement.

It's not unusual to find AIR chefs featured in The New York Times, Garden & Gun, The Local Palate, and Southern Living or earning national recognition for their food, hospitality, and pioneering work in sustainability. Thanks to the creativity and inventiveness of AIR members, Asheville consistently ranks as one of the nation's finest foodie cities.

In recent years, AIR's work with the Green Restaurant Association (GRA) and the Blue Ridge Sustainability Institute (BRSI) resulted in Asheville being named the first city in the U.S. to be named a Green Dining Destination™. In 2014, three AIR members made GRA's list of the Greenest Restaurants in America — The French Broad Chocolate Lounge, Green Sage Café, and Luella's Bar-B-Q.

AIR commitment to supporting a new generation of culinary innovators and entrepreneurs extends beyond the ordinary to programs that inspire leadership and prepare staff for culinary careers. In addition to ongoing professional development for its members, AIR also supports GO! Kitchen Ready, a program that prepares adult students to enter the culinary field, and the Chefs of Tomorrow Scholarship Fund at Asheville-Buncombe Tech's nationally acclaimed culinary program.

Roasted Brussels Sprouts

—Wicked Weed Brewing

MAKES 2 TO 3 SERVINGS

10 ounces Brussels sprouts

1 to 2 tablespoons olive oil blend

2 tablespoons unsalted butter, divided

1 1/2 tablespoons sugar

1 teaspoon kosher salt

1 tablespoon cider vinegar

COOK'S NOTE:

Wicked Weed Brewing recommends not trimming too much off the bottoms of the Brussels sprouts or they will fall apart and not sear properly.

We asked for a popular recipe from this brewhouse and were surprised to learn that this is the most asked-for dish. We can't help but think it would be excellent drizzled with a touch of aged balsamic instead of the cider vinegar, unless you make the Cider Vinegar (page 199) yourself, of course!

Preheat the oven to 450° F. Trim the stems of the Brussels sprouts; cut in half from top to bottom.

Meanwhile, pour the oil into a large, heavy skillet and brush evenly over the bottom. Arrange the Brussels sprouts, cut sides down, in the skillet. Place the skillet over medium-high heat. Sprinkle the tops of the Brussels sprouts evenly with the sugar and salt. Once the skillet is hot, put 1 tablespoon of the butter in the center of the Brussels sprouts and let it melt.

When the butter is melted, place the skillet in the hot oven. Cook until they are tender and the bottoms are nicely caramelized but not burning; check after 10 to 12 minutes, depending on the size of the Brussels sprouts.

Place the skillet on the stovetop over medium heat. Add the vinegar and the remaining 1 tablespoon of the butter; toss them around to deglaze the skillet.

1 tablespoon vegetable oil

1 teaspoon salt

2 to 2 1/2 pounds broccolini, stems trimmed

1/4 Dried Cherry Vinaigrette (page 200)

1/2 cup chopped walnuts, toasted

COOK'S NOTE:
The vinaigrette can be prepared up to 24 hours ahead of serving. Bring to room temperature and whisk before drizzling vegetables with the vinaigrette and tossing with walnuts.

Steamed Broccolini *with* Dried Cherry Vinaigrette *&* Walnuts

—Traci Taylor, FIG

Chef Traci Taylor suggests serving the vinaigrette with roasted or steamed broccolini, carrots, sweet potatoes, cauliflower, asparagus, green beans, and Brussels sprouts.

Fill a large skillet halfway with water; bring to a boil. Add the oil and salt; add the broccolini. Cover, reduce heat, and simmer until the broccolini is crisp-tender, 4 to 5 minutes, turning pieces once during cooking. Drain and place in a shallow serving dish.

Toss the broccolini with the vinaigrette, and then sprinkle with the walnuts.

Sesame Kale

—Miki Kilpatrick, HOMEGROWN

We love the way Homegrown serves fresh kale; it's very flavorful and tender-crisp. For a vegetarian main dish, serve it in bowls with cooked kasha or quinoa and a sprinkling of chopped peanuts or sesame seeds.

Heat a large, heavy skillet over medium-high heat; add the olive oil and heat until it is hot but not smoking. Add the ginger and garlic, and sauté for 30 seconds. Add the kale, in 2 batches, tossing the first batch with tongs until it is softened before adding the next. Continue to cook, tossing with the tongs, until the kale is wilted, about 4 minutes.

Add the stock and tamari sauce; cook until the liquid is mostly evaporated, tossing with the tongs. Remove from the heat and drizzle with the sesame oil, tossing to coat the greens.

MAKES 2 TO 3 SIDE DISH SERVINGS

1 tablespoon olive oil

1 tablespoons minced fresh ginger

1/2 tablespoon minced garlic

1 bunch kale, tough stems removed and chopped

1/4 cup vegetable stock

2 tablespoons tamari sauce

2 teaspoons dark sesame oil

Rattlesnake Beans *with* Mushrooms *&* Thyme-Infused Honey Drizzle

—Chef Mary Collins-Shepard, SEASONAL SCHOOL OF CULINARY ARTS

When chef Mary Collins-Shepard mentioned to the Warren Wilson garden manager that she needed beans for her class on cooking with honey, he came back with several pounds of "rattlesnake" pole beans. (See below, Seasonal School of Culinary Arts) A drizzle of thyme-infused honey gave a kiss of sweetness to the quick-cooked fresh vegetables.

MAKES 8 SERVINGS

FOR THE HONEY:

3/4 cup local honey

4 full sprigs thyme

1/4 teaspoon sea salt

FOR THE VEGETABLES:

1 1/2 pounds fresh "rattlesnake" green beans

3 tablespoons unsalted butter

2 medium shallots, thinly sliced

8 ounces mixed mushrooms (shiitake, cremini, oyster), sliced

1/4 teaspoon sea salt, or to taste

1/4 teaspoon freshly ground pepper, or to taste

To prepare the honey, warm the honey to just below a simmer in a small saucepan over medium heat. Remove from the heat and stir in the thyme and salt. Cover and let stand for at least 1 hour.

To prepare the beans, remove any strings from the beans, if necessary. Snap the beans in half if they are over about 4 inches long. Cook the beans in a large saucepan over boiling, salted water until they are crisp-tender, 3 to 4 minutes. Drain and place them in a large bowl of ice water to stop the cooking. Drain and pat dry.

Remove the thyme stems (the leaves can stay), and place over low heat to warm them.

Place the butter in a large, heavy skillet over medium-high heat, and let it melt. Add the shallots; sauté until they are translucent, about 2 minutes. Add mushrooms; sauté until just tender, about 4 minutes. Add the blanched beans and cook, stirring occasionally until they are hot, about 5 minutes. Transfer to a bowl and drizzle with the honey.

Seasonal School of Culinary Arts

Teaching chefs in Western North Carolina consider the Seasonal School of Culinary Arts at Warren Wilson College a rewarding journey of culinary education. Run by chef Susi Seguret Gott, this annual, weeklong cooking school requires chefs to commit one day to teaching a class to attendees, who come to enjoy the incredible foods and wines as well as learn how to cook.

The week runs concurrent with the Swannanoa Gathering, a well-known music-filled workshop series conducted elsewhere on campus. Each weeklong session of the Seasonal School of Culinary Arts brings together students and renowned chefs to classes by day. In the afternoons and evenings, students enjoy the musical offerings at the Swannanoa Gathering. All in attendance enjoy the wine, beer, food tastings, and lovely meals that highlight our local cuisine.

Warren Wilson: A Different Crop of College Town

At 18, most kids dream of going off to school in a bustling big city or a college town known for its clubs and coffeehouses. Freshmen come to Warren Wilson College's Sustainable Agriculture Concentration pick Asheville — nay, the relaxed and rural Swannanoa — for its sprawling farmland and a farming way of life.

The college is home to a working 275-acre mixed-crop and livestock operation, as well as a three-acre garden and one-acre apple orchard. Its farm is fully student-run; a manager helps a student-crew maintain the garden's crops, small apiary, and composting program. In other words, both the farm and garden provide students with hands-on farming experience, a perfect complement to courses that cover a range of agricultural practices, terminology, and important issues. By the end of their four years, graduates are ready to carry out the mission of the Environmental Studies Department: to prepare leaders who are able to critically assess, develop, and promote sustainable futures for life on Earth.

Fortunately for us, many don't go far. Numerous alumni are now established Asheville-area farmers, growing the crops and raising the animals that feed their community. And they don't stop there: Many pay it forward and open up their farms via internships and apprenticeships to current Warren Wilson students. Now that's sustainable ag!

Appalachian Homegrown

Simmered & Stewed

PBR Mussels • 124

Cream of Mussel Soup • 125

Spinach & Split Pea Soup • 126

Celeriac Bisque • 127

PBR Mussels
on page 124

PBR Mussels

—The Admiral

In a community that loves perfectly tender-cooked mussels bathed in creatively seasoned broths, this one is legendary.

Cook the bacon in a large, heavy saucepan over medium-high heat until softened and fat is rendered. Add the onion, peppers, and garlic; sprinkle with 1/2 teaspoon of the salt and 1/2 teaspoon of the pepper. Cook, stirring occasionally, until the onions begin to caramelize, about 5 minutes.

Stir in the tomato paste and cook until the mixture is a dark red brick color. Add the beer; bring to a boil, scraping the bottom of the saucepan to loosen the clinging particles. Add 1 cup of water and the tomatoes, crushing the broth with a fork to break up the tomatoes. Bring to a boil, stirring; cover, reduce heat, and simmer about 1 hour, stirring occasionally.

Remove the saucepan from the heat and stir in the vinegar, brown sugar, and hickory smoke powder; cook until the sugar dissolves. Season to taste with additional salt and pepper.

Return the broth to a boil. Add the mussels and cover tightly; cover and cook 2 minutes. Shake the saucepan and cook another 2 minutes. Uncover and use tongs to transfer all of the mussels that have opened to shallow soup bowls. Cover the saucepan and cook until all the mussels have opened, 1 to 2 more minutes. Use tongs to add them to bowls with other mussels, and discard any mussels that have not opened. Cover the bowls to keep the mussels warm.

If desired, strain the broth, pressing on the solids; reserve the broth. Discard the solids. Ladle the broth over the mussels, dividing evenly. Arrange bread slices on the mussels in the shallow bowls.

MAKES 4 TO 6 SERVINGS

1/4 cup diced smoked bacon

1 small yellow onion, sliced

1 poblano pepper, seeded and sliced

3 cloves garlic, sliced

Kosher salt

Freshly ground pepper

2 tablespoons tomato paste

1 (12-ounce) can Pabst Blue Ribbon beer

1 (28-ounce) can San Marzano tomatoes, undrained

3 tablespoons apple cider vinegar

2 tablespoons firmly packed brown sugar

1 to 1 1/2 teaspoons hickory smoke powder, or to taste

3 to 4 pounds fresh mussels, scrubbed and debearded

Artisan bread loaf, thickly sliced and grilled

Cream of Mussel Soup

—**Brian Ross,** DOUGH

An elegant soup, this creamy concoction draws influences from the French classic version. Using both the cooking broth from the mussels and the whole mussels, the soup is delicately concentrated with the flavor of seafood. Chef/owner Brian Ross replaces the traditional celery in the saffron and cream broth with fresh fennel, adding a slight sweet anise nuance that complements the flavors.

To prepare the mussels, combine the wine, water, shallots, and thyme in a large saucepan. Bring to a boil; boil until the liquid is reduced by half, 15 to 25 minutes.

Add the mussels and cover tightly; cook for 2 minutes. Shake the saucepan and cook for another 2 minutes. Uncover and use tongs to transfer all of the mussels that have opened to shallow soup bowls. Cover the saucepan and cook until all the mussels have opened, 1 to 2 more minutes. Use tongs to add them to bowls with other mussels, and discard any mussels that have not opened.

Strain and reserve the broth. Remove the mussels from their shells and discard the shells.

To prepare the soup, melt the butter with the oil in a large saucepan over medium-high heat. Add the onion, fennel, and leek; cook, stirring frequently, until they are translucent, 5 to 6 minutes. Stir in the chicken stock, cream, saffron, salt, pepper, and reserved mussel liquid. Add the potatoes and bring to a boil. Cover, reduce heat, and simmer, stirring frequently, until the vegetables are tender, about 20 minutes.

MAKES 4 SERVINGS

FOR THE MUSSELS:

1 1/2 cups dry white wine

1 cup water

1/2 cup sliced shallots

3 sprigs fresh thyme

3 pounds mussels, scrubbed and debearded

FOR THE SOUP:

2 tablespoons unsalted butter

2 tablespoons extra-virgin olive oil

1 large yellow onion, thinly sliced

1 large fennel bulb, thinly sliced

1 medium leek, white and light green part only, thinly sliced

4 cups chicken stock

1 cup heavy whipping cream

Large pinch of saffron threads

1/2 teaspoon salt, or to taste

1/2 teaspoon freshly ground pepper, or to taste

1 1/2 cups peeled and finely diced Yukon gold potatoes

7 cups water

1 pound (2 cups) dried green split peas, rinsed

1 tablespoon oil

1 onion, finely diced

2 cloves garlic, minced

2 tablespoons minced fresh thyme

1 tablespoon minced fresh rosemary or sage

1 tablespoon minced wfresh oregano

2 teaspoons sea salt

1 teaspoon freshly ground pepper

10 ounces fresh spinach leaves, chopped

Spinach & Split Pea Soup

—**Cathy Cleary,** WEST END BAKERY

"This is a really easy soup to make," says chef/owner Cathy Cleary. "It takes a little time for the peas to cook, but the active time is only about 10 minutes! We make it at the bakery when we are really busy cooking other things because it is satisfying and delicious. But we can also get tons of other stuff done while it cooks."

Place the water and peas in a large, heavy saucepan. Cover and bring to a boil; reduce the heat and simmer until the peas are very tender, about 45 to 60 minutes.

Meanwhile, heat a large, heavy skillet over low heat; add the onion and garlic; cook until tender, stirring occasionally, about 15 minutes. Add the herbs, salt, and pepper; sauté 2 minutes. Add to the soup, stirring well. Add the spinach; cook, stirring frequently, until the spinach is wilted, 4 to 5 minutes.

Celeriac Bisque

—Duane Fernandes, ISA'S BISTRO

We met at different restaurants for our initial book planning meetings. On one brisk, breezy day, we ducked into Isa's for lunch and ordered this soup…and it was a given that we'd ask chef Duane Fernandes for the recipe. This globe-shaped root vegetable has a celery-like flavor; it is starchy and, when puréed, thickens soup like a potato. At Isa's, they garnish the soup with organic rye bread crumbs, a drizzle of sage oil, and a few celery leaves.

MAKES 10 SERVINGS

10 cups vegetable stock

2 bulbs celeriac, peeled and chopped

1 stalk celery, chopped

1/2 large russet potato (4 to 5 ounces), peeled and chopped

1/2 onion, chopped

1 teaspoon salt, or to taste

1/2 teaspoon ground white pepper

1 cup heavy whipping cream

Combine the stock, celeriac, celery, potato, onion, salt, and pepper in a large, heavy saucepan. Bring to a simmer over medium heat; cover, reduce the heat, and simmer until the celeriac is fork tender, about 25 minutes. Add the cream and simmer an additional 20 minutes. Let the soup cool.

In a blender, purée the soup in batches until smooth. Reheat before serving.

Appalachian Homegrown

Pasta, Grains & Beans

Penne a la Vodka • 130

Pasta with Mushrooms &
Saffron Cream Sauce • 131

Farro Risotto • 132

Smoky Mac "N Cheese • 133

Ricotta Gnudi with Porcini Ragout • 134

Vegan Pesto • 136

Roasted Garlic • 136

Veggie Burger • 137

Chef Jeremy Elliot presents Vinnie's pasta recipe on page 130

MAKES 3 TO 4 SERVINGS

8 ounces dried penne pasta, uncooked

1/3 cup finely diced pancetta

1 tablespoon olive oil

1/3 cup finely diced red onion

1/4 cup vodka

1 cup heavy whipping cream

1/2 cup marinara sauce

Salt and freshly ground pepper to taste

About 1 tablespoon thinly sliced green onion

Penne *a la* Vodka

—Jeremy Rae Elliott, VINNIE'S NEIGHBORHOOD ITALIAN

Vinnie's is a popular neighborhood spot in North Asheville where families gather after soccer games, friends meet after work, and couples enjoy a night out. The food is reliably tasty, and the owner greeting you night after night is a friend to all. Chef Elliott shares this classic Italian dish.

Cook the pasta in boiling, salted water according to package directions to al dente. Drain and keep warm.

Meanwhile, heat a large, heavy skillet over medium-high heat; add the oil and pancetta. Sauté until the pancetta is crispy and the fat is rendered, about 2 minutes. Add the red onion; cook until its edges are brown, about 2 minutes. Remove the skillet from the heat; pour in the vodka and carefully light the alcohol with a long match. Once the alcohol has burned off, return to medium-high heat; add the cream and cook to thicken it slightly, about 1 minute. Stir in the marinara; cook and stir until hot, about 30 seconds.

Toss the pasta and sauce together. Scatter a little green onion on each serving.

Pasta *with* Mushrooms *&* Saffron Cream Sauce

—**Michael Gentry,** EVERYONE COOKS

Chef Michael Gentry, aka The Sustainable Gourmet, teaches a series of cooking classes called "Everyone Cooks." Students prepare a family-style meal of vegetarian, vegan, and raw recipes using local, organic, and wild sources. While it's a favorite class at Warren Wilson College, Gentry also teaches at different locations. Find more information at "Everyone Cooks" on Facebook.

You'll see chef Gentry often at the Seasonal School of Culinary Arts each July at the Swannanoa Gathering on the Warren Wilson campus. Here he shares one of his cooking class recipes.

Cook the pasta in boiling, salted water according to the package directions. Drain, reserving 1/4 cup of the pasta cooking liquid. Return the pasta and the cooking liquid to the saucepan; toss with the butter. Cover and keep warm.

Dissolve the saffron in 1 tablespoon of warm water in a small bowl. Stir in the cream.

Heat a large, heavy skillet over medium heat; add the coconut oil and simmer. Add the garlic and sauté for 20 seconds. Add the mushrooms; cook, stirring frequently, until they are tender, about 5 minutes. Add the squash, nutmeg, crushed red pepper, salt, and pepper; cook, stirring occasionally, until the squash is just tender, 2 to 3 minutes. Add the wine and cook until the liquid evaporates, about 3 minutes. Stir in the cream mixture; cook, stirring constantly, just until hot, about 1 minute.

Remove from the heat and stir in the cheese and basil; pour over the pasta and toss well.

MAKES 4 SERVINGS

8 ounces dry orrechiette, bucatini, linguini, or fettucini pasta

1/4 teaspoon saffron threads

3/4 to 1 cup heavy whipping cream

2 tablespoons coconut oil

8 cloves garlic, peeled and crushed

1/2 pound shiitake mushrooms, trimmed and sliced

1/2 pound yellow squash, cut into 1/2-inch cubes

1 teaspoon freshly ground nutmeg

1/2 teaspoon crushed red pepper

1/2 teaspoon sea salt

1 teaspoon freshly ground pepper

1/2 cup dry white wine

1 tablespoon butter

1/2 cup freshly grated Parmigiano-Reggiano cheese

1/3 cup torn fresh Thai basil leaves

Farro Risotto

—**Mark Demarco,** CEDRIC'S TAVERN

1 cup cauliflower florets

1 cup broccoli florets

1 cup shelled garden peas

1/4 cup extra-virgin olive oil

1/4 cup finely diced carrots

1/4 cup finely diced celery

1/4 cup finely diced yellow onion

4 cups cooked farro or arborio rice

1/2 cup dry white wine

Grated zest and juice of 1 lemon, divided

2 roasted red bell peppers, roasted and sliced

1/2 cup (2 ounces) freshly grated Parmesan cheese

1 bunch fresh parsley leaves, finely chopped

1 stick (1/2 cup) cold unsalted butter, diced

COOK'S NOTE:
To roast the red peppers, chef Demarco recommends charring them over an open flame. Then place them in a bowl and cover with plastic wrap. The peppers will sweat and the skin will loosen and be easy to peel. Do not rinse, as this will rinse away flavor.

Farro is rather a novelty to American cooks, entering our food lexicon only recently with availability in major grocery stores. But Italians have been eating this chewy, non-wheat grain for over 2,000 years. Chef Mark Demarco has substituted farro for the more bland, but still chewy arborio rice, adding an earthy nuttiness to the dish. By the way, the rice is less trouble to cook, too.

Bring a large saucepan of water to a boil; add the cauliflower florets and cook until just tender, 2 to 4 minutes. Remove the florets with a slotted spoon and place in a large bowl of ice water to stop the cooking process.

Return the water to a boil; add the broccoli florets and cook just until tender, 2 to 4 minutes. Meanwhile, add more ice to the ice water bath if needed; remove the florets with a slotted spoon and add to the ice water. Drain the vegetables and place in a bowl to reserve. Prepare another ice water bath.

Return the water to a boil. Add the peas and blanch for 2 minutes; drain the peas in a colander and place them in the ice water bath. Drain the peas and add them to the broccoli and cauliflower.

Place a large, heavy skillet over medium-high heat; add the olive oil and heat until hot but not smoking. Add the carrots, celery, and onion; sauté until they are just tender, 3 to 5 minutes. Stir in the farro. Add the wine and lemon juice; boil until the liquid is reduced by half, about 3 minutes. Stir in the peas, broccoli, cauliflower, and roasted peppers; cook, stirring constantly, until the vegetables are hot, about 1 minute.

Remove the skillet from the heat and stir in the lemon zest, Parmesan, parsley, and butter until the butter melts.

Smoky Mac 'N Cheese

—**Miki Kilpatrick,** HOMEGROWN

One look at the website domain name of Greg and Miki Kilpatrick's neighborhood spot, and you get the personality of the restaurant: slowfoodrightquick. com. This is the place where we go to get a home-cooked meal that's about as good as it gets. They know that "out here in the real world, people are in a hurry. So we serve up "slow food"…good, clean, local food "right quick!" They make food from local farmers into meals that are affordable, convenient, delicious, and healthy. With a constantly rotating menu, the food they make is inspired by what's fresh from the famers they support.

Cook the pasta in a large saucepan of boiling water according to the package instructions until the pasta is al dente. Drain in a colander. Wipe the saucepan dry.

Preheat the oven to 350° F. Butter a 13 x 9-inch baking dish.

Combine the butter and garlic in the saucepan; cook over medium-high heat until the butter melts, stirring constantly. Reduce the heat to medium and add the flour; cook, stirring constantly, until the mixture is smooth. Continue cooking and stirring for 1 minute more.

Gradually pour in the milk, stirring with a whisk until the sauce is smooth. Whisk in the salt and pepper; bring to a simmer and cook, stirring constantly, until the sauce is smooth and thickened. Add the Cheddar and smoked pepper jack cheeses; reduce the heat to low and cook, stirring constantly, until cheese is melted. Remove from heat and stir in the pasta.

Pour the pasta mixture into the prepared casserole dish; sprinkle with the breadcrumbs. Bake until the sauce is bubbly and breadcrumbs are browned, about 20 minutes.

MAKES 8 SERVINGS

1 pound macaroni

2 sticks (1 cup) unsalted butter

2 tablespoons minced fresh garlic

3/4 cup all-purpose flour

6 cups whole milk

1/2 teaspoon salt

1/2 teaspoon freshly ground pepper

2 cups (8 ounces) shredded Cheddar (or smoked Cheddar) cheese

2 cups (8 ounces) shredded smoked (or regular) pepper jack cheese

Additional salt and freshly ground pepper to taste

1 cup fresh breadcrumbs

COOK'S NOTE:
Homegrown smokes their pepper jack cheese at the restaurant. To get smoky flavor, you can use smoked Cheddar cheese and regular pepper jack cheese.

Ricotta Gnudi
with Porcini Ragout

—**Brian Ross**, DOUGH

Gnudi are pillowy nuggets similar to gnocchi, but lighter and tenderer because they are made with less flour. Chef/owner Brian Ross uses OO flour to make fluffy, light gnudi; OO is the Italian designation for the finest ground flour with the lowest gluten content. OO flour is often used for making thin and crisp (not chewy) pizza crust as well as tender gnudi.

FOR THE GNUDI:

1 pound fresh ricotta cheese

1 large egg

1/3 cup finely grated Parmesan cheese

1/2 teaspoon salt

Large pinch of ground white pepper

2 cups OO flour or all-purpose flour, divided

Sea salt

FOR THE RAGOUT:

2 tablespoons unsalted butter

1/2 cup sliced porcini mushrooms

1/2 clove garlic, minced

1/2 medium shallot, minced

1 sprig fresh thyme

1 cup chicken stock

1 cup heavy whipping cream

Sea salt and freshly ground pepper to taste

Additional freshly grated Parmesan cheese for serving

COOKS NOTE:
You'll need about a 1-ounce piece of Parmesan to measure 1/3 cup finely grated. For the porcini mushrooms, you can use fresh or dried and rehydrated.

To make the gnudi, line a large fine-mesh sieve with several layers of paper towels or cheesecloth; place over a medium bowl. Spoon the ricotta into the sieve. Let it drain for up to an hour.

Beat the egg, Parmesan cheese, salt, and pepper in a large bowl. Stir in the drained ricotta. Sprinkle 1 cup of the flour into the bowl and stir gently to blend. Cover and refrigerate the dough for 1 hour or up to 24 hours.

Line a baking sheet with plastic wrap. Place about a cup of the additional flour in a wide shallow bowl or on a work surface. Scoop out about a cup of the dough and shape it into a ball. Add to the flour and toss to coat lightly, then roll the flour out to shape it into a short log. Place it on the baking sheet; cut it to make 1-inch dumplings.

Prepare an ice water bath. Bring a large pot of boiling water to a boil; add 1 to 2 tablespoons of sea salt. Cook the gnudi, in batches, until very tender, about 8 minutes. Remove from the boiling water and transfer to the ice water bath to stop the cooking process; remove and drain on paper towels.

To make the ragout, melt the butter in a large skillet over medium heat; add the mushrooms, garlic, shallot, and thyme; cover and cook until the mushrooms are just tender, about 3 to 5 minutes. Add the stock and boil uncovered until the liquid is reduced to about 1/2 cup, about 5 minutes.

Stir in the cream; bring to a simmer. Reduce the heat and simmer until thickened, if necessary.

To serve, reheat the gnudi in boiling water; drain and transfer to a buttered serving dish. Pour the ragout over the gnudi and sprinkle generously with Parmesan cheese.

Vegan Pesto

—Aaron Thomas, NINE MILE

3/4 cup plus 2 tablespoons
raw sunflower seeds

3 tablespoons mashed
Roasted Garlic
(recipe follows)

1 1/2 teaspoons fresh
lemon juice

1 1/2 teaspoons
kosher salt

3/4 teaspoon freshly
ground pepper

3 cups firmly packed fresh
basil leaves, divided

1 1/4 cups canola or
olive oil, divided

1 tablespoon water

This Caribbean-inspired restaurant has 2 locations: in Montford and in West Asheville. They have quickly become neighborhood gathering spots for locals, and the signature pasta and rice dishes have drawn loyal fans from all over Asheville. Owner Aaron Thomas shared his popular pesto, and recommends using "a non-GMO canola oil instead of olive oil if you refrigerate this pesto. Canola oil won't solidify and separate when it is chilled."

Process the sunflower seeds in a food processor until very finely ground, 1 to 2 minutes. Add the garlic, lemon juice, salt, and pepper; pulse until well combined, 5 times. Add half of the basil and half of the oil; process until finely chopped, about 10 seconds. Scrape the sides of the bowl and add the remaining basil, oil, and water; process until smooth, thick, and creamy.

Roasted Garlic

—Aaron Thomas, NINE MILE

1 large bulb garlic

1 tablespoon olive oil

Preheat the oven to 400° F. Peel away the outer, papery layers surrounding the garlic bulb, leaving the skin of the individual cloves intact to hold them together. Using a sharp knife, cut 1/4 to 1/2 inch off the top of the bulb, exposing the garlic cloves.

Place the garlic bulbs in a loaf pan; drizzle the oil over the tops of the exposed garlic to coat. Cover the pan snugly with foil; bake until the cloves feel soft when pressed, about 30 to 35 minutes. Let the garlic cool.

Use a small, sharp knife to make small slits in the skin outside each clove; pull or squeeze the cloves out of their skins.

Veggie Burger

—**Traci Taylor,** FIG

We asked chef Traci Taylor how she served the tasty burgers: "We cook with the seasons, so in winter we do grilled red onion, goat cheese, and tomato jam on the burgers; in summer, fresh tomatoes, Bibb lettuce, grilled onions, choice of cheeses."

Sauté the mushrooms in the olive oil in a large heavy skillet over medium-high heat until they are tender, about 5 minutes. Remove from the skillet and place in a bowl. Add the shallots, jalapeño, and garlic to the skillet; cover, reduce heat to low, and cook until the shallots are tender, stirring frequently, about 5 minutes.

Combine the egg, 4 cups of the chickpeas, lime juice, ginger, cumin, and coriander in a food processor; process until the chickpeas are mashed and the mixture is blended. Turn the mixture out into a large bowl. Add the remaining chickpeas to the processor; pulse until they are mashed, scraping the bowl as needed. Scrape the chickpeas into the bowl and stir the mixture to blend.

Add the mushrooms and shallot mixture to the chickpea mixture; stir well. Form into 4-inch patties; place on a rimmed baking sheet lined with parchment paper. Cover and refrigerate at least 4 hours.

To cook, place the flour, beaten egg mixture, and breadcrumbs in separate dishes. Heat a large heavy skillet over medium heat; add 1/8 inch of oil and heat until hot but not smoking. Dip the patties, one at a time, in the flour, then the egg, then the breadcrumbs. Fry, in batches, until browned and cooked through, 2 to 4 minutes on each side. Serve in buns with desired toppings.

MAKES ABOUT 12 BURGERS

1 1/2 cups sliced mushrooms

1 tablespoon extra-virgin olive oil

1/2 cup minced shallots

1/2 cup minced seeded jalapeño

1 clove garlic, minced

1 large egg

8 cups cooked, drained chickpeas, divided

1/2 cup fresh lime juice

1 tablespoon minced ginger

1 1/2 teaspoons ground cumin

1 1/2 teaspoons ground coriander

1/2 cup toasted pumpkin seeds

All-purpose flour

1 additional large egg, beaten with 2 teaspoons water

Plain dry breadcrumbs

Market
Mains

Farmer & Chef Asheville

For the Love *of* Meat

Asheville-area protein producers are a wise, intrepid, and resourceful pack. Lacking the exceedingly flat, vast ranges of the ranching West, they perch their lamb and cattle, as well as pigs, on the mountainous terrain they have in WNC. They maximize small acreage by raising chickens and rabbits. And they cultivate cool streams for trout the way other farmers cultivate rows of veggies.

They're also an innovative herd, offering much more than chops and chuck to chefs and customers. They turn their raw products into one-of-a-kind charcuterie creations from salami to trout jerky.

But perhaps above all, our farmers are a respectful brood: They shuck most modern-day methods for a return to sustainable, humane Appalachian ways that honor the earth and their livestock. Their animals are pasture-raised with ample space to roam, sun to soak up, and grass and natural forages aplenty — forget hormones and antibiotics.

They implement time-honored practices like rotational grazing to keep their pastures pristine, and they use low-stress handling methods when preparing and transporting animals for processing. What's more, they work their fields year-round. They do it all in order to provide quality, safe products at tailgates, farm stands, and stores — ready to serve as the stars of our meals.

The result of their labor is Asheville's unique carnivore culture. Our area chefs pride themselves on whole-animal cooking, finding creative uses for every part from nose to tail, leaving no waste. And here, it's not the bar where everyone knows your name, but rather our thriving independent butcher shops.

—Maggie Cramer, writer and editor

Market Mains

Beef & Lamb

Lamb Kabobs with Mint Pesto Sauce • 142

Fresh Gnocchi with Spicy Lamb Sausage,
Tomato & Coconut • 143

Roasted Tomatoes Stuffed with
Ground Lamb • 144

Sloppy Jai • 145

Bourbon Honey Marinated Hangar Steak
with Blackberry BBQ Sauce • 146

Rolled Flank Steak • 147

Corned Beef • 150

Beef Bacon • 150

Duck Confit & Crepinettes • 151

Lamb Kabobs with
Mint Pesto on page 142

Lamb Kabobs *with* Mint Pesto Sauce

—**Wendy Brugh,** DRY RIDGE FARM

One of Wendy and Graham Brugh's favorite ways to enjoy lamb, she adapted this recipe from the book, Garde Manger, 4th Edition.

MAKES 4 TO 6 SERVINGS

1/4 cup extra-virgin olive oil

2 tablespoons fresh lemon juice

1 teaspoon kosher salt

1/2 teaspoon freshly ground pepper

2 tablespoons chopped fresh mint

3 cloves garlic, crushed

2 1/2 pounds leg of lamb, cut into 3/4-inch cubes

Mint Pesto
(page 209)

1 cup sour cream

15 slices bacon
(about 1 pound)

10 water-soaked skewers

COOK'S NOTE:
For a variation, add
2 teaspoons grated fresh ginger to the marinade and 1 teaspoon to the pesto.

Combine the olive oil, lemon juice, salt, and pepper in a large bowl; whisk to blend. Stir in the mint and garlic; add the lamb cubes and toss to coat well. Cover and refrigerate, stirring occasionally, at least 4 hours and up to overnight.

Combine the Mint Pesto and sour cream in a bowl and stir well.

Preheat the oven to 450° F. Or preheat a grill for medium-high heat.

To assemble the kabobs, run a skewer through a piece of bacon about 1/2 inch from the end of the slice. Push a lamb cube onto the skewer, and wrap the long end of the bacon slice around the top of the lamb cube, skewering it to secure. The bacon should snake around the cubes in an S shape. Repeat this process to fill all skewers.

If roasting, arrange the skewers on a rack in a rimmed baking sheet and bake until the lamb is browned but still pink on the inside or to the desired doneness, 8 to 12 minutes for medium-rare. If grilling, grill the skewers, turning, 8 to 10 minutes for medium-rare. Serve with Mint Pesto sauce.

Fresh Gnocchi *with* Spicy Lamb Sausage, Tomato, *&* Coconut

—**Dawn and Stephen Robertson,** EAST FORK FARM

Shop for East Fork Farm sausage at the Asheville City Market on Saturdays. Then stroll down several tents to Rio Berolini's table for the homemade gnocchi and other fresh pasta. At home, Dawn serves this dish with sautéed kale.

MAKES 4 SERVINGS

1 pound bulk East Fork Farm Spicy Lamb Sausage

1 large onion, chopped

1 large clove garlic, finely chopped

1 (28-ounce) can stewed tomatoes, undrained

1 (12-ounce) can coconut milk

1 bunch Italian parsley, leaves chopped

1/2 teaspoon salt

1 pound fresh gnocchi

Cook the sausage, onion, and garlic in a large, heavy saucepan over medium heat until the sausage is browned, breaking up the sausage with a wooden spoon as it cooks. Stir in the stewed tomatoes, coconut milk, parsley, and salt. Bring to a boil; reduce the heat and simmer for 30 minutes.

Meanwhile, cook the gnocchi in boiling, salted water until all of the gnocchi is floating, 2 to 3 minutes. Drain well and add to the lamb mixture.

Slow Food Asheville: A Pleasure and Commitment

The Asheville chapter, or "convivium," of the global Slow Food movement links the pleasure of food with a commitment to the community and environment. Through locally created programs and events, the convivium aims to support and sustain the people who grow our food sustainably and the people who eat consciously — to attain the larger goal of caring for our planet.

Slow Food Asheville is not sitting still with our blessings: an abundance of tailgate markets, organic growers, food artisans, and incredible restaurants. The chapter is actively promoting relationships between farmers, cooks, families, and the community through programs and events initiated by restaurant owners, chefs, and citizens. Events include: FEAST (page 38); Heritage Foods Education, which preserves food traditions and the Appalachian Food Storybank; Slow Food on Campus, which works with students to educate them about sustainable food systems; and Slow Food Events in WNC, which gathers together to enjoy food.

For more information: slowfoodasheville.org.

Roasted Tomatoes Stuffed *with* Ground Lamb

—**Wendy Brugh,** DRY RIDGE FARM

"This is my mom's recipe," says Wendy Brugh, "one that I'm sure has been passed on down generations. She emigrated to the US from Belgium, and I grew up making and eating many dishes that embody Belgian cuisine: simple dishes made from fresh ingredients, topped with light sauces, that all come together in a satisfying meal," explains Wendy. "Since childhood, I've enjoyed making this dish. It's a celebration of the tomato season, and I love the messiness of its creation — from scooping out juicy tomato insides to kneading the lamb stuffing with my hands."

MAKES 4 TO 6 SERVINGS

4 to 6 large fresh tomatoes

1 pound ground lamb

1 large yellow onion, diced

2 cloves garlic, minced

1 large egg

About 1/4 cup minced fresh herbs, such as thyme, oregano, and parsley, divided

Salt and freshly ground pepper

Preheat the oven to 350° F.

Cut a thin slice from blossom end of each tomato so you can hollow them; reserve the slices. Using a small spoon, scoop out the flesh into a small saucepan, leaving shells for stuffing. Arrange the tomatoes in a roasting pan.

Combine the lamb, onion, garlic, egg, 3 tablespoons of the herbs, 1/2 teaspoon of the salt, and 1/4 teaspoon of the pepper in a bowl; mix lightly but well.

Spoon the stuffing into the tomatoes, dividing evenly; the lamb mixture will sit up above the rims. Top with the tomato slices. Roast, uncovered, until the lamb is cooked, about 45 minutes.

About 10 minutes before the end of roasting, bring the saucepan of tomato flesh to a simmer over medium heat, breaking up the large pieces; stir in the remaining tablespoon of herbs, and season to taste with salt and pepper. Reduce heat and simmer for 5 to 10 minutes. Drizzle the sauce over the stuffed tomatoes.

1/4 cup oil

1 tablespoon cumin seed

1 teaspoon coarsely ground black peppercorns

2 cups diced yellow onion

1 tablespoon kosher salt

1 tablespoon finely diced fresh ginger

1 teaspoon minced fresh chilies, such as serrano

2 tablespoons ginger garlic paste

2 tablespoons ground coriander

2 tablespoons ground cumin

1 tablespoon ground turmeric

1 teaspoon chili powder

1/4 cup coarsely chopped cilantro leaves

2 pounds ground lamb (preferably coarse ground)

1 tablespoon garam masala

1/2 cup plain yogurt

2 cups canned crushed tomatoes, undrained

1 tablespoon brown sugar

1 tablespoon cider vinegar

Hawaiian rolls, split and lightly buttered on cut sides

Sweetened yogurt, cilantro leaves, and diced onion (as toppings)

Sloppy Jai (*Kheema Paay*)

—Meherwan Irani, CHAI PANI

"This dish captures the essence of the playfulness of Chai Pani, yet pays a multi-layered homage to my roots," says chef/owner Meheran Irani. *"The recipe is originally a 15th century Mughal recipe with its heavy use of aromatic spices and a touch of yogurt, but updated with a distinctly Parsi touch of vinegar and brown sugar and then repurposed into a familiar American sandwich."*

Heat a 12-inch or other very large, deep skillet over medium-high heat; add the oil and heat until hot but not smoking. Add the cumin seed and peppercorns; let the seeds sputter for about 30 seconds, but do not burn them. Add the onion and salt; cook, stirring until onions are golden brown, 2 to 4 minutes. Stir in the ginger and chilies; sauté until softened, about 1 minute. Stir in the garlic ginger paste; sauté until paste is browned, about 1 minute.

Add the coriander, cumin, turmeric, chili powder, and chopped cilantro; sauté 1 minute. Add the lamb and garam masala; cook, stirring to break up meat, until the lamb is completely cooked. The lamb must brown and not boil, which is why the skillet should be very large. Reduce the heat and stir in the yogurt; cook, stirring until the lamb is glossy, about 10 minutes. Stir in the tomatoes, sugar, and vinegar; cover and simmer for 15 minutes, stirring occasionally.

To serve, toast the cut sides of the rolls on a grill pan; the buns should still be soft with golden, grill-marked interiors. Spoon the lamb mixture onto the roll bottoms; drizzle with a little sweetened yogurt, sprinkle with cilantro and diced onions, and lean the roll tops on the Sloppy Jai.

145

Bourbon Honey Marinated Hangar Steak *with* Blackberry BBQ Sauce

—**Mary Collins-Shepard,** SEASONAL SCHOOL OF CULINARY ARTS

MAKES 4 SERVINGS

1/4 cup bourbon

2 tablespoons soy sauce

2 tablespoons honey

2 tablespoons extra-virgin olive oil

4 (4- to 5-ounce) strips trimmed beef hangar steaks

1 teaspoon freshly ground pepper, or to taste

Blackberry BBQ Sauce (page 217)

Challenged to teach a cooking class using honey as an ingredient, chef Mary Collins-Shepard instructed the group in grilling this earthy, smoky, lightly salty and sweet steak, served with a spicy fresh blackberry-based sauce. A little bourbon goes a long way to distinguishing the taste of the marinade and sauce, so use quality bourbon for best flavor.

Combine the bourbon, soy sauce, honey, and olive oil in a zip-top plastic bag; seal the bag or shake it to blend the marinade ingredients. Add the steaks to the bag; seal and turn to distribute the marinade evenly around the steaks. Refrigerate 2 to 4 hours, turning the bag occasionally.

Remove the steaks from the marinade, allowing the excess marinade to drip off. Discard the marinade. Sprinkle the steaks with pepper, to taste.

Preheat a grill for medium-high heat; oil the grill rack. Grill the steaks until desired doneness, about 4 to 6 minutes on each side for medium-rare. Serve with the Blackberry BBQ Sauce.

Chefs at Welcome Table: A Means of Grace

Welcome to the white tablecloth dining spot at the Haywood Street Congregation in downtown Asheville. Take a seat at a table lushly set with linens, flowers, china, and fine flatware. Enjoy the beautifully presented, delicious, nutritious, and substantial meal cooked by chefs from our finest local independent restaurants.

This is no ordinary soup kitchen. The community program, piloted by the Heirloom Hospitality Group owners and staff, brings restaurant-quality food to families and individuals in need. Currently, 16 restaurants individually prepare a meal from their menu one Wednesday per month. Collectively, they feed over 450 guests.

Says Liz Button, organizer and co-owner of Curate, "By our actions and our food, we're delivering a clear message: Regardless of who you are or your circumstances, you deserve the very best." Chefs at Welcome Table are indeed a means of grace.

Read more at haywoodstreet.org/2010/07/the-welcome-table/.

Rolled Flank Steak

—Hickory Nut Gap Farm

Flattening the steak with a meat mallet serves to tenderize the steak, make it easier to roll, and allow it to cook evenly.

Preheat the grill to medium-high heat or preheat the oven to 400° F. Brush the steak with the oil and sprinkle with the salt and pepper, to taste. Let it stand for 20 minutes to take the chill off the meat.

Combine the egg, garlic, cheese, breadcrumbs, onion, watercress, and parsley in a medium bowl; mix thoroughly. Season lightly with salt and pepper, as desired.

Pound the steak on a work surface with a meat mallet to flatten it evenly to about 1/2-inch-thick. Place it so that the long side is nearest you. Spread the cheese mixture over the meat, leaving a 1-inch border. Roll the flank steak up and over the cheese mixture like a jellyroll. Tuck in the ends of the steak and tie it in 4 or 5 places with butcher's twine.

Grill the rolled steak, turning as it browns, until it is medium-rare or an instant read thermometer inserted in the center of the inside of the roll reads 125° F., 15 to 20 minutes. Alternatively, you can roast the rolled steak on a rack in a roasting pan until it cooks to your desired doneness, 15 to 20 minutes. Let it stand for 5 to 10 minutes before slicing.

MAKES 6 SERVINGS

1 (1.5-pound) flank steak

2 tablespoons olive oil

3/4 teaspoon kosher salt, or to taste

3/4 teaspoon freshly ground pepper, or to taste

1 large egg, lightly beaten

4 cloves garlic, minced

1 ounce (1/4 cup) shredded farmer's cheese or other mild white cheese

1/2 cup fine, dry plain breadcrumbs

1/4 cup finely chopped onion

1/4 cup chopped fresh watercress or spinach

1 teaspoon minced fresh parsley

Butcher's Specials

Old-Time Butcher Revival

The old-school craft of butchery is finding its chops in a new generation of food artisans. What farmers markets have done for produce, Asheville butchers are doing for local, pasture-raised meats. Meet two local men who've taken up the cleaver to do more than give us perfectly delicious traditional cuts. They also make incredible sausages, salamis, hot dogs, and more. They're not only versed in our food culture, they are helping drive it.

Bringing Back the Butcher of Yore:
Foothills Deli and Butchery

Meat lovers, meet your new playground: Foothills Farm & Butchery's full-service, whole-animal butcher shop and deli from the McKissick family farmers of Foothills Pasture Raised Meats. Meredith and Casey McKissick sell meats ready for your culinary magic. They have specialty house-made sausages and hot dogs made the right way with only what you would eat in the form of meat — no fillers or mystery meats. And they make lunch sandwiches in the kitchen and sell complete to-go dinners made by their chefs. All the meats are locally and pasture raised. Foothills' own meats are stocked and on the menu, with offerings from other area farms with the same quality commitment.

Says Casey McKissick, "I've always loved the idea of the old school, full-service butcher shop. The butcher of yore took responsibility for the whole animal and had to have the skills to turn each pound of lean, fat, bone, skin, and offal into a marketable product that could make money — and find or create a buyer for each item. The renaissance of the local butcher is playing out across the country, riding the wave of the local food movement. We're one of the very few owned and operated by the farmers themselves. We bring in top-notch food professionals, chefs, and butchers to turn our animals into delicious and nutritious foods. A big part of the inspiration was also to be able to make a hot dog we wanted for our kids: the perfect dog made out of good, clean meat. Turns out, lots of other parents also want this for their families."

For more information, go to: www.foothillslocalmeats.com.

Meet the Butcher, and What the Heck is a Crepinette?

Chris Reed is the friendly guy at the helm, as knowledgeable about each meat and fowl in the display case as his local sources. A fourth-generation butcher, Reed learned the craft from his grandfather and father at an early age. He inherited their cooking techniques, too; just ask him how to cook anything in the case.

Reed is known for his spicy, creatively seasoned bacon. He won top prized at the North Carolina Baconfest in 2014 for Best Bacon, with his Maple Rosemary, Wakin' Bacon, and Fire Belly pork bacon flavors, as well as a Maple Chipotle duck bacon.

Chatting as he wraps up duck bacon one morning, he mentions his latest crepinette concoction — duck confit with cranberries and pistachios — and gives me a sample to test. Never having seen one in my life, I leave to go home and sauté it for breakfast, adding a poached egg on top as he suggests. It was incredible.

The patty was wrapped in pig's caul fat, web-like pieces of what looks like cheesecloth with large pores. Reed pulls off pieces and wraps it around the meat; at home, pan-fry it until that fat layer melts into the confit mixture and crisps like lean bacon.

"You should be able to get caul fat from your local butcher shop. To play it safe, ask for at least a pound," says Chris. "Don't worry about having extra; after you eat crepinettes, you will want to wrap all your meats in caul fat!"

Corned Beef

—**Meredith and Casey McKissick,** FOOTHILLS DELI & BUTCHERY

MAKES ABOUT 16 SERVINGS

2 1/2 quarts distilled water

1/4 cup plus 1 tablespoon kosher salt

1/4 cup plus 1 tablespoon evaporated cane juice crystals (raw sugar)

2 tablespoons cure #1

1 tablespoon black peppercorns, coarsely ground

1 tablespoon crushed allspice berries

3/4 teaspoon crushed red pepper

1/2 teaspoon minced fresh garlic

1 bay leaf, crushed

1 (5-pound) beef brisket

Pour the water into a large glass bowl; stir in the salt, cane crystals, cure #1, peppercorns, allspice, crushed red pepper, garlic, and bay leaf until the crystals dissolve. Cover and refrigerate until the brine is chilled to 40° F.

Place the beef brisket in a nonreactive container just large enough to hold the meat submerged in the brine. For the quickest results, inject the brine, using a meat syringe, into the beef brisket. Cover and refrigerate for 3 days. Alternately, place the brine and brisket in a large, nonreactive container that will hold the meat submerged in brine; cover and refrigerate for at least 10 days.

Remove the brisket from the container and rinse well; place it in a large, heavy saucepan. Pour in enough cold water to cover the brisket. Bring to a boil, spooning off any scum that rises to surface; cover, reduce heat, and simmer for 5 hours or until very tender. Remove the meat and let cool slightly before serving.

Beef Bacon

—**Meredith and Casey McKissick,** FOOTHILLS DELI & BUTCHERY

Resist the urge to trim all the fat off of the meat. It will provide flavor and assist in the curing process. You may trim away to create a nice, square slab of meat, which will cure and smoke more evenly. Rub salt and sugar liberally over the meat. Wrap tightly in plastic wrap and refrigerate one week.

Unwrap and rinse the meat; smoke the meat at 180° for 8 hours. Cool and refrigerate until cold, at least 6 hours or overnight before slicing and cooking.

MAKES ABOUT 1 1/2 POUNDS

2 1/2 pounds beef plate meat or brisket, untrimmed

1 1/2 tablespoons kosher salt

1 tablespoon sugar

COOK'S NOTE:
It is helpful to use a kitchen scale and measure the salt and sugar in grams to get the correct portions of salt and sugar for curing the beef.

Duck Confit & Crepinettes

—**Chris Reed,** KATUAH MARKET

MAKES 8 SERVINGS

Finely ground sea salt

6 to 8 fresh duck legs

2 tablespoons ground
white pepper

36 whole cloves

6 finely crushed bay leaves
or chopped leaves from
6 sprigs rosemary

10 whole juniper berries,
crushed and minced,
optional

About 3 to 4 pounds
rendered duck fat

1 tablespoon plus
2 teaspoons chili powder

2 1/2 teaspoons sea salt

2 teaspoons each dried
oregano, crushed red
pepper, ground red pepper

1 1/2 teaspoons each
ground cumin and
chipotle powder

3 cloves garlic,
crushed and minced

1/2 cup rendered duck fat

1/4 cup red wine vinegar

Pour a 1/4-inch-thick layer of salt in a 13 x 9-inch baking pan. Cut 10 small slits in the duck leg skin. For each leg, push 2 cloves in three of the slits; sprinkle with pepper and arrange on salt, skin sides up. Sprinkle with bay leaves and juniper. Cover completely with another layer of salt.

Place another pan on the duck legs and weight it down with bricks or cans. Refrigerate 24 hours to cure. Rinse thoroughly and place on a rack in a baking dish; refrigerate, uncovered, 12 hours.

Preheat the oven to 200° F. Melt the duck fat in a heavy, ovenproof pot over low heat. Submerge the duck legs in the fat, covering by 1/2 inch. Cover and bake 6 to 7 hours. Let it cool. Place the duck legs in a covered container and pour the fat over them to submerge. Cover and refrigerate at least 1 week and up to 2.

To make 15 Crepinettes with the Duck Confit:

Mix the spices and garlic in a bowl. Chop the duck meat very finely with some of the skin (optional) and add to the spices. Add the rendered fat and vinegar, mixing well. Cover and chill.

Form 3-inch diameter patties. Cut sections of the caul fat that appear large enough to wrap the patties. Wrap each patty completely, stretching the caul fat and piecing together smaller sections of caul fat, if necessary. Cook in a heavy oiled skillet over medium heat until browned.

Market Mains

Pork

Roast Pork Shoulder • 154

Pork Butt Rub • 154

Pork Tenderloin with
Orange Blossom Honey Mustard • 155

Bahn Xeo
(Vietnamese Coconut Crepe) • 156

Nouc Cham • 157

BBQ Carnitas Tacos • 158

Grilled Pork & Pineapple with
Poblano Coulis • 160

Chorizo-Stuffed Pork Chops • 161

Roast Pork Shoulder
on page 154

Roast Pork Shoulder

—**William Dissen,** THE MARKET PLACE RESTAURANT

Chef/owner William Dissen shares an oven-roasting technique for the Wood Grilled Pork Shoulder he featured at an Outstanding in the Field dinner (page 184). He served it with a bean and kale ragout with roasted tomatoes.

MAKES 16 SERVINGS

Preheat the oven to 300° F. Line a large rimmed baking sheet with aluminum foil; place a rack on the foil.

Tie the pork butt into a shape that is an even thickness with butcher's twine. Rub the meat all over with the Pork Butt Rub and place it on the rack. Melt the butter with the thyme; rub that all over the meat too.

Roast until a meat thermometer reads 185° F., about 5 hours. Let the meat stand for 10 minutes before slicing.

1 (8-pound) boneless pork shoulder

1 cup Pork Butt Rub (recipe follows)

3/4 stick (6 tablespoons) butter, cubed

4 thyme sprigs

Pork Butt Rub

MAKES 3 CUPS

1 cup kosher salt

1/2 cup firmly packed light brown sugar

1/4 cup ground mustard

2 tablespoons each garlic powder, paprika, smoked paprika, & dried rosemary, thyme, basil, marjoram, oregano

1 tablespoon freshly ground black pepper

1 1/2 teaspoons ground cumin

Combine all the ingredients in a pint jar; shake to blend the ingredients well. Cover tightly and store up to 6 months.

Pork Tenderloin *with* Orange Blossom Honey Mustard

—Laurey Masterton, LAUREY'S

We are grateful for permission to reprint this recipe from Laurey Masterton's book The Fresh Honey Cookbook. *In Laurey's words, "Pork is well complemented by sweet things. On a trip to Tuscany, I was wowed by a dinner of local pork chops served with a sweet onion confit made with sugar. The flavor stayed with me and after making my version of that dish a number of times, I decided to play with it using honey and fresh fruit. Here's what I came up with."*

MAKES 6 TO 8 SERVINGS

2 (1-pound)
pork tenderloins

2 tablespoons extra-virgin olive oil, divided

1/2 teaspoon
granulated garlic

1/2 teaspoon kosher salt

1/2 teaspoon freshly ground pepper

2 tablespoons
Dijon mustard

2 tablespoons honey, preferably orange blossom honey

1 navel orange, unpeeled and thinly sliced

1 Meyer lemon, halved

Preheat the oven to 375° F. Drizzle the pork with 1 tablespoon of the olive oil and season with garlic, salt, and pepper.

Heat a large cast-iron skillet over medium-high heat. Add the remaining 1 tablespoon of the oil and swirl to coat the surface of the skillet. Add the tenderloins and sear on both sides, turning, about 2 minutes. For ideal browning on all sides, curve each tenderloin close to the sides of the skillet, leaving a space in the center. Remove from the heat.

Combine the mustard and honey in a small bowl; blend well and then spoon the mixture over the pork. Layer the orange slices under the pork, lining them up in the center of the pan and over-lapping to fit. Place the tenderloins, side by side, on top of the oranges.

Place the skillet in the oven and roast until the internal temperature reads 145° F. on an instant-read meat thermometer. Remove the skillet from the oven and squeeze the lemon over the pork. Let stand 5 minutes and transfer the pork to a cutting board.

Cut the meat into diagonal, 1-inch-thick slices. Arrange a slice or two of the oranges on each plate and fan the sliced pork on top. Spoon the pan juices over the pork.

"Oh my!" said chef Laurey Masterton.

Bahn Xeo
(Vietnamese Coconut Crepe)

—**Eric Kang,** THE ADMIRAL

"Traditional fillings are pork and shrimp. Crepes are served with a mixture of herbs, such as cilantro, shiso (an herb in the mint family), and mint," explains sous chef Eric Kang. "The dipping sauce is called Nouc Cham."

To prepare the crepe batter, combine the rice flour, turmeric, and salt in a large bowl. Combine 1 3/4 cups warm water and coconut milk; add to the rice flour mixture and whisk to blend. Stir in the scallions. Cover and refrigerate 2 hours or overnight.

To prepare the filling, combine the pork, 2 tablespoons of the oyster sauce, and 1 teaspoon of the fish sauce in a medium bowl, tossing well. Combine the shrimp and remaining oyster sauce and fish sauce in another bowl.

MAKES 4 TO 6 SERVINGS

FOR THE CREPES:

2 cups rice flour

1/4 teaspoon
ground turmeric

1 teaspoon salt

3/4 cup coconut milk

3 scallions, sliced

FOR THE FILLING:

1/2 pound very thinly sliced
pork belly or pork shoulder

3 tablespoons
oyster sauce, divided

2 teaspoons
fish sauce, divided

1/2 pound peeled and
deveined shrimp, halved

2 tablespoons vegetable
oil, divided

FOR SERVING:

Nouc Cham (recipe follows)

Leaf lettuce leaves

2 cups bean sprouts

Cilantro, shiso, and mint
leaves (as garnish)

Heat the 1 tablespoon of the oil in a large, heavy skillet over medium-high heat; add the pork mixture and sauté until no longer pink, 2 to 3 minutes. Remove from the skillet and wipe the skillet dry.

Heat the remaining tablespoon of the oil in the skillet over medium-high heat; add the shrimp mixture and sauté until shrimp are firm and opaque, about 2 minutes. Remove from the skillet.

To prepare the crepes, heat a medium nonstick skillet over medium-high heat; lightly oil the skillet. Pour in about 3 tablespoons of batter, tilting the pan in a circular motion so that the batter coats the surface of the skillet evenly in a very thin layer. Sprinkle some of the pork, shrimp, and bean sprouts evenly over the crepe. Cover and cook until the bottom is crispy and the crepe is cooked through, about 2 minutes.

Gently fold the crepe in half with a spatula and slide onto a plate. Repeat with the remaining batter and filling.

Serve with the desired herbs on each plate with a small bowl of Nouc Cham. To eat, pull off pieces of the crepe; wrap up the lettuce with the desired herbs; dip it in the sauce.

MAKES ABOUT 1 1/4 CUPS

1/2 cup sugar

Juice and grated zest of 6 limes

1/2 cup fish sauce

1/2 serrano chile with seeds

3 cloves garlic, minced

Nouc Cham

—**Eric Kang,** THE ADMIRAL

Nouc Cham is a traditional dipping sauce for Bahn Xeo.

Whisk the sugar in 1 cup warm water until the sugar is dissolved. Add the remaining ingredients, stirring well. Let it stand for 15 minutes; stir before serving.

BBQ Carnitas Tacos

FOR THE PORK:

1 (4 to 6-pound) boneless or (5 to 7-pound) bone-in pork shoulder

1 1/2 tablespoons ground cinnamon

1 1/2 tablespoons chili powder

2 teaspoons kosher salt

2 teaspoons freshly ground pepper

FOR THE COLESLAW:

1/4 cup mayonnaise

2 tablespoons sugar

2 tablespoons distilled white vinegar

1/2 teaspoon dried oregano

1/4 teaspoon garlic powder

1/4 teaspoon onion powder

1/4 teaspoon freshly ground pepper

1/8 teaspoon salt, or to taste

1 (16-ounce) bag coleslaw mix

FOR THE BAKED BEANS:

2 strips bacon, chopped

1 (16-ounce) can baked beans

2 teaspoons molasses

3/4 teaspoon ground cumin

Freshly ground pepper, to taste

Salt, to taste

FOR THE TACOS:

16 corn tortillas, warmed

Carnitas BBQ Sauce (page 218)

—**Laura and Ben Mixson,** WHITE DUCK TACO SHOP

We braise 4 pork shoulders at a time for about six hours, let them sit for one, then pull it for the day's tacos," says chef/owner Laura Mixson.

To roast the pork, preheat the oven to 350° F. Mix the cinnamon, chili powder, salt, and pepper; rub all over the pork. Place the pork in an ovenproof Dutch oven with a tight-fitting lid; alternatively, place in a roasting pan and cover with a piece of heavy-duty aluminum foil, sealing the edges to the rim of the pan. Roast 5 to 6 hours or until the pork shreds easily.

Let the pork stand 1 hour; lift out the pork and place it in a large dish. Spoon the fat off the meat juices, reserving the meat juices in the Dutch oven. Pull the pork and add it back to the juices to keep it moist. (You can refrigerate leftovers up to 4 days.)

To make the coleslaw, whisk the mayonnaise, sugar, vinegar, oregano, garlic powder, onion powder, pepper, and salt in a large bowl. Add the cabbage and toss; cover and refrigerate up to 1 hour.

To make the baked beans, cook the bacon in a medium saucepan over medium-high heat until crisp, 4 to 5 minutes. Reduce the heat to low and add the beans, molasses, cumin, salt, and pepper. Cover and simmer, stirring frequently, 10 minutes.

For each serving, layer 2 tortillas on a serving plate; layer the beans, pork, and coleslaw on the tortillas. Top with Carnitas BBQ Sauce.

Grilled Pork *and* Pineapple *with* Poblano Coulis

—**Michael Fisera**, LEXINGTON AVENUE BREWERY

MAKES 8 SERVINGS

FOR MARINADE:

2 cups olive oil blend

2 tablespoons minced fresh cilantro

1 1/2 tablespoons brown sugar

1 1/2 tablespoons minced fresh garlic

1 1/2 tablespoons ground cinnamon

1 tablespoon toasted cumin seeds, ground

1 tablespoon ground coriander

1 tablespoon ground ginger

1 teaspoon ground allspice

1/2 teaspoon ground cloves

1 1/2 tablespoons fresh orange juice

FOR THE MEAT:

2 large pork tenderloins (about 1 1/2 pounds)

1 fresh pineapple, peeled, cored, and cut into 8 slices

Poblano Coulis (recipe follows)

TASTING NOTES:
LAB's beers rotate quite often, but chef Michael Fisera recommends serving an IPA. "Bitter and floral, IPA pairs great with the sweet/spicy combo of that dish."

This tasty pork dish was a course at their first beer pairing dinner in the brewery room; a beautiful chef's table was set in front of the gleaming tanks of brew, and each course was well-paired with a pour of the chef and brewmaster's choice.

Combine the oil, cilantro, brown sugar, garlic, spices, and juice in a large shallow baking dish; mix well. Add the pork and turn to coat with the marinade. Arrange the pineapple slices around the tenderloins. Cover and refrigerate overnight, turning the pork occasionally.

Remove the pork and the pineapple slices from the marinade and place them on a platter. Cover and refrigerate until you are ready to cook.

Pour the marinade into a saucepan; bring to a boil for 30 seconds. Pour it into a bowl set over a larger bowl of ice so it will chill rapidly. Add additional ice to the large bowl if it melts before the marinade is cooled at least to room temperature. Clean the baking dish.

Preheat the oven to 300° F. Preheat a grill for high heat, or alternatively use a grill pan. Sear the pork on the grill or (grill pan over high heat) until well marked. Place the seared pork in the shallow baking dish; pour the cooled marinade over it. Place it in the oven and cook until the pork reaches 145° F. on an instant-read meat thermometer, about 20 minutes or so. While the pork cooks, carefully lower the grill heat. If you are using charcoal, move the coals to one side. Grill the pineapple slices until they are well marked and caramelized.

Put the pork on a serving platter; let stand 5 minutes before slicing. Discard the marinade. Plate the pork and pineapple together; drizzle with Poblano Coulis.

Chorizo-Stuffed Pork Chops

—Amy and Jamie Ager, HICKORY NUT GAP FARM

Owners Amy and Jamie Ager are the fourth generation to work the land of this nearly century-old farm. They humanely raise livestock free to roam the pasture. If you are serving more than 2, you can double or triple the recipe.

Preheat the oven to 350° F. Set aside an ovenproof skillet or wrap the handle with foil.

Rub the pork chops with the salt and pepper; squeeze the lime on both sides of the chops.

Heat a large, nonstick skillet or grill pan over medium-high heat. Add the olive oil and heat until hot but not smoking. Add the pork chops and sear on both sides, 30 seconds per side. Remove from the skillet and place on a cutting board; let stand until cool enough to touch.

Make a 2-inch incision along the side of the pork chop (along the fat cap). Do not go all the way through the chop. Lay the sliced brie inside the pork chop; follow with chorizo and arugula, pushing them as far into the chop as you can. Return the chops to the skillet; cover and place in the oven. Roast until an instant meat thermometer inserted into the pork registers 155 degrees F., about 15 to 20 minutes. Let stand for 5 to 10 minutes before serving.

MAKES 2 SERVINGS

- 2 (12-ounce) bone-in pork chops, about 1 inch thick
- 3/4 teaspoon kosher salt
- 3/4 teaspoon freshly ground pepper
- 1 lime
- 2 tablespoons olive oil
- 1/2 cup thinly sliced, rind-trimmed brie-style cheese
- 1/2 cup crumbled, cooked chorizo
- 1/2 cup loosely packed fresh arugula, chopped
- 4 ounces fresh asparagus, ends snapped off

Market Mains

Poultry

Roast Chicken • 163

Paprika Chicken with
Krimzon Lee Peppers • 164

Coronation Chicken Salad • 165

Coconut Turkey with Quinoa • 165

Chicken Black Bean with Chèvre
Enchiladas with Salsa Verde • 166

Malabar Chicken Curry • 167

Roast Chicken

—**Ann Araps,** HICKORY NUT GAP FARM

MAKES 4 TO 6 SERVINGS

1 (5 to 6-pound) chicken

1 lemon, cut into 6 pieces

1/2 onion, chopped

3 sprigs fresh rosemary

About 3 tablespoons
extra-virgin olive oil

3/4 teaspoon kosher salt,
or to taste

3/4 teaspoon freshly
ground pepper, or to taste

1 tablespoon chopped
fresh or 1 teaspoon
dried oregano

1 tablespoon chopped
fresh rosemary

*Sales & Relations Manager Ann Araps gave us
this simple, but perfect recipe she uses when
roasting Hickory Nut Gap Farm's pasture-raised
chicken for dinner.*

Preheat the oven to 425° F. Rinse the chicken, inside and out, and
pat dry with paper towels. Squeeze the lemons inside the chicken,
and place the lemons, onions, and rosemary inside the chicken.
Tie the legs together with butcher's twine.

Place the chicken on the rack of a roasting pan; rub the outside
with olive oil and season with salt, pepper, and chopped herbs.
Roast uncovered for 10 minutes. Reduce the oven temperature to
325° F; cover with foil and roast until the juices run clear,
1 1/2 to 2 hours. Let stand at least 10 minutes before serving.

Make stock with the bones
Place a chicken carcass (from a 5 to 6-pound chicken) in a large,
heavy saucepan or slow-cooker, and cover with 6 to 8 cups of
water. Add 1 cup chopped onion, 3 stalks celery, and 2 carrots;
simmer 8+ hours. Strain and store in an airtight container in
the refrigerator or freezer.

Paprika Chicken *with* Krimzon Lee Peppers

—**Mark Rosenstein,** SMOKY PARK SUPPER CLUB

"Krimzon Lee peppers are a variety grown by Mountain Harvest Organics in Madison County," tells chef Mark Rosenstein. *"They have a unique blend of long, slow heat and sweetness in perfect balance. Every year, I preserve 10 pounds, first charring them over a wood grill." Typically 6 to 8 inches long, the thick-fleshed peppers hold heat in their ribs.*

COOK'S NOTE:
1 whole chicken breast from a 5 1/2 pound chicken will easily serve 4 to 6 people.

MAKES 4 SERVINGS

1/2 cup Krimzon Lee peppers, charred

1 tablespoon chopped fresh dill

1 whole, skin-on boneless chicken breast, halved

3 tablespoons olive oil, divided

1 teaspoon sweet Hungarian paprika

1/4 teaspoon salt, or to taste

1/4 teaspoon freshly ground pepper, or to taste

1/2 pound kale

1/2 pound bok choy

8 garlic scapes, sliced

1 lemon

Build a wood fire in the grill or pit. You will need to position a large griddle over the embers for grilling over high heat, with a cooler spot for finishing the chicken. Lightly oil a large cast-iron or other heavy griddle.

Chop the peppers with the dill on a cutting board; drain off as much liquid as possible and place the peppers and dill in a small bowl.

Make a pocket in each chicken breast half: Lay the breast flat on a cutting board. Working on the rounded edge of the breast and using a sharp knife, start slicing parallel to the surface of the cutting board, leaving a 1 to 1 1/2-inch uncut edge around all but the rounded side.

Stuff the pockets with the pepper mixture. Using a bamboo skewer, thread the skewer through the outer edge of the stuffed breast to close it.

Place 2 tablespoons of the olive oil and paprika in a mixing bowl. Add the kale, bok choy, and garlic scapes; toss well. Season with 1/4 teaspoon salt and 1/4 teaspoon pepper.

Rub the chicken with the remaining 1 tablespoon olive oil. Preheat the griddle set over a wood fire with the embers glowing. Place the chicken on the hottest part of the griddle, skin sides down; grill until it is very golden, 5 to 7 minutes. Turn and move the chicken breast haves to a cooler spot on the griddle to finish cooking, 7 to 9 minutes.

Grill the greens on the hottest part of the flat pan over the fire. Move to the edge of the grill until the chicken is cooked. Serve with the chicken.

Coronation Chicken Salad

MAKES 6 TO 8 SERVINGS

—**Mark Demarco,** CEDRIC'S TAVERN

Chef Mark Demarco recommends dark meat for the salad, so we poached 5 pounds boneless, skinless chicken thighs for 12 minutes, then let them cool in the cooking liquid.

Heat a large skillet over medium heat; add the olive oil and heat until hot but not smoking. Add the onion and sauté until tender, about 4 minutes. Stir in the curry powder; remove from the heat and scrape into a large bowl.

Add the mayonnaise, yogurt, ginger, salt, and pepper to the bowl; stir well. Fold in the chicken, cherries, pecans, and cilantro. Cover and refrigerate up to 3 days.

Serve with pita bread and sautéed greens.

1 tablespoon
extra-virgin olive oil

1 medium-size yellow
onion, diced

1 tablespoon
curry powder

1/2 cup mayonnaise

1/2 cup plain yogurt

2 tablespoons chutney

2 quarter-size pieces
peeled ginger, minced

1/2 teaspoon kosher salt

1/2 teaspoon freshly
ground pepper

4 cups roughly chopped
cooked chicken

1/2 cup dried cherries

1/2 cup chopped
pecans, toasted

1 bunch cilantro
leaves, chopped

Coconut Turkey *with* Quinoa

—**Dawn Robertson,** EAST FORK FARM

MAKES 6 TO 8 SERVINGS

2 turkey wings,
about 2 1/2 pounds

1 large onion, chopped

1 (13-ounce)
can coconut milk

1 1/2 cups quinoa

1 tablespoon curry powder

1 teaspoon dried sage

1/2 teaspoon
ground turmeric

3/4 teaspoon salt,
or to taste

1/2 teaspoon freshly
ground pepper

The Robertson's turkeys forage for wild greens and grains with plenty of fresh air. That makes a healthier product," says owner Dawn Robertson. Also delicious!

Combine the turkey, onion, and salted water to cover in a 4-quart slow cooker and cook on low heat for 6 to 8 hours. Lift the turkey legs from the water and place in a large dish; let them stand until the turkey is cool enough to handle. Strain the broth into a large saucepan, disgarding the solids. Chop or shred meat; add the bones to the broth and simmer 30 minutes.

Strain the broth again, discarding the solids; measure out 4 1/2 cups for the recipe. Reserve the remaining broth for other uses.

Combine the 4 1/2 cups broth, coconut milk, quinoa, curry powder, sage, turmeric, salt, and pepper in the slow cooker; cover and cook on low heat for 4 hours.

Chicken, Black Bean, *and* Chèvre Enchiladas *with* Salsa Verde

MAKES 8 TO 10 SERVINGS

1 jalapeno, seeded and chopped

1/2 medium onion, chopped

2 cloves garlic, minced

2 (16-ounce) cans black beans, drained with liquid reserved

Meat from 1 rotisserie-cooked chicken, shredded

1/2 pound Looking Glass Creamery Plain Chèvre, divided

1/2 pound Looking Glass Creamery Chipotle Chèvre, divided

About 1 1/2 cups, oil for frying

20 corn tortillas

Salsa Verde (page 80)

Handful of cilantro, chopped (as garnish)

SERVE WITH:

1 head chopped lettuce

2 cups salsa fresco or pico de gallo

2 cups sour cream

—**Jennifer Perkins,** LOOKING GLASS CREAMERY

This recipe is every bit worth the effort to make. But if you need a shortcut, you can use good quality store-bought salsa verde. When Looking Glass Creamery Chipotle Chèvre is not available, substitute their plain chèvre and add 1/2 of a chipotle chili in adobo sauce, finely minced.

Sauté the pepper and onion in a large, heavy skillet over medium heat until just tender, about 3 minutes. Add the garlic and sauté another 30 seconds. Spoon the vegetables into a blender container; wipe the skillet clean.

Add the black beans to the blender and pulse to chop coarsely, scraping the side of the blender and adding back the reserved black bean liquid as needed. Scrape the black bean mixture into a bowl and stir in the chicken. Gently fold in half of each flavor of chèvre.

Preheat the oven to 350° F. Heat 1 inch of oil in the skillet until it is hot but not smoking. Using tongs and working with one at a time, dip the tortillas into the hot oil until soft, about 5 seconds. Drain on paper towels.

Cover the bottom of a 13 x 9-inch baking dish with a thin layer of the Salsa Verde. Spoon 2 to 3 tablespoons of the chicken mixture into the center of each tortilla; roll up and fit them snuggly into the baking dish. Cover with the remaining Salsa Verde and sprinkle the remaining chèvre on top.

Bake until the filling is hot, 20 to 25 minutes. Transfer the enchiladas to serving plates and garnish with cilantro; serve with lettuce, sour cream, and salsa fresco on the side.

Malabar Chicken Curry

—**Meherwan Irani,** CHAI PANI

"I love this dish since it's the antithesis of the aromatic, cream- and butter-laden dishes of North India that most Americans are familiar with," tells chef/owner Meherwan Irani. "Curry leaves, coconut milk, and tamarind make this South Indian dish funky, smoky, and tangy, and it's delicious served with rice. It's usually made with prawns or fish, but make it with chicken too."

To prepare the chicken, place the chicken in a bowl; combine the spices and sprinkle over the chicken. Rub the spices all over the chicken, coating evenly.

To prepare the curry, heat 1/4 cup of the oil in a large, heavy saucepan over medium heat. Add the curry leaves, red chilies, mustard seeds, and fenugreek seeds; sauté until fragrant, about 1 minute. Add the onion and ginger; reduce the heat to medium-low and cook, stirring frequently, until the onions are browned and very soft, 25 to 30 minutes. Stir in the cilantro, coriander, chili powder, and turmeric.

Increase the heat to medium; add the tomatoes, lime juice, tamarind pulp, and salt. Simmer, stirring occasionally, until the tomatoes are soft and the oil separates out, 15 to 20 minutes. Stir in the coconut milk and 1/2 cup water; bring to a boil, stirring frequently. Reduce the heat so that the mixture simmers.

Heat the remaining oil in a large, heavy skillet over medium-high heat. Add the chicken, in batches, and brown on all sides, leaving the centers pink, 2 to 4 minutes. Place on a plate as you cook the batches.

Add the chicken to the curry and simmer until the chicken is cooked through, 5 to 7 minutes. Serve over the rice.

COOK'S NOTE:
Curry leaves can be ordered online.

MAKES 8 TO 10 SERVINGS

FOR THE CHICKEN:
2 pounds boneless chicken breast, cut into bite-size pieces

1 teaspoon chili powder

1 teaspoon ground turmeric

1 teaspoon kosher salt

1 teaspoon coarse ground pepper

FOR THE CURRY:
1/2 cup vegetable oil, divided

12 to 15 curry leaves, finely chopped

2 to 3 dried red chilies

1 1/2 teaspoons mustard seeds

1/2 teaspoon fenugreek seeds

4 cups chopped red onion

2 1/2 tablespoons grated fresh ginger

1/2 cup chopped cilantro

1 1/2 tablespoons ground coriander

1 teaspoon chili powder

1 teaspoon turmeric

3 cups chopped fresh tomatoes or crushed canned tomatoes

2 tablespoons fresh lime juice

2 tablespoons tamarind pulp

1 teaspoon salt

1 cup well-stirred canned unsweetened coconut milk

Hot, cooked basmati rice

Seven Sows Bourbon & Larder

Best Southern Fried Chicken Dinner

Chef/owner Mike Moore shared his wildly popular, award-winning entree, including the Mac 'N Cheese and gravy. Both Yahoo and Lee Brian Schrager, Miami/NYC Wine & Food, ranks the dish in the top 10 Best Fried Chicken in the United States.

Fried Chicken

—Mike Moore,
SEVEN SOWS BOURBON & LARDER

To prepare the buttermilk marinade, combine 1/2 cup water with the buttermilk, hot sauce, thyme, and garlic in a large, nonreactive bowl. Add the chicken, turning to coat and submerging in the buttermilk mixture. Cover and refrigerate 48 hours.

To prepare the chicken breading, combine the flour and spices in a large bowl, whisk to blend.

Heat the oil in a large heavy saucepan or fryer to 350° F. Lift the chicken pieces out of the buttermilk mixture, allowing it to drip back into the bowl for 4 to 5 seconds. Add the chicken to the breading and use your hands to coat the pieces well.

Cook the chicken — in batches so as not to crowd them while they cook — until they are browned and crispy, 4 to 5 minutes or until an instant-read meat thermometer registers 165° F. at thickest part of meat. Transfer the pieces to a rack placed over a baking sheet to rest for at least 2 minutes before serving with Carlie's Giblet & Egg Gravy and Macaroni & Cheese.

FOR THE BUTTERMILK MARINADE:

3 cups fresh-churned buttermilk, preferably from Cruze Dairy

1 cup Texas Pete hot sauce

Handful of fresh thyme sprigs

4 cloves garlic, smashed

3 pounds bone-in chicken pieces

FOR THE CHICKEN BREADING:

2 cups all-purpose flour

2 tablespoons paprika

1 teaspoon garlic powder

1 teaspoon onion powder

1 teaspoon ground thyme

2 tablespoons salt

2 teaspoons pepper

TO COOK AND EAT:

Peanut oil for deep-frying

Carlie's Giblet & Egg Gravy (recipe follows)

Macaroni & Cheese (recipe follow)

COOK'S NOTE:
The 48-hour marinade tenderizes and slightly par cooks the chicken prior to deep-frying. However, If you have a sous vide (a water bath cooker popular with chefs) at home, you can skip the marinating step and cook the chicken, sealed in a vacuum bag with the buttermilk mixture, submerged in the hot water bath (immersion circulator) set at 63° C for 2 1/2 hours.

Mac N Cheese

—**Mike Moore,** SEVEN SOWS BOURBON AND LARDER

Cut a 1-inch-deep slit in the onion and insert the bay leaf in the onion. Stud the onion with the cloves.

Cook the macaroni in a large saucepan of boiling, salted water according to package directions. Drain and keep warm.

Meanwhile, melt the butter in a heavy, medium saucepan over medium-high heat; add the flour and stir until the mixture is smooth. Cook the roux until it is light brown, stirring frequently, 5 to 6 minutes. Whisk in the cream, milk, and wine until the mixture is smooth. Whisk in the thyme, salt, and pepper. Add the onion; reduce the heat to low and simmer 10 minutes, stirring occasionally.

Strain the sauce and return to the saucepan over low heat. Add the cheese; stir until melted and smooth. Stir in the hot, drained macaroni and lemon zest. If desired, top each serving with a handful of arugula.

MAKES 4 TO 6 SERVINGS

1 medium-size red onion, peeled

1 bay leaf

3 cloves

5 tablespoons unsalted butter

5 tablespoons all-purpose flour

2 cups heavy whipping cream

1 cup whole milk

2 tablespoons dry white wine

1 tablespoon chopped fresh thyme

salt & pepper to taste

2 cups (8 ounces) shredded white Cheddar cheese

1/2 pound elbow macaroni, uncooked

1 teaspoon grated lemon zest

Carlie's Giblet & Egg Gravy

—**Mike Moore,** SEVEN SOWS BOURBON AND LARDER

MAKES ABOUT 4 CUPS

1/2 stick (1/4 cup) butter

1 chicken neck bone

2 chicken gizzards, chopped

1 chicken liver, chopped

1/2 medium onion, chopped

2 cloves garlic, minced

1/4 cup all-purpose flour

1 teaspoon minced fresh thyme

1/2 teaspoon salt, or to taste

1/2 teaspoon freshly ground pepper, or to taste

3 cups chicken stock

3 hard-cooked eggs

Melt the butter in a large, heavy saucepan over medium heat. Add the neck bone, gizzards, and liver, and sauté until the meat is browned, about 6 minutes. Add the onion and garlic and cook until they are beginning to brown, 2 to 3 minutes. Sprinkle the flour, thyme, salt, and pepper over the mixture and stir until no lumps of flour remain. Cook, stirring constantly, 2 minutes. Gradually add the chicken stock, stirring well. Simmer, stirring frequently, until the mixture has thickened to desired gravy thickness. Remove the neck bone and discard.

Ladle the gravy over your chicken and sprinkle with egg and pimiento.

Market Mains

NC Trout & Sea

Quick, Easy, and Lusty Trout • 171

Lime Basil Grilled Trout • 171

Blackened Salmon with Candied Apricots
& Grand Marnier-Bacon Vinaigrette • 172

Grand Marnier-Bacon Vinaigrette • 173

Roasted Cod, Cabbage,
& Shiitakes with Wasabi Sauce • 173

Seared Trout on Wilted Greens Salad with
Smoked Tomato Vinaigrette • 174

NC Flounder with Rock Shrimp in
Coconut Carrot Lemongrass Broth • 175

Quick, Easy, *and* Lusty Trout

—**Former Research and Development Charles Hudson,** SUNBURST TROUT FARMS

MAKES 4 SERVINGS

4 (6 to 8-ounce) Sunburst Trout fillets

Juice of 1 lemon

1 teaspoon seasoned salt, such as Lawry's

1 teaspoon seafood seasoning, such as Old Bay

1/4 cup Lusty Monk Mustard

Former Chef Charles Hudson uses Lusty Monk Original Sin Mustard in this recipe. Lusty Monk makes fresh-ground mustards "full of flavor and fire" including: Original Sin, Burn in Hell Chipotle, and Altar Boy Honey Mustard.

Position the oven rack so that the trout cooks 4 to 6 inches from the heat source. Preheat the oven broiler. Line a rimmed baking sheet with nonstick foil or a piece of parchment paper.

Place the trout fillets on the baking sheet; squeeze the lemon over them and sprinkle with the seasonings. Spoon 1 tablespoon of mustard on each of the fillets, and spread gently to the edges.

Broil until the fish barely flakes when you insert a fork in the thickest part and slightly twist it.

Lime Basil Grilled Trout

—**Charles Hudson,** SUNBURST TROUT FARMS

Former Research and Development Chef Charles Hudson shared this quick and easy way to cook trout.

Finely chop the basil; mix with the lime juice, garlic, olive oil, seasoned salt, and pepper in a shallow dish. Add the trout and turn to coat in the marinade. Cover and refrigerate 1 hour, turning fillets occasionally.

Preheat the grill to medium-high heat. Remove the trout from the marinade and place them, flesh-sides-down, on a well-oiled grill rack. Grill 3 minutes, then flip and cook until the fish barely flakes when you insert the fork in the thickest part and slightly twist it, about 2 minutes.

MAKES 4 SERVINGS

Handful of fresh basil leaves, about 1 ounce

Juice of 1 lime

2 cloves garlic, minced

1/4 cup extra-virgin olive oil

1 teaspoon seasoned salt, such as Lawry's

1 teaspoon freshly ground pepper

4 (6 to 8-ounce) Sunburst Trout fillets

171

Blackened Salmon *with* Candied Apricots *&* Grand Marnier-Bacon Vinaigrette

—**Michael Fisera**, LEXINGTON AVENUE BREWERY

MAKES 4 SERVINGS

FOR THE BLACKENING SEASONING MIX:

2 cups cornstarch

1/2 cup paprika

1/2 cup Old Bay Seasoning

2 tablespoons plus 1 teaspoon dry mustard

2 tablespoons celery salt

2 tablespoons salt

1 tablespoon each of the following: chili powder, ground sumac, smoked paprika, ground turmeric, gumbo file powder, garam masala, ground coriander, ground red pepper

FOR THE SALMON:

4 (5 to 6-ounce) salmon fillets

2 tablespoons peanut or safflower oil

1 tablespoon unsalted butter

1 tablespoon minced garlic

Candied Apricots, as garnish (page 209)

Chef Michael Fisera served this dish at a beer-pairing dinner in the brewery room behind the bar, pouring the LAB's "Hop Burst" with the course. He recommends a very light, late-addition hopped ale to complement the flavors in the dish.

Keep what you don't use of the blackening coating for pan-frying other types of fish. Store in a spice jar or freezer zip-top plastic bag in a cool, dark place.

To prepare the blackening seasoning mix, combine all the ingredients in a bowl; whisk to blend. Measure out and reserve 1 cup for coating the fish. Pour the remaining mixture into a covered jar and store in a cool, dark place for other uses.

To prepare the salmon, dredge the filets in the blackening seasoning mix. Heat a large cast iron skillet over medium-high heat; add the oil and heat until hot but not smoking. Add the fillets to the skillet; lift and turn the fillets about 90 degrees with a spatula to prevent sticking. Cook until the fillets have turned white about 1/2 inch from the bottom, about 2 minutes. Flip the fillets and immediately remove from the heat. Drop in the butter and garlic, swirling the pan. Let it stand until the fish is cooked to desired doneness, about 2 minutes.

Use the spatula to lift the fillets onto serving plates. Garnish with the Candied Apricots and drizzle with the Grand Marnier-Bacon Vinaigrette.

MAKES ABOUT 1 3/4 CUPS

Grand Marnier-Bacon Vinaigrette

—**Michael Fisera,** LEXINGTON AVENUE BREWERY

Juice and grated zest of 1/2 orange

1/2 cup rice wine vinegar

1 1/2 teaspoons Grand Marnier

1 1/2 teaspoons chopped fresh herbs

1 1/2 teaspoons honey

1 1/2 teaspoons minced garlic

3/4 teaspoon Dijon mustard

1 1/4 cups strained, warm bacon fat

Salt and freshly ground pepper to taste

Process the orange juice and zest, rice wine vinegar, liqueur, herbs, honey, garlic, and mustard in a blender until smooth. With the machine running, gradually add the warm bacon fat, processing until emulsified. Season with salt and pepper.

Roasted Cod, Cabbage, & Shiitakes *with* Wasabi Sauce

—**Debby Maugans,** AUTHOR

Coming home from an ASAP Farm Tour trip to the Mushroom Hut at Fox Farm, I devised this recipe to use the shiitakes I'd gathered.

Preheat the oven to 450° F. Mix the mayonnaise, yogurt, wasabi paste, and half of the ginger and garlic in a small bowl.

Drizzle 2 teaspoons of the olive oil on the fish fillets; sprinkle with 1/4 teaspoon salt and 1/4 teaspoon pepper. Toss the cabbage and mushrooms with the remaining 4 teaspoons olive oil, ginger, garlic, 1/4 teaspoon salt, and 1/4 teaspoon pepper in a large bowl, mixing well.

Place a foil-lined, rimmed baking sheet in the oven for 5 minutes or until very hot. Quickly arrange the fish on one side of the hot baking sheet; scatter the vegetables on the other side. Roast, stirring the vegetables occasionally, until fish is cooked through, about 12 minutes. Divide on serving plates and serve with the wasabi mixture.

MAKES 2 SERVINGS

2 tablespoons mayonnaise

1 tablespoon plain Greek yogurt

1/2 teaspoon wasabi paste

1 (1-inch) piece ginger, finely grated, divided

1 or 2 large cloves garlic, finely grated, divided

2 tablespoons extra-virgin olive oil, divided

2 (6-ounce) cod fillets, about 1 inch thick

Sea salt

Freshly ground pepper

2 cups (packed) very thinly sliced green cabbage

3 ounces shiitake mushrooms, sliced

Seared Trout *on* Wilted Greens Salad *with* Smoked Tomato Vinaigrette

—Charles Hudson, SUNBURST TROUT FARMS

Former Chef Charles Hudson developed Hudson's Smoked Tomato Jam as a value-added condiment for trout, and there are many ways to use it: on biscuits, baked brie, and goat cheese; in dressings and marinades; and as a glaze for chicken, pork, and fish.

To prepare the trout, season the trout with salt and pepper. Heat a large heavy skillet over medium heat; add the oil and heat until hot but not smoking. Add the seasoned fillets, flesh sides down, and cook 3 minutes. Flip and continue to cook until the fish barely flakes when you insert a fork in the thickest part and slightly twist it. Remove the fillets from the heat and let the soil drip away; keep warm.

To prepare the salad, thoroughly wash and dry the greens; remove the tough stems and cut or tear into 1/2-inch-wide strips. Place the greens in a large, heatproof bowl.

Heat a large skillet over medium heat; add the olive oil and heat until hot but not smoking. Add the onion and sauté until transparent, 2 to 3 minutes. Stir in the vinegar and Smoked Tomato Jam; bring to a boil, stirring to loosen clinging particles. Pour over the greens and toss with tongs. Add salt and pepper, to taste.

Place the salad on serving plates, dividing evenly. Top with the trout.

MAKES 4 SERVINGS

FOR THE TROUT:

4 (6 to 8-inch) trout fillets

1/2 teaspoon kosher salt, or to taste

1/2 teaspoon freshly ground pepper, or to taste

1/4 cup olive or vegetable oil

FOR THE SALAD:

1 pound spinach, mustard greens, or turnip greens

1/4 cup extra-virgin olive oil

1 small red or yellow onion, thinly sliced

1/4 cup Hudson's Smoked Tomato Jam

1/4 cup cider vinegar

1/4 teaspoon kosher salt, or to taste

1/4 teaspoon freshly ground pepper, or to taste

NC Flounder *with* Rock Shrimp *in* Coconut Carrot Lemongrass Broth

—Traci Taylor, FIG

You can substitute thin snapper fillets or trout fillets for this Asian-style flounder dish from chef/owner Traci Taylor.

To prepare the broth, place a large saucepan over medium heat. Add the oil and heat until hot but not smoking. Add the shallots and salt; cover and cook until tender, about 5 minutes. Add the lemongrass and carrots; sauté 5 minutes. Add the kaffir lime leaves, carrot juice, and ginger; bring to a boil, stirring. Add the coconut milk and return to a boil; cover, reduce heat, and simmer until the carrots and lemongrass are very tender, 20 to 30 minutes. Remove from the heat; stir in the fish sauce, salt and pepper, and lime juice. Keep warm.

Meanwhile, sprinkle the cucumber slices lightly with salt and let stand while preparing the shrimp and flounder.

Rinse the flounder and pat dry with paper towels. Sprinkle lightly with salt and pepper.

Heat a large, heavy-bottom skillet over medium-high heat; add 1 tablespoon of the oil and heat until hot but not smoking. Add the rock shrimp and sauté until opaque, 2 to 3 minutes. Remove from the skillet and place them on a plate. Wipe the skillet clean.

Place the skillet over medium-high heat for 1 minute; add 2 more tablespoons of the oil to the skillet and heat until just smoking. Quickly add the fish fillets, skin sides down, and press lightly with a flat spatula to crisp the skin. Cook until you see a golden brown color on the edges, about 2 minutes; gently slide a spatula under the skin of each fillet to loosen them and flip. Let them cook until done, about 1 minute. Remove from the skillet and gently place them on a plate.

Drain the cucumber slices. Ladle 1/2 to 3/4 cup of the broth into each shallow serving bowl; gently place a fish fillet, skin side up, in the center of each bowl. Arrange 4 shrimp and several cucumber slices in each bowl; scatter the mint over each serving.

MAKES 6 SERVINGS

FOR THE BROTH:

1 tablespoon canola oil

5 shallots, minced

1/4 teaspoon salt

5 lemongrass stalks, finely chopped

1/2 pound carrots, coarsely chopped

4 kaffir lime leaves

1 cup carrot juice

2 tablespoons fresh grated ginger with juice

2 (13 1/2-ounce) cans coconut milk

1/4 teaspoon kosher salt, or to taste

1/4 teaspoon freshly ground pepper, or to taste

2 teaspoons fish sauce

2 to 3 teaspoons fresh lime juice, or to taste

1 seedless cucumber, diagonally sliced

2 tablespoons thinly sliced fresh mint (as garnish)

FOR THE SEAFOOD:

6 (4 to 6-ounce) NC-caught flounder or trout fillets

Kosher salt, to taste

Freshly ground pepper, to taste

3 tablespoon canola oil, divided

16 peeled and deveined rock shrimp

Farm Dinners

We joined three chef-prepared outdoor dinners, held in different counties surrounding Asheville: one set in a barn, one under a tent by a river, and one creekside on the porch of a water-powered mill, all with extraordinary views of the Blue Ridge Mountains.

EAST FORK FARM:

Dawn and Stephen Robertson, owners of the farm, host four dinners a year by the creek that powers the grain mill designed by Stephen. This meal was created and cooked over a wood fire by chef Mark Rosenstein with Kikkoman Shaw, a graduate of the Go-Kitchen Ready culinary program piloted by Rosenstein. For a schedule of future dinners, go to eastforkfarm.net.

HICKORY NUT GAP FARM DINNER:

We were on hand for the first dinner of its kind held on the farm: a slow-roasted barbecue pork dinner prepared by chef Steven Goff, paired with specialty beers by Catawba Brewing. Starting with music and appetizers in the party shed cross the road from the farm store, we moved into the barn — decorated with party lights strung from the rafters and elegantly but informally set tables — for an incredible meal.

GREEN TOE GROUND

Galen Delcogliano is both chef and farm owner with his wife, Nicole. On this cool October evening, they and their 2 daughters hosted a dinner by the Toe River, cooking the meal in the handmade clay, wood-fired oven that Galen built. They slow-roasted a delicious leg of lamb ahead to serve as the entree. As guests arrived, they watched Gaelen grill this fig and arugula pizza for the first course. Nicole and her daughters pickled the vegetables from their expansive garden.

Lamb Tacos

—Mark Rosenstein

Chef Mark Rosenstein makes his own blend of spices to make the red pepper chili spice used extensively in Ethiopian cooking. "I usually make a year's worth of Berbere spice and store it in mason jars," says Rosenstein. You can order it online or purchase at the Spice and Tea Exchange or other spice companies.

Heat a large cast-iron skillet over medium-high heat; add the oil and heat until hot but not smoking. Add the lamb and cook until browned on all sides, about 3 minutes. Reduce the heat to medium; add the onion and bell pepper. Season with the Berbere, salt, and pepper; cook, stirring until the onion and pepper are tender, about 5 minutes.

Heat another skillet over medium-high heat; brush with some of the remaining oil. Working with one at a time, toast the tortillas in the skillet just until warmed, about 10 seconds; fill with about one eighth of the lamb mixture. Repeat heating and filling the tortillas with the lamb mixture, brushing the skillet with some of the remaining oil if needed.

MAKES 4 SERVINGS

2 tablespoons corn oil, divided

12 ounces lean lamb trimmings

1 small onion, diced

1 red bell pepper, seeded and sliced

1/4 teaspoon salt

1/4 teaspoon freshly ground pepper

3 tablespoons Berbere spice

8 corn tortillas

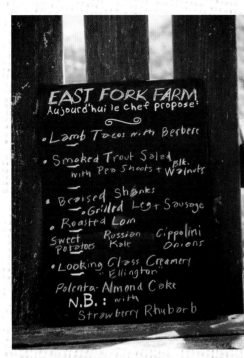

EAST FORK FARM
Aujourd'hui le chef propose:

• Lamb Tacos with Berbere

• Smoked Trout Salad
    with Pea Shoots + Blk. Walnuts

• Braised Shanks
    • Grilled Leg + Sausage

• Roasted Loin
Sweet   Russian   Cippolini
Potatoes   Kale   Onions

• Looking Glass Creamery
        "Ellington"

Polenta-Almond Cake
    N.B. : with
        Strawberry Rhubarb

HICKORY NUT GAP FARM

Catawba Stout BBQ Sauce

—**Steven Goff,** KING JAMES PUBLIC HOUSE

Chef Steven Goff created this sauce for a Hickory Nut Gap Farm dinner with courses paired with Catawba Brewing Company beers. He spit-roasted and smoked a whole pig for the dinner, and finished the pulled pork with this beer BBQ sauce. At the end of cooking the sauce, Goff puréed it with rendered pork fat "for sheen and body, and to layer up the pork flavor," he says.

Heat the fat in a large, heavy saucepan over medium-low heat. Add the onions and garlic; cook until they are caramelized, stirring occasionally, 8 to 10 minutes. Stir in the brown sugar; cook, stirring constantly, until the sugar is dissolved and caramelized, 4 to 5 minutes. Stir in the wine and lemon juice; simmer until the liquid is almost evaporated, about 5 minutes. Stir in the stout. Increase the heat and boil, stirring occasionally, until the mixture reduces by about three-fourths, 10 to 15 minutes.

Stir in the tomatoes, cumin, coriander, and fennel and caraway seeds. Reduce the heat and simmer uncovered until the mixture is reduced by half, 30 to 45 minutes. Stir it frequently so that the mixture doesn't stick to the bottom and burn.

Let the sauce cool and process, in batches, in a blender until it is smooth.

MAKES 5 1/2 TO 6 CUPS

1/4 cup rendered bacon or pork fat, or canola oil

2 medium-size yellow onions, finely diced

3 cloves garlic, minced

1 cup firmly packed brown sugar

1/4 cup dry white wine

1/4 cup fresh lemon juice

4 cups Catawba Stout

2 (28-ounce) cans crushed tomatoes

1 1/2 teaspoons ground cumin

1 1/2 teaspoons ground coriander

1/2 teaspoon fennel seeds, crushed

1/2 teaspoon caraway seeds, crushed

GREEN TOE GROUND

Grilled Fresh Pear
and Mozzarella Pizza

—Nicole and Galen Delcogliano, GREEN TOE GROUNDS

Galen Delcogliano, both chef and farmer, held a farm dinner by the Toe River one cool October evening. This is the pizza Galen put together with fresh pears and cheese and homemade crust, as guests gathered to watch their first course cooking in the wood-burning oven he built by hand. If you have a wood-fired oven, slide the pizza into the oven and cook until the crust is browned, 5 to 7 minutes.

2 pounds fresh tomatoes, cored and peeled

2 tablespoons unsalted butter

3 to 4 cloves garlic, crushed and minced

3 tablespoons minced fresh herbs: basil, oregano, thyme

1/2 teaspoon salt

1/4 teaspoon freshly ground pepper

1 store-bought or home-made pizza dough ball

6 to 8 ounces thinly sliced fresh mozzarella

1 to 2 pears, thinly sliced

Cornmeal

Chop the tomatoes, reserving the juices. Melt the butter in a heavy, medium saucepan over medium heat. Add the garlic and sauté for 30 seconds. Add the tomatoes with their juices and the herbs; reduce the heat and simmer uncovered until the sauce is thick but pourable, about 1 hour. Add water if it becomes too dry. Season with the salt and pepper. Let it cool.

To make the pizza, place a pizza stone on the lowest rack in the oven and preheat the oven to 450° F. If you don't have a pizza stone, stack 2 heavy baking sheets together and line the top one with a piece of parchment paper.

Sprinkle a pizza peel or the parchment on the prepared baking sheet lightly with the cornmeal. Roll the pizza dough ball to a 14-inch round; lift and place it on the pizza peel, directly on the cornmeal. Spread about 1/2 cup of the sauce over the dough; top with the mozzarella and pear slices.

Slide the pizza onto the preheated stone or place onto the baking sheet stack in the oven. Bake until the crust is golden brown, 10 to 15 minutes. Transfer to a cutting board, slice, and serve.

Outstanding in the Field Dinner

Since 2010, Outstanding in the Field's vintage red bus has rolled each year into our area stocked with all the accoutrements for feast in a local farm field. Chef William Dissen creates and cooks a multi-course meal, with the help of his kitchen crew from The Market Place Restaurant. "He's kind of a hero to us," says OITF founding chef and artist Jim Denevan. "Partly because he's so nice and partly because we love his passion for good, local food." Read more at ourstandinginthefield.com.

Hors d'oeuvres
spinach & ricotta fritters, romesco sauce looking glass creamery chocolate lab cheese, lavender honey, lavash crispy pork belly, pickled pink ladies, sorghum

1st
smoked sunburst farm trout, peas,
cornbread (p.42) croutons, heirloom tomatoes & arugula

2nd
lamb merguez, pickled ramps, foraged
mushroom farro, gem lettuce, jalapeno
buttermilk aioli, feta

3rd
wood grilled pork shoulder (p. 154), preserved strawberry relish,
butter bean & kale ragout, roasted tomatoes

Dessert
lemon verbena custard (p. 246),
preserved blackberries, basil

Lamb Merguez *with* Jalapeño Aioli *and* Pickled Ramps

—William Dissen, THE MARKET PLACE RESTAURANT

MAKES 12 TO 13 LINKS

2 pounds boneless lamb shoulder, cut into 3/4-inch dice

1/2 pound pork fatback, cut into 3/4-inch dice

3/4 cup roasted red peppers, cut into 1/2-inch dice

1 1/2 tablespoons kosher salt

1 tablespoon paprika

1 tablespoon minced fresh oregano

1 tablespoon minced fresh garlic

1 teaspoon sugar

3/4 teaspoon freshly ground pepper

1/4 cup red wine, chilled

1/4 cup ice water

20 feet sheep casing

Jalapeño Aioli (page 203)

Pickled Ramps (recipe follows)

"Ask a butcher for sheep casings or you can order then online," says chef/owner William Dissen.

Combine the lamb, fatback, roasted peppers, salt, paprika, oregano, garlic, sugar, and pepper in large mixing bowl; mix well. Cover and refrigerate until you are ready to grind the meat.

Grind the meat mixture through the small die into a medium mixing bowl; place the mixing bowl into a larger bowl of ice. Add the water and wine to the lamb mixture, and beat with a hand-held electric mixer at medium speed until it has a uniform sticky appearance, about 1 minute. Stuff the mixture into sheep casing and twist into 10-inch links. Refrigerate links in a covered container until ready to cook. Pan-fry or grill the sausage over medium heat until browned and cooked through.

Pickled Ramps

—William Dissen, THE MARKET PLACE RESTAURANT

MAKES 4 CUPS

2 pounds ramps, cleaned, and green leaves cut off 1-inch above its red stem

1 tablespoon black peppercorns

1 teaspoon mustard seeds

1/2 teaspoon fennel seeds

1/2 teaspoon ground cumin

1 cup white wine vinegar

1 cup sugar

1 tablespoon kosher salt

2 bay leaves

Bring a medium saucepan of water to a boil; add enough kosher salt to make it taste like the ocean. Add the ramps and cook until crisp-tender, about 30 seconds. Use a slotted spoon to remove the ramps from the water and place them in a large bowl of ice water. When they are cool, remove them from the ice water and drain well on paper towels. Place them in a sterilized quart jar with a tight-fitting lid.

Heat a medium saucepan over medium-high heat. Add the peppercorns, mustard seeds, fennel seeds, and cumin seeds, and toast until fragrant, moving the saucepan over the heat, about 30 seconds. Add the vinegar, sugar, salt, and bay leaves; bring to a boil, stirring constantly until the sugar dissolves, about 2 minutes.

Pour the hot mixture over the ramps, and seal the jar. If you aren't canning them at this point, let the jar cool to room temperature, then store it in the refrigerator.

Blind Pig:
A Supper Club

With A Conscience

Chef Mike Moore of Seven Sows Bourbon and Larder believes in giving back.

Upon moving back home to Western North Carolina from San Francisco, he brought with him the concept of an underground supper club similar to some in California. But Moore had in mind a worthy focus and mission: bringing together chefs and artisan craftsmen to create unique and fascinating dining experiences for guests while ultimately improving our community. With the vision that some proceeds from the cost of the meal would go directly to a designated local charity, he started the Blind Pig Supper Club in Spring 2011.

Each Blind Pig's menu and dinner concept is drafted to raise the bar on normal restaurant dining with sensually appealing — and sometimes

outrageous —food, art, and music contributing to a party in an undisclosed location. As with most underground supper club concepts, location and menu are a mystery to guests until the last possible moment, adding to the adventure.

Blind Pig serves strictly local and seasonal vegetables and pasture-raised organic meats from area farmers to support sustainable agriculture. The event also supports environmental and species-sustainable fish and seafood, as well as respectfully hunted game and foraged wild foods. Meanwhile, as often as possible, the event organizers prepare food on wood fires with old-time Appalachian cooking ways.

A reputable host of Southern Appalachia's best chefs, cooks, servers, designers, artists, farmers, foragers and hunters contribute their craft and talents...all with the benefit of giving back to causes with personal mean- ing. And as always, the event adheres to the philosophy of " waste not-want not" when it comes to food.

Aztec-Inspired Hot Chocolate

—**Jael and Dan Rattigan,** FRENCH BROAD CHOCOLATE LOUNGE

MAKES 6 CUPS

Cook's Note: We tested this recipe with dried rose petals and anise seeds from the Spice and Tea Exchange.

Bring the cream just to a boil in a heavy, medium saucepan. Remove from the heat and stir in the chilies, vanilla bean, rose petals, and anise seeds. Cover and steep 15 minutes. Strain through a sieve into a bowl, pressing on solids to extract 1 cup infused cream.

Place the chocolate, almonds, and cinnamon in a food processor; process until the mixture is finely ground. With the processor running, pour the hot cream through the feed tube and process until smooth and blended.

Scrape the ganache into the saucepan; whisk in the milk. Bring to a simmer, stirring constantly; remove from the heat and serve.

1 1/4 cups heavy whipping cream

1 1/2 arbol chilies, ground in a blender or spice grinder

1 vanilla bean, split

1 cup dried rose petals

1 1/2 teaspoons anise seeds

8 ounces (65 to 75% cacao) dark chocolate, finely chopped

1/2 cup slivered almonds, toasted

1 teaspoon ground cinnamon

5 cups whole milk

187

How Chefs Cook
at Home

Intrigued by the idea of taking a peek inside the home kitchens of successful Asheville restaurateurs, we asked them: "How do you cook at home? What do you like to fix during your downtime? Would you mind if we tell the world?"

The answers we received would provide enough fodder for a book of its own. But two families replied immediately, and we couldn't resist adding the lively family cooking photos to their recipes.

MARTHA & PETER POLLAY,
POSANA CAFÉ

"This is how we eat," says chef Peter Pollay. The whole family is involved with weeknight cooking, with the children arguing on a regular basis over who gets to cook. Turning to Fedora and Parker, Peter asks, "What part of the meal do you want to cook?"

Fedora wins the plating task, while Parker's job is manhandling the kale. "Squeeze the life out of it, Parker." The Pollays offer encouragement. "Kids, look at the salad. Do you think we need more currants or pumpkin seeds?" They all assess the dishes during the preparation, developing an early appreciation for refined tastes.

The Pollay's philosophy of eating and cooking is the same at home as in the restaurant: "We eat foods that are as close to their natural state as possible, and we buy greens by the case." Both kitchens are totally gluten-free.

Kale Salad *with* Manchego, Pumpkin Seeds, *and* Currants

MAKES 4 SERVINGS

1 bunch kale, stemmed and cut into thin julienne strips

2 lemons

1/2 cup (4 ounces) extra-virgin olive oil, divided

1 cup (4 ounces) freshly grated Manchego cheese

1/4 cup (2 ounces) toasted pumpkin seeds

1/4 cup (2 ounces) currants

1/4 to 1/2 teaspoon salt, or to taste

1/4 to 1/2 teaspoon freshly ground pepper, or to taste

—**Chef Peter Pollay,** POSANA CAFÉ

The Pollay's children love to cook and have been helping in the kitchen since they were each old enough to hold a spoon. Fedora, the older daughter, peels away the stems from the kale as the younger son Parker squeezes lemons.

Place the kale in a large bowl. Cut the lemons in half and remove the seeds; squeeze the juice over the kale. Drizzle 1/4 cup of the olive oil over the kale; using clean hands, massage the kale well with the dressing to "wilt" it. Add the cheese, pumpkin seeds, and currants; toss well. Season with the salt and pepper.

Divide the salad between 4 serving plates; drizzle each with a tablespoon of the remaining olive oil; garnish with additional pumpkin seeds, if desired.

JAEL & DAN RATTIGAN,
FRENCH BROAD CHOCOLATE LOUNGE

Locals and visitors stand in line waiting for a taste of the couple's extraordinary cacao concoctions. What would the Rattigans pull together for dinner on a Sunday evening? Surely they don't feed their children chocolate for dinner. We couldn't wait to find out.

Even after long days spent at the lounge and factory, it's priority for them to feed the family well and healthfully. Dan is usually the dinner chef, gathering ingredients from area farmers and, in this case, from their own backyard. Jael, who professes "chocolate makes me happy," works her dessert magic. The boys passed the time with homework and reading — just another family meal.

Ginger Coconut Meatballs

—**Jael and Dan Rattigan,** FRENCH BROAD CHOCOLATE LOUNGE

MAKES 4 TO 6 SERVINGS

1 pound ground pork

3 tablespoons all-purpose flour

1 tablespoon grated fresh ginger

2 to 3 green onions, white and green parts, finely chopped

1 tablespoon fish sauce

1 tablespoon soy sauce

1 large egg, lightly beaten

Grated unsweetened coconut

2 to 3 tablespoons olive oil

Chickweed Pesto Aioli (page 208)

Chef Dan Rattigan used Dry Ridge Farm pork for the meatballs. He suggests serving the meatballs with Chickweed Pesto Aioli, stone-ground grits, and a spring garden salad.

Combine the pork, flour, ginger, green onion, fish sauce, soy sauce, and egg, mixing well. Shape into 12 balls; roll in the grated coconut.

Heat a large, heavy skillet over medium heat; add the olive oil and heat until hot but not smoking. Add the meatballs and cook, turning until browned on all sides, 4 to 5 minutes. Reduce the heat and continue cooking, turning until they are cooked through, 8 to 10 minutes. Serve with the Chickweed Pesto Aioli.

Sustainability at
The Biltmore Estate

George Vanderbilt came to Asheville to pursue a dream: building a sustainable, working estate in the Blue Ridge Mountains, supported by forestry and agriculture.

He was aided by Frederick Law Olmsted, who designed and conceived the first program of forestry management as a model for the country. More than a century later, this interest in stewardship of our natural resources continues throughout the Biltmore Estate.

Biltmore's current sustainability projects include solar panels to generate the estate's own renewable energy source. Plus, solar fields serve as pasture for more than 300 chickens that lay eggs daily that are served in estate restaurants.

Biltmore also raises beef and lamb that are free-range pastured and fed natural grains that are free of hormones and antibiotics. Vegetables, herbs, and fruit are grown to supply estate restaurants with year-round fresh produce. Partnerships with farmers in Western North Carolina promote the use of locally sourced food for estate restaurants.

An estate vineyard produces Chardonnay, Riesling, Viognier, Cabernet Franc, Cabernet Sauvignon, and Merlot grapes. Another effort is canola plantings. Biltmore planted 50 acres of non-GMO canola, which is converted to more than 5,000 gallons of biodiesel oil annually to power various farm machinery.

As a family-owned business, Biltmore's top priority is preserving and protecting the estate for future generations. Using sustainable practices ensures that vision is carried on.

Oyster Chowder "Purse" *in* Lobster Broth

—**Kirk Fiore,** LIONCREST AT BILTMORE ESTATE

Chef Kirk Fiore prepared this soup for the Movable Feast farm-to-table dinner on the grounds of the Biltmore Estate. Now he shares it with you.

MAKES 4 SERVINGS

FOR THE LOBSTER AND LOBSTER STOCK:

1 cup heavy whipping cream

1 cup dry sherry

2 celery stalks, cut up

1 onion, quartered

1 bay leaf

1/2 vanilla bean

1 (1 to 2-pound) lobster

Salt and freshly ground pepper, to taste

FOR THE CREAM FILLING:

1 1/2 cups heavy whipping cream

3 shallots, minced

2 stalks celery, minced

1 bay leaf

FOR THE DUMPLINGS:

2 cups all-purpose flour

12 freshly shucked oysters

Minced chives (as garnish)

To prepare the lobster and lobster stock, combine the cream, sherry, celery, onion, bay leaf, and vanilla bean with 1 quart of water in a large stockpot. Bring to a boil; reduce heat to maintain a simmer. Add the lobster; poach 12 minutes. Remove the lobster using tongs and place in a shallow dish.

Bring the cooking liquid to a boil; boil until reduced by half, 10 to 15 minutes. Strain the broth through a wire mesh sieve, discarding solids. Season the broth with salt and pepper, to taste.

Remove the meat from the lobster and roughly chop. Refrigerate the lobster meat.

To prepare the cream filling: combine the cream, shallots, celery, and bay leaf in a medium saucepan; bring to a boil. Reduce heat and simmer until reduced to 3/4 cup, about 30 minutes. Pour into a shallow pan and refrigerate until completely cold.

Meanwhile, prepare the dumplings: place the flour in a large mixing bowl. While running an electric mixer fitted with the dough hook, slowly pour in 3/4 cup boiling water; knead 5 minutes with the dough hook, until smooth. Scrape the dough onto a piece of plastic wrap; wrap and refrigerate until the filling is chilled, at least 30 minutes.

Line a baking sheet with wax paper and coat with cooking spray. Divide the dough, by tablespoons, into 12 portions; gently roll out each into 2-inch disks on the wax paper. Spoon the cream mixture, by tablespoons, into the center of each dough disk; place an oyster on top of each. Fold the dough disks over to enclose the filling; crimp the edges with a fork. Refrigerate until ready to cook.

To serve, bring the lobster broth to a simmer; poach the dumplings until cooked, 3 to 5 minutes. Remove the dumplings with a slotted spoon and place in warm serving bowls. Ladle the remaining broth over the dumplings; top with the chopped lobster and garnish with minced chives.

A Little Something Extra

"Lagniappe"

That most thoughtful touch that sets a dish apart. A burst of this, a pop of that. A little dab of something extra that — often quite unexpectedly — brings the flavor complexity of a dish to new, spectacular heights. It can be tangy, spicy, sweet, or savory. Too much might overpower, but just enough…perfection.

"Lagniappe," pronounced "LAN-yap," loosely translates as "a little something extra." It comes from Spanish and French/Creole origins. The term simply conveys a small gift — or more simply put, something to nicely round things out.

Oddly enough, a "bakers dozen," the uneven number thirteen, was also sourced from this concept. Prime numbers aside, who would complain about an extra donut or other scrumptious, doughy treat? Not even the baker.

There is also something particularly homey, roots-oriented, and essentially Southern about lagniappe. It is the picked-fresh, farmer's market berries that go into canned preserves, saved for months and opened after the first frost for a taste of summer at its peak. It is Great Aunt Mabel's pickle recipe that packs a punch and leaves friends lip-smacking and begging for a jar of their own.

It is the savory gravy you look forward to as part of the over-the-top holiday spread or — even better — during a weeknight home-cooked meal of meatloaf, paired with (as my husband likes to refer to them) "creamed 'taters." That little something that brings back a visceral memory connected with home and comfort. An extra element to a dish that makes a restaurant, BBQ joint, or food truck one you can't forget.

In this chapter, we have curated some of best lagniappes found in Western North Carolina. Our chefs and farmers have contributed recipes for pestos, chutneys, salsa, and more: from gravies and dressings all the way to compotes and regionally inspired BBQ sauce. Because if you didn't already know it, we North Carolinians take those little extra somethings rather seriously. After trying some of these lagniappes, you will discover why they inspire such pride.

—**Christine Sykes Lowe, Author**

A Little Something Extra

Dressings & Drizzles

Cider Vinegar • 199

Citrus Dressing • 199

Maple Sherry Vinaigrette • 200

Chipotle-Citrus Vinaigrette • 200

Dried Cherry Vinaigrette • 200

Balsamic Vinaigrette • 201

Blue Cheese Dressing • 201

Curry Dijon Vinaigrette • 202

Poblano Coulis • 202

Aioli & Smoked Paprika Aioli • 203

Jalapeño Aioli • 203

Cider Vinegar

—Steven Goff, FORMERLY OF KING JAMES PUBLIC HOUSE

Chef Steven Goff ferments his own flavored vinegars and uses them as a base for sauces and marinades, as well as to season food. His cooking relies completely on local ingredients, and his passion for making vinegars comes from the desire to "use even the air we breathe in this place" in his food — thus fermenting the apples, water, and sugar in this perfectly balanced cider vinegar.

Process the apples, in batches, in a food processor to chop; place the apples in a wide-mouth glass container.

Heat 1 quart of the water and sugar in a medium saucepan, stirring until the sugar dissolves. Remove from the heat and let cool; stir in the remaining water and the vinegar. Pour the sugar solution over the apples.

Cover the jar with a piece of cloth and secure with a rubber band. Let it stand at room temperature to ferment until bubbling activity ceases, 1 to 2 weeks. Strain the solids and place in sterilized bottles. Cover and keep in a cool, dark place for 3 weeks to 2 months to ferment to your desired taste.

MAKES 3 1/2 QUARTS

8 local apples, stems removed and cut up

3 quarts filtered water, divided

3/4 cup sugar

1/4 cup Braggs raw vinegar or homemade

COOK'S NOTE:
Use the whole apple, cores and peels too, to flavor the vinegar. The Braggs raw vinegar is a "starter" for the fermentation process. But if you make batches of vinegar, you can save out a little to use as the starter for the next batch instead of the Braggs.

Citrus Dressing

—Randy Talley, THE GREEN SAGE COFFEEHOUSE AND CAFÉ

Fresh-squeezed orange and lemon juices balance the vinegar in the dressing for Raw Citrus Kale Salad on page 102. Drizzle it on other green salads or use it as a marinade.

Combine all the ingredients in a jar; cover tightly, and shake to blend. Store in the refrigerator.

MAKES 2 CUPS

1/2 cup apple cider vinegar, such as Bragg's

1/2 cup canola oil (expeller pressed)

1/2 cup extra-virgin olive oil

1/4 cup fresh lemon juice

1/4 cup fresh orange juice

1/2 teaspoon sea salt

1/2 teaspoon freshly ground pepper

Maple Sherry Vinaigrette

—**Eric Kang,** THE ADMIRAL

MAKES 1 1/3 CUPS

1/3 cup sherry vinegar

1/3 cup maple syrup

1/3 cup canola oil

Kosher salt

Freshly ground pepper

Here's the "secret" dressing for The Admiral's arugula salad. Now you can get rave reviews, too.

Combine the vinegar, syrup, and oil in a squeeze bottle or jar; shake well before drizzling on your greens. Season the salad with salt and pepper to taste.

Chipotle-Citrus Vinaigrette

—**Michelle Kelley,** THE CANTINA

MAKES 2 1/2 CUPS

1/4 cup canned chipotle chilies in adobo sauce

1/4 cup fresh lime juice

1/4 cup orange juice (no pulp)

1/4 cup red wine vinegar

1 1/2 cups olive oil

1 teaspoon salt, or to taste

Smoky heat comes together with bright citrus to add kick to chef Michelle Kelley's popular salad dressing at The Cantina in Biltmore Village.

Combine the chilies and sauce, lime juice, orange juice, and vinegar in a blender; pulse to blend. With the processor running, gradually add the olive oil until the dressing is emulsified. Stir in salt to taste; store in a covered jar in the refrigerator.

Dried Cherry Vinaigrette

—**Traci Taylor,** FIG

MAKES ABOUT 1 1/4 CUPS

1/2 cup extra-virgin olive oil

3 tablespoons white balsamic vinegar

2 tablespoons minced shallots

2 tablespoons minced fresh mint or thyme

1 teaspoon sugar

1/2 teaspoon coarse salt, or to taste

1/2 teaspoon freshly ground pepper

1/2 cup dried tart cherries

Try drizzling the vinaigrette over roasted or steamed broccolini, carrots, sweet potatoes, cauliflower, asparagus, green beans, or Brussels sprouts, then sprinkle with chopped walnuts.

Whisk the olive oil, vinegar, shallots, mint, sugar, salt, and pepper in a medium bowl; stir in the dried cherries. Store in a covered jar in the refrigerator.

Balsamic Vinaigrette

—**John Stehling,** EARLY GIRL EATERY

Chef John and Julie Stehling drizzle this house vinaigrette over their Fried Green Tomato Napoleon (page 68), but you can use it for salads or whenever you need a balsamic vinaigrette dressing.

Combine the mustard and vinegar in a food processor bowl or blender. With the processor running, gradually pour in the oils in a slow, steady stream; process until emulsified, scraping the bowl as necessary. Mix in the salt and pepper; store in a covered jar in the refrigerator.

MAKES ABOUT 2 CUPS

1/4 cup Dijon mustard

2 tablespoons balsamic vinegar

1 cup vegetable oil

3/4 cup extra-virgin olive oil

1 teaspoon salt

1/5 teaspoon ground white pepper

Blue Cheese Dressing

—**Jake Schmidt,** EDISON CRAFT ALES + KTCHEN

Chef Jake Schmidt serves this creamy salad dressing as a nice contrast to the bright flavors in Fried Green Tomato Salad with Watercress, Pepper Jelly & Blue Cheese Dressing p. 103.

Combine the mayonnaise, half-and-half, 1/2 cup of the blue cheese, crème fraîche, lemon juice, vinegar, Worcestershire sauce, salt, and pepper in a food processor; process until the dressing is smooth. Scrape into a bowl and stir in the remaining blue cheese. Cover and refrigerate until serving time.

MAKES ABOUT 2 1/4 CUPS

2 cups mayonnaise

1 cup half-and-half

1 cup crumbled Maytag blue cheese, divided

1/4 cup crème fraîche

2 tablespoons fresh lemon juice

2 tablespoons red wine vinegar

1/2 teaspoon Worcestershire sauce

1/2 teaspoon salt, or to taste

1/2 teaspoon freshly ground pepper, or to taste

Curry Dijon Vinaigrette

—**Traci Taylor,** FIG

MAKES ABOUT 1/2 CUP

1/4 cup plus 3 tablespoons extra-virgin olive oil

2 tablespoons white balsamic vinegar

1 teaspoon Madras curry powder

2 teaspoons Dijon mustard

1 teaspoon honey

1/8 teaspoon kosher salt

1/4 teaspoon freshly ground pepper

White balsamic vinegar and honey give a lightly sweet taste to the dressing, complementing the curry flavor. To make a delicious, Indian-inspired chicken salad, mix it with pulled chicken, toasted chopped almonds, celery, and raisins.

Combine all the ingredients in a small jar or bowl; shake to blend or whisk well.

Poblano Coulis

—**Michael Fisera,** LEXINGTON AVENUE BREWERY

Chef Michael Fisera balanced grilled pork and pineapple with a mildly hot purée. It's delicious with fish, pork, chicken, or lamb, especially served with grilled fruit.

MAKES ABOUT 1 1/4 CUPS

6 medium-size poblano peppers

1 bunch cilantro leaves, chopped

1/4 cup minced garlic

1 teaspoon ground cinnamon

About a tablespoon oil

Salt and freshly ground pepper

1 1/2 teaspoons brown sugar

Preheat the oven to 450° F. Fill a 2-quart saucepan with water; bring to a boil and salt the water. Meanwhile, remove the stems and seeds from 5 of the poblanos; dice and add to the boiling water and cook until tender, about 5 minutes. Drain, reserving the peppers.

Remove the stem and seeds of the remaining poblano, keeping the pepper mostly whole. Toss the cilantro, garlic, cinnamon; stuff the pepper with the mixture, rub outside with oil and sprinkle with salt and pepper. Place the pepper on a baking sheet and roast until tender, about 15 minutes, turning once.

Placed the stuffed pepper, diced peppers, and brown sugar in a blender or food processor; process until smooth, scraping the container as necessary. If necessary, add water, by tablespoons, to reach a sauce texture you can drizzle. Season to taste with salt and pepper.

Aioli *and* Smoked Paprika Aioli

—**Sam Etheridge,** AMBROZIA

Chef/owner Sam Etheridge uses half of this lemony Hollandaise-like sauce to bind the egg yolks in Deviled Eggs with Smoked Paprika Aioli, Bacon Jam, and Fried Sage (page 64); the other half is blended with smoked paprika for a lovely finishing garnish on the plate.

Combine the egg yolks, egg, lemon juice, and mustard in a food processor; pulse a few times to blend, and scrape down the sides of the processor bowl. With machine running, gradually pour in the oil, processing until the mixture is blended and thick. Measure out 1/2 cup and reserve for mixing with the egg yolks in the deviled eggs.

Scrape the remaining basic Aiol into a small bowl, and stir in the paprika. The basic Aioli and Smoked Paprika Aioli can be made ahead and refrigerated in an airtight container for up to 1 week.

MAKES 1/2 CUP BASIC AOLI AND 1 CUP SMOKED PAPRIKA AIOLI

2 large egg yolks

1 large egg

Juice of 1 lemon

1 teaspoon Dijon mustard

1 cup blended olive oil

Salt and freshly ground pepper to taste

1 tablespoon smoked paprika

Jalapeño Aioli

MAKES 2 CUPS

3 jalapeños

1 3/4 cups Duke's mayonnaise

1 cup packed fresh basil leaves

1 tablespoon roasted garlic

1 tablespoon fresh lemon juice

Kosher salt

Freshly ground pepper

—**William Dissen,** THE MARKET PLACE RESTAURANT

Roasting the jalapeños before blending with the basil, roasted garlic, and mayonnaise mixture gives chef/owner William Dissen's sauce smoky heat.

To roast the the jalapeños, spear one jalapeño at a time crosswise onto the end of a long-handled meat fork. Hold it over a high flame on a gas stovetop until it is blackened and blistered on one side, 1 to 2 minutes; turn it over to blister the other. (Alternately, you can broil the jalapeños close to the heat source.) As they finish roasting, place them in a small paper bag; seal the bag and let the peppers steam to loosen the skin, about 5 minutes.

Peel the jalapeños; remove the stems and seeds. Place in a blender container; puree until smooth. Add the mayonnaise, basil, roasted garlic, lemon juice, 1/4 teaspoon salt, and 1/4 teaspoon pepper; cover and process the aioli until smooth, scraping the sides of the blender as necessary. Season to taste with additional salt and pepper, if desired.

A Little Something Extra

Condiments

Lemon Chutney • 205

Pepper Jelly • 206

Apple Butter • 206

Bacon Jam • 207

Peach Chutney • 207

Mint Pesto • 209

Remoulade • 208

Candied Apricots • 209

Lemon Chutney

—Traci Taylor, FIG

At Fig, the Lemon Chutney is served with grilled chicken and a small head of grilled organic romaine drizzled with curry vinaigrette. It is also nice as a refreshing glaze for grilled pork tenderloin.

Cut the lemons in half vertically; cut into paper-thin slices (or as close as you can!) with a sharp knife, then remove the seeds; place in a large bowl. Cut the onions vertically into thin, julienned strips; add to the lemons.

Sprinkle the salt over the lemons and onions; toss to mix well. Cover and let stand for at least 4 hours and up to 24 hours.

Drain and rinse the lemons and onions; place in a large, heavy saucepan. Add 2 cups water and bring to a boil. Cover, reduce heat, and simmer until the lemon rind is tender, about 20 minutes.

Add the sugar, vinegar, raisins, mustard seeds, ginger, and red pepper; bring to a simmer over medium heat, stirring constantly until the sugar dissolves. Reduce heat to low, maintaining barely a simmer until thick, stirring frequently, 1 to 1 1/2 hours. Let the mixture cool completely; chutney will thicken as it cools. Spoon into sterilized jars and seal tightly. Refrigerate for up to 6 weeks.

MAKES 8 (1/2-PINT) JARS

2 pounds firm, thin-skinned lemons

1 pound sweet onions

3 tablespoons sea salt

2 cups water

4 cups sugar

1 cup cider vinegar

1 cup golden raisins

1/4 cup yellow mustard seeds

2 teaspoons ground ginger

1/8 teaspoon ground red pepper

COOK'S NOTE:
Look for plump, smallish to medium fresh lemons that have smooth, shiny peel. The rind typically contains less bitter pith under the peel.

Pepper Jelly

—**Jake Schmidt,** EDISON CRAFT ALES + KITCHEN

Chef Jake Schmidt strategically spreads Pepper Jelly between slices of crisp-battered fried green tomatoes in his Fried Green Tomato Salad (page 103) for a surprise taste of sweet and hot.

Process the peppers in a food processor; scrape into a large, nonreactive saucepan. Stir in the vinegar and 2 cups of the sugar; bring to a boil, stirring constantly until the sugar melts. Skim the surface as needed; reduce heat and boil gently for 10 minutes. Remove from the heat; stir in 1 teaspoon salt and 1 teaspoon crushed red pepper flakes.

Stir together the remaining 1 1/2 cups sugar and pectin; add to the pepper mixture. Bring to a boil, stirring constantly until the sugar melts; boil gently, stirring constantly, until thickened, about 2 minutes.

Ladle the hot jelly into jars, leaving 1/4 inch headspace. Wipe the rim and center the lid on the jar. Screw the band tight. Process in a boiling water canner for 10 minutes. Remove the jars and let cool.

MAKES ABOUT 10 PINTS

3 1/2 pounds banana peppers, stemmed and seeded

2 quarts apple cider vinegar

3 1/2 cups sugar, divided

5 ounces pectin

1 teaspoon kosher salt, or to taste

1 teaspoon crushed red pepper flakes, or to taste

Apple Butter

MAKES ABOUT 3 CUPS

4 sticks (2 cups) unsalted butter, divided

4 cups local apple cider, such as Noble Cider

1 cup sorghum

1 (1-pound) box firmly packed light brown sugar

1/2 teaspoon salt, or to taste

5 pounds local apples, such as Mutsu, cored and sliced

1 vanilla bean, halved

—**Jake Schmidt,** EDISON CRAFT ALES + KITCHEN

Mutsu apples are also called crispin apples. Much of the intense apple flavor comes from using Noble Cider, our area's first hard cider beverage company.

Melt 2 sticks of the butter in a large, heavy saucepan over medium heat. Continue cooking, stirring occasionally, until the butter is browned. Immediately add the cider, sorghum, sugar, and salt, stirring constantly until the sugar is dissolved. Add the apples; scrape the vanilla bean seeds into the mixture and add the pod halves. Stir well; cook the mixture, reducing the heat as necessary to maintain a low simmer, until almost no liquid remains, 1 to 2 hours. If the mixture starts to stick, transfer it right away to another pot or it will burn.

Let the apple mixture cool and remove the vanilla pod halves. Then process the apple mixture, in batches, in a blender until it is smooth. Scrape it into a bowl and stir in the remaining 2 sticks of butter. If desired, strain the mixture; store in covered containers in the refrigerator.

Bacon Jam

—Sam Etheridge, AMBROZIA

MAKES ABOUT 1 1/2 CUPS

1 pound premium-quality bacon, chopped

1/2 cup chopped yellow onion

1 teaspoon minced garlic

1 cup firmly packed brown sugar

1 cup chicken stock

We love this sweet, savory, smoky dollop on the deviled egg appetizer (page 64) from chef/owner Sam Etheridge at Ambrozia. Don't miss the classic bacon and egg combo with a twist. The jam is also good on biscuits and morning toast.

Cook the bacon in a large skillet over medium heat until crisp, stirring frequently. Drain bacon on paper towels; pour off all but 1 tablespoon of the drippings in the skillet.

Add the onion and garlic to the drippings and cook over medium heat until translucent. Stir in the brown sugar and stock; bring to a boil over medium-high heat, stirring constantly until the brown sugar is dissolved. Reduce heat and boil gently, uncovered, until reduced by one third, about 15 to 20 minutes.

Let the mixture cool completely; pour into a blender container. Process until just smooth, scraping the sides of the container as necessary. Store in a covered container in the refrigerator for up to 1 week. Serve at room temperature.

Peach Chutney

—Jennifer Perkins, LOOKING GLASS CREAMERY

When fresh peaches hit the markets, don't miss out on making chutney. Technically, it will last for several weeks in the refrigerator; but you'll want to use it often for the Baked Pack Square with Peach Chutney (page 79) or on grilled meats and chicken.

MAKES ABOUT 6 CUPS

4 pounds fresh peaches

4 green onions, finely chopped

4 cloves garlic, chopped

2 cups cider vinegar

2 cups firmly packed light brown sugar

1 cup minced fresh ginger

2 tablespoons yellow mustard seeds

1 tablespoon minced dried chipotle chili peppers

1/2 teaspoon ground cardamom

1/2 teaspoon kosher salt, or to taste

1/4 teaspoon freshly ground pepper, or to taste

Peel the peaches and remove the pits; chop coarsely and place in a large, nonreactive saucepan. Add the onions, garlic, vinegar, brown sugar, ginger, mustard seeds, chili peppers, and cardamom.

Bring to a boil, stirring constantly until the sugar melts. Reduce the heat and simmer until the mixture is thickened, stirring occasionally, 50 to 60 minutes. Adjust the heat as necessary to maintain a gentle simmer; watch carefully after 30 minutes and stir more frequently to make sure the chutney does not burn. Stir in salt and pepper to taste. Ladle into sterilized jars and store in the refrigerator.

Remoulade

—**Denny Trantham,** FORMERLY OF THE GROVE PARK INN

Remoulade is a cold sauce with origins in France, recognized in America for saucing Louisiana seafood dishes. Chef Denny Trantham picks up the traditional flavors of tangy and salty in the mayonnaise base, and he adds layers of fresh herbs to complement his Jumbo Crab Cakes (page 65).

Place the mayonnaise in a medium bowl. Combine the cornichons, vinegar, capers, mustard, chives, dill, cilantro, shallots, garlic, and anchovies in a blender; purée until smooth, scraping the sides of the blender as necessary. Add to the mayonnaise and stir well. Cover and refrigerate for 1 hour and up to 2 weeks.

MAKES ABOUT 2 3/4 CUPS

2 cups mayonnaise

1/3 cup chopped cornichons

1/4 cup red wine vinegar

1/4 cup drained capers

2 tablespoons Dijon mustard

2 tablespoons chopped fresh chives

2 tablespoons chopped fresh dill

1 tablespoon chopped fresh cilantro

2 teaspoons minced fresh shallots

2 teaspoons minced fresh garlic

6 anchovies or 1 1/2 teaspoons anchovy paste

Chickweed Pesto Aioli

MAKES ABOUT 1 1/2 CUPS

—**Jael and Dan Rattigan,** FRENCH BROAD CHOCOLATE LOUNGE

For the chickweed pesto:

1 cup chickweed or arugula, washed and dried

1/2 cup toasted pumpkin seeds

2 green onions, white and green parts, sliced

1/4 cup olive oil

FOR THE AIOLI:

1 large egg

1 1/2 teaspoons lemon juice

1/2 teaspoon salt

3/4 cup olive oil

"Chickweed is a spring yard weed that is delicious when young and picked before it has flowered," says chef/owner Jael Rattigan. "It makes a great pesto, which we use for the aioli served with the Ginger Coconut Meatballs (page 193)."

Purée the chickweed, pumpkin seeds, green onion and olive oil in a blender, scraping down the sides of the blender as needed. Scrape the pesto into a bowl.

Add the egg, lemon juice, and salt to the blender; process until combined, about 10 seconds. With the blender running, gradually add the olive oil in a slow, steady stream, processing until the mixture is emulsified, scraping the sides of the blender as needed. Add to the pesto and stir well. Cover and refrigerate any leftovers.

Mint Pesto

—**Wendy Brugh,** DRY RIDGE FARM

Wendy and Graham Brugh raise sheep, meat chickens, laying hens, rabbits, and heritage breed hogs on their farm in Mars Hill. Wendy blogs regularly about farm goings-on and what they'll have at farmers markets: www.dryridgefarm.org

When we tested this recipe, we made it again with lime juice instead of lemon juice and added 2 teaspoons grated fresh ginger to it. Served on grilled salmon, it was yummy!

Combine the olive oil, mint, parsley, Parmesan, pine nuts, lemon juice, salt, and pepper in a food processor or blender; process until a coarse paste forms, scraping the container as needed.

MAKES ABOUT 2 1/2 CUPS

1/2 cup extra-virgin olive oil

2 1/4 cups lightly packed fresh mint leaves

1 1/4 cups lightly packed fresh parsley leaves

2/3 cup freshly grated Parmesan cheese

1/2 cup pine nuts, walnuts, or pecans

2 tablespoons fresh lemon juice

1/2 teaspoon sea salt

1/2 teaspoon freshly ground pepper

Candied Apricots

—**Michael Fisera,** LEXINGTON AVENUE BREWERY

MAKES ABOUT 4 CUPS

2 cups dried apricots

3 cups sugar plus additional for coating, divided

COOK'S NOTE:
Save the sugar syrup when you drain it off the cooked apricots to:

• Pour it over vanilla (or peach) ice cream or fresh berries.

• Add a tablespoon to homemade vinaigrette.

• Use as a sweetener for ice tea or fresh lemonade.

Chef Michael Fisera used the apricots as a garnish for Blackened Salmon with Candied Apricots and Grand Marnier-Bacon Vinaigrette (page 173).

Sprinkle a thin layer of sugar in a rimmed baking sheet.
Put 1 1/2 cups of the sugar in a large bowl.

Place the apricots in a medium bowl; add enough water to cover them. Let stand for 10 minutes. Drain the apricots and discard the water.

Finely dice the apricots and place them in a 2-quart saucepan.
Add 2 cups water and 1 1/2 cups sugar; bring to a boil, stirring until the sugar dissolves. Boil gently until a thick syrup forms, 25 to 30 minutes. Pour through a wire mesh sieve, reserving the apricot syrup for other uses. Immediately toss the apricots into the large bowl with the sugar. Pour onto the baking sheet and separate the apricots using 2 forks; let them cool completely. Store the apricots in the sugar in an airtight container for 1 week.

A Little Something Extra

Pickled

Natural Pickles • 211

Pickled Ramps • 212

Quick Fennel Pickles • 213

Asian-Style Pickled Cucumbers • 213

Chow Chow • 214

Refrigerator Garlic Pickles • 215

Natural Pickles

—**Steven Goff,** FORMERLY OF KING JAMES PUBLIC HOUSE

Chef Steven Goff shares this method for lactic acid fermentation; by using a pickling liquid with a high concentration of salt, harmful bacteria are prevented from multiplying while the lactic acid dominates and stops other cultures from thriving. You get a wonderful tang from these pickles.

Combine the water, salt, pepper, crushed red pepper, thyme, garlic, and bay leaves in a saucepan; bring to a boil, stirring until the salt is dissolved. Cover, remove from the heat, and let cool completely.

Pack the vegetables tightly into the jars. Pour the cooled water mixture over the vegetables, taking care to submerge them in the liquid and leaving 1-inch headspace from the jar rim. Cover tightly and shake to mix the brine and vegetables; make sure the ingredients are submerged.

Let the pickles stand in a cool, dark place for 1 to 2 weeks or until they have pickled to your desired taste.

MAKES 6 PINTS

2 cups plus 2 tablespoons filtered water

3 1/2 teaspoons coarse salt

1 tablespoon whole black peppercorns

1 teaspoon dried crushed red pepper

8 sprigs thyme

6 cloves garlic, crushed

2 bay leaves

Small pickling cucumbers

COOK'S NOTE:
Also try pickling kohlrabi and carrot sticks, onion wedges, beet wedges, seeded peppers, garlic, and radishes.

Pickled Ramps

—**Denny Trantham,** FORMERLY OF GROVE PARK INN

MAKES 1 QUART

1 pound ramp bulbs (or whole ramps), trimmed

1 cup sugar

1 cup rice wine vinegar

1 cup water

1 tablespoon kosher salt

1 tablespoon Japanese 7 seasoning (shichimi togarashi)

1 1/2 teaspoons Korean crushed red pepper (kochukaru) or other mild crushed chili pepper

COOK'S NOTE:
Ramps may have become the "it" vegetable of NYC chefs, but here we've always celebrated this fresh spring outcropping of white tubers, burgundy stems, and floppy green leaves — similar to young leeks. With the aroma and strong flavor of garlic and leeks when they're raw, many prefer to sauté, roast, or grill them. And if you're from the mountains, pickling is tops for making sure the ramp season stays around for a while.

Chef Denny Trantham grew up in Haywood County and made his way to become Executive Chef at the Grove Park Inn. He cut his teeth on the rich traditions of the Appalachian South, and so he is a living, cooking tribute to our WNC culture.

Blanch ramp bulbs in boiling, salted water to soften, 30 seconds; drain and plunge into a bowl of ice water. Drain. (If using very young ramps, blanch them whole with the bulb, stem, and leaves.)

Combine the sugar, vinegar, water, salt, seasoning, and crushed red pepper in a large saucepan; bring to a boil, stirring until the sugar dissolves. Remove from the heat and add the ramps to the mixture, pressing down to submerge them. Let the brine and ramps cool to room temperature.

Use tongs to remove the ramps from the brine and place in a non-reactive container; pour the brine over the ramps. Cover and refrigerate overnight and up to 3 days.

Top Chefs: AB Tech Culinary Arts Program

Asheville-Buncombe Technical College, known locally as AB Tech, offers a Culinary Arts Program that continues to gain exposure on the national scene. As a result, graduates of the program are well prepared to join the growing culinary industry. Students and graduates have won numerous national and regional culinary competitions, and many have risen to prestigious leadership ranks at top culinary institutions throughout the country.

Accredited by the American Culinary Federation, the program offers five state-of-the-art, professionally equipped kitchens in which to train, co-op education positions in the field, training in an on-campus restaurant with a banquet room and five dining rooms, performing chef demonstrations in the demo kitchen and in the community, and much more real life experience.

Many local renowned chefs have graduated from the program. Many, including Steven Goff of King James Public House, return to AB Tech to teach, giving back the gifts and skills he received there.

Quick Fennel Pickles

—Chef Steven Goff, FORMERLY OF KING JAMES PUBLIC HOUSE

You can pickle other vegetables using this method too: carrots, cucumbers, peppers, kohlrabi, and cauliflower. Try adding other aromatics to the brine before heating: whole fennel, cardamom pods, coriander, and strips of orange rind (minus the white pith).

Combine the vinegar, sugar, salt, peppercorns, mustard seeds, thyme, and shallots in a large, nonreactive saucepan. Bring to a boil, stirring until the sugar dissolves. Let the mixture cool to room temperature, then strain it, discarding the solids.

Pack the fennel tightly into the jars. Pour the vinegar mixture over the vegetables, taking care to submerge them in the liquid; leave 1-inch headspace from the jar rim. Cover tightly and shake to mix the brine and vegetables; make sure the ingredients are submerged.

Cover and let the pickles stand in a cool, dark place for 2 days; then refrigerate up to 1 month.

MAKES 3 TO 4 PINTS

4 cups rice vinegar

1 cup sugar

4 tablespoons salt

1 tablespoon whole black peppercorns

1 tablespoon yellow mustard seeds

8 sprigs thyme

2 shallots, minced

2 medium fennel bulbs, trimmed and cut into wedges

Asian-Style Pickled Cucumbers

MAKES ABOUT 2 CUPS

1 1/2 cups rice vinegar

1 cup water

1 cup sugar

1/4 cup garlic-chili sauce

2 tablespoons minced pickled ginger

2 European cucumbers, thinly sliced

—Denny Trantham, FORMERLY OF THE GROVE PARK INN

We like these sweet, spicy, gingery pickles in fish tacos and with in the buns with homemade hot dogs from Foothills Farm and Butchery.

Combine the vinegar, water, sugar, garlic-chili sauce, and ginger in a large, sterilized wide-mouth jar. Cover and shake until the sugar dissolves. Add the cucumbers; cover and refrigerate overnight, turning the jar occasionally.

Drain the cucumbers and toss with the cilantro.

Chow Chow

—**Traci Taylor,** FIG

MAKES 4 PINTS

2 red bell peppers,
finely chopped

2 large onions,
finely chopped

4 cups finely
chopped cabbage

4 cups finely chopped
green or red tomatoes

1/4 cup salt

2 cups firmly packed
light brown sugar

1 1/2 cups apple cider
vinegar

1 1/2 cups water

1 teaspoon each:
 dry mustard, turmeric,
celery seed, & ground
cinnamon, allspice,
cloves, yellow
mustard seeds

3 bay leaves

1 jalapeño, halved
and seeded

In the South, whether you like it XXX hot or mild, chow chow is as important as salt and pepper on the supper table. It's a must to go on dishes of pinto beans with cornbread, and it turns a pan-fried pork chop into a 5-star dish. In chef Traci Taylor's kitchen, chow chow raises the Pork Schnitzel several notches. Her version is mostly mild, relying on the brine's spices and a delicious pairing of cabbage, green tomatoes, peppers, and onions to set it apart.

Combine the peppers, onion, cabbage, and tomatoes in a large, non-reactive bowl; toss well with salt. Cover and let stand 12 hours or overnight.

Line a colander with a double thickness of cheesecloth; add the vegetables and let them drain well.

Combine the brown sugar, vinegar, water, spices, bay leaves, and jalapeño in a large, non-reactive saucepan; bring to a boil, stirring constantly until the sugar melts. Reduce heat to medium and boil uncovered, 5 minutes. Add the vegetables; remove from the heat and let cool in the brine, to room temperature. Pack in sterilized jars. Store in the refrigerator.

Refrigerator Garlic Pickles

—Bill Hunt, KAY FARM

At his Asheville City Market booth, Bill Hunt, owner of Kay Farm, sells his homemade pickles alongside his perfect cucumbers, potatoes, beans, and gorgeous heads of romaine. If you are lucky enough to spot a jar before he runs out, grab it. Next time, you'll want to get to the market earlier for more.

Although he had trouble searching the farmhouse for this recipe during the chaos of renovating his home and moving back to this third-generation farm, he knew he'd better get a hold of it before it was time to pickle. Couldn't disappoint his fans!

Combine 2 cups of the water, vinegar, salt, sugar, and garlic in a clean container; stir or shake until the sugar and salt are totally dissolved An empty one gallon vinegar jug is perfect for this.

Trim the ends, and slice about 1/4-inch thick as desired or cut lengthwise into spears.

Place 1 clove of garlic in each clean pint jar. Add a slice of hot pepper or peppercorns, if using. Pack the cucumbers into the jars, but not too tightly.

Ladle the brine over the cucumbers, filling to the top rounded edges; screw on the lids. Store overnight and up to 2 weeks in a cool place but not in the refrigerator. After opening the jars, store in the refrigerator.

MAKES 24 PINTS

5 to 6 pounds of pickling cucumbers

11 cups water, divided

3 cups white vinegar

1 cup kosher salt

1/2 cup white sugar

24 small cloves garlic (1 clove per pint)

Slice of hot pepper or a few peppercorns (optional)

COOK'S NOTE:
This much brine will make around 24 pints. If you aren't pickling that many cucumbers, you can cut the recipe in half. The pickles will store up to 2 weeks, but nobody waits that long to eat them.

A Little Something Extra

Sauced

Blackberry BBQ Sauce • 217

Scooter's BBQ Sauce • 218

Carnitas BBQ Sauce • 218

Vinegar-Based BBQ Sauce • 219

East Carolina BBQ Sauce • 219

Blackberry BBQ Sauce

—**Mary Collins-Shepard,** SEASONAL SCHOOL OF CULINARY ARTS

Berry sweet and lightly tart with mild chili heat, this BBQ sauce was a hit with the SSCA class on cooking with honey. Chef Mary Collins-Shepard added a splash of bourbon to give it an earthy, smoky nuance to partner with the Bourbon Honey Marinated Hangar Steak (page 146).

Purée the blackberries in a blender and scrape into small, non-reactive saucepan. (If you don't want seeds in the sauce, press the purée through a fine-mesh sieve into the saucepan.) Add the honey, orange juice and rind, ketchup, chili powder, and vinegar.

Bring to a simmer over medium heat, stirring frequently. Simmer uncovered, 2 minutes. Remove from the heat and whisk in the butter until the sauce is smooth; stir in the bourbon. Season with the salt and pepper. Store in a covered container in the refrigerator up to 1 week; serve warm or at room temperature.

MAKES 1 1/2 CUPS

2 cups fresh blackberries

1/3 cup honey

Juice and grated zest of 1 orange

1 tablespoon ketchup

1 teaspoon chili powder

1 teaspoon balsamic vinegar

2 tablespoons unsalted butter, softened

2 tablespoons bourbon

1/4 teaspoon sea salt, or to taste

1/4 teaspoon freshly ground pepper, or to taste

Down East BBQ Sauce

1 cup honey

2 cloves of garlic, separated and peeled

3 tablespoons whole fennel seeds

2 tablespoons dried crushed red pepper

4 teaspoons celery seeds

4 teaspoons yellow mustard seeds

4 teaspoons ground coriander

1 tablespoon dried thyme

6 1/4 cups distilled white vinegar

3 1/4 cups cider vinegar

1 1/4 cups canned diced tomatoes, undrained

1/2 cup plus 2 tablespoons kosher salt

—Jeff Miller, LUELLA'S BAR-B-QUE

"We create sauces that best complement our meats without overpowering the flavors that we've worked so hard to get just right," says chef/owner Jeff Miller. This is a homecook version of Luella's flagship sauce.

Combine the honey and garlic in a large, non-reactive saucepan; bring just to a simmer. Reduce the heat to very low and barely simmer for 20 minutes, stirring occasionally.

Meanwhile, grind next four ingredients in a spice grinder or blender. Scrape into honey mixture; stir in coriander and thyme.

Whisk in the vinegars, tomatoes, and salt, and bring just to a simmer. Simmer 30 minutes, stirring occasionally, adjusting the heat as necessary to keep the honey barely simmering.

Remove from the heat and let the sauce cool. Use an immersion blender to purée the sauce or process, in batches, in a blender. Store in covered jars in the refrigerator.

Carnitas BBQ Sauce

—Laura & Ben Mixson, WHITE DUCK TACO SHOP

This thick, sweet and tangy barbecue sauce goes on White Duck's Carnitas Tacos p. 158. It's not just sweet and tangy; lime, chipotle, and thyme add unique layers of flavor that complement the cinnamon-chili rub on the pork.

Combine all of the ingredients in a large, heavy saucepan, stirring well. Bring to a simmer over medium-high heat, stirring constantly until the sugar dissolves. Cover, reduce the heat to low, and cook for 4 hours, stirring occasionally. Adjust the heat if necessary.

Let the sauce cool; purée in a blender until the sauce is smooth. Store in a covered jar in the refrigerator.

1 medium onion, finely chopped

3 cups ketchup

1/2 cup apple cider vinegar

1/2 cup sugar

3 tablespoons fresh lime juice

3 tablespoons soy sauce

2 tablespoons dry mustard

4 1/2 teaspoons ground chipotle powder

4 1/2 teaspoons pepper

2 teaspoons liquid smoke

2 teaspoons dried thyme

1 teaspoon granulated garlic

1 teaspoon ground cloves

Vinegar-Based BBQ Sauce

—Steve Bardwell and Gale Lunsford, WAKE ROBIN FARM BREADS

Wake Robin Farm has been recognized by the state as a "century farm;" it has been farmed by owners Steve Bardwell and Gail Lunsford's family since the early 1800s. Today, after over 150 years of farming, the land is under a forest management plan dedicated to the reintroduction of the American chestnut. The couple supports the farm by baking European-style and whole-grain breads, with local grains grown and ground in NC, in their wood-fired oven.

They share their spirited no-cook BBQ sauce for sandwiches. Says Bardwell, "Once you try this sauce, you will never put tomatoes in BBQ sauce again."

Combine 2 tablespoons of the vinegar with the black pepper, crushed red pepper, liquor, sorghum, sugar, and salt in a jar; cover and shake to blend it well. Let the mixture stand at room temperature for 24 hours. ("The alcohol is working its magic," says Bardwell.)

Add the remaining vinegar and shake well. Let the sauce stand at room temperature for 1 week, shaking the jar occasionally. Store in the refrigerator.

MAKES ABOUT 1 1/2 CUPS

1 1/4 cups apple cider vinegar, divided

3 tablespoons freshly ground (fine) black pepper

3 tablespoons crushed red pepper

2 tablespoons bourbon or moonshine

2 tablespoons sorghum or molasses

2 tablespoons sugar

1 tablespoon salt

East Carolina BBQ Sauce

—Steven Goff, KING JAMES PUBLIC HOUSE

Chef Steven Goff makes this sauce with his homemade vinegar to dress chopped barbecue; the spicy tang of the vinegar sauce complements the smoky meat.

Combine the vinegar, crushed red pepper, garlic, salt, and pepper in a non-reactive saucepan; bring to a boil. Reduce the heat and simmer 15 minutes. Refrigerate until you are ready to serve.

MAKES 2 CUPS

2 cups Cider Vinegar (page 199)

2 tablespoons dried crushed red pepper

1 1/2 teaspoons minced fresh garlic

1 1/2 teaspoons salt

1 tablespoon freshly ground pepper

Sweet Cravings

Chocolate Mousse with
Candy Roaster Cream
on page 248

Gimme Some Sugar

What do 18 pastry chefs, professional bakers, chefs and restaurateurs, and dessert artisans have in common? Food, certainly — this is a cookbook, after all. But beyond food, beyond gathering the ingredients and putting them together in surprising ways, these 18 individuals share one important trait, one vital art… one all-consuming devotion. In a word, seduction.

In this chapter, you'll discover cravings you never realized you had as page after page reveals the recipe secrets of the legendary cakes, homestyle pies, cookies, custards and puddings, and ice creams served in Asheville eateries. There's not another collection like this, corralling the wisdom, training, and skills of 18 dessert gurus.

And yet, all the recipes are accessible enough that even the first-time baker can make them. They will tempt your palate with unique flavor combinations:

Peach and rhubarb. Fragrant vanilla bean and coconut. Strawberry and basil. Toasted nuts and exotic spices. Chocolate and beets. Citrus ginger mint, rosewater, and bright liqueurs. Bourbon and mascarpone. Every luscious flavor you can imagine — and some you'd never thought of — right here in these gorgeous pleasures. Get ready to be seduced.

—**Debby Maugans,** AUTHOR

Sweet Cravings

Cakes

Olive Oil Apple Cake • 224

Lane Cake • 225

Buttermilk Chocolate Cake • 227

World's Best Tropical Carrot Cake • 228

Chocolate Beetroot Cake • 229

Coconut Cake • 230

Olive Oil Apple Cake
on page 224

Olive Oil Apple Cake

—**Cynthia Pierce,** YUZU PATISSERIE

Pastry chef/owner Cynthia Pierce offers this apple cake in the fall, when local apples are in season.

MAKES 8 TO 12 SERVINGS

2 large eggs

1 cup sugar

1/4 cup extra-virgin olive oil

1 teaspoon vanilla extract

1/2 cup all-purpose flour

2 teaspoons baking powder

1/2 cup whole milk, divided

4 small or 3 large Granny Smith apples

Grated zest of 1/2 lemon

Confectioners' sugar

Preheat the oven to 375° F. Butter an 8-inch square baking pan. Cut 2 (14 x 8-inch) strips of parchment paper and lay them in the pan, crisscrossed and overlapped, so that the sides are lined and there is overhang on each side. (You'll use the overhang to lift the cool cake out of the pan.)

Combine the eggs and sugar in a large mixing bowl of a stand mixer fitted with the whisk attachment. Beat until the eggs are thick and pale, 3 to 4 minutes. Beat in the olive oil and vanilla.

Change to the paddle attachment on the mixer. Whisk the flour and baking powder together in a small bowl. Add the flour mixture alternately with the milk mixture, beginning and ending with the dry ingredients; beat at low speed after each addition, just until blended. Scrape the bowl as needed.

Peel, core, and thinly slice the apples; mix gently with the grated zest. Fold the apples into the batter gently, using a rubber spatula. Scrape the batter into the prepared pan.

Bake until the top is deeply browned and the cake starts to pull away from the pan, 45 to 50 minutes. Let the cake cool completely in the pan on a wire rack. Use the parchment overhanging edges to lift the cake from the pan and let it cool on the wire rack. Dust slices with confectioners' sugar.

Lane Cake

—**Kathleen Purvis,** AUTHOR OF *BOURBON*, FOOD EDITOR OF *THE CHARLOTTE OBSERVER*

*This classic Southern cake from Kathleen Purvis'
book,* Bourbon, *was the dessert at a Farmer and Chef
South event. The bourbon and food tasting featured
a book discussion with Purvis, food prepared by chefs
Mike Moore and Peter Pollay using Foothills Deli and
Butchery meats, dessert prepared by author Debby
Maugans, a flight of bourbons and a cocktail for
tasting, and a book signing presented by
Malaprops Bookstore/Café.*

*For the event, Maugans adapted the Bourbon
Mascarpone Cream Icing (on page 233) from her
book,* Small-Batch Baking, *and added chopped, dried
cherries and chocolate to the filling instead of the
traditional raisins.*

To prepare the cake, position the oven racks in upper and lower
thirds of the oven. Preheat the oven to 350° F. Coat 3 (8- or 9-inch)
cake pans with cooking spray; line the bottoms with circles of
parchment paper. Dust the insides of the pans with flour and tap
out the excess.

Whisk the flour, baking powder, and salt in a medium bowl to
blend the dry ingredients. Stir together the milk and vanilla in a
small bowl.

Place the egg whites in a large mixing bowl. Beat at medium speed
of an electric mixer until foamy, 45 to 60 minutes. Increase the
speed to medium-high and beat them until the egg whites form
stiff peaks.

Combine the butter and sugar in another large mixing bowl;
beat at medium speed until it is fluffy, 1 to 2 minutes. Add the
flour mixture in three batches alternately with the milk mixture,
beginning and ending with the dry ingredients; beat at low speed
after each addition, just until blended. Fold one-third of the beaten
whites into the batter; fold in the remaining egg whites. (The batter
may appear curdled.) Scrape the batter into the prepared cake pans.

COOK'S NOTE:
To measure the flour
correctly, first sift about
3 1/4 cups flour into a
large bowl or onto a sheet
of wax paper. Then spoon
the sifted flour into the
measuring cups, and level
the top with the flat edge
of a knife. Return any
extra sifted flour back into
the flour container.

MAKES 12 TO 16 SERVINGS

FOR THE CAKE:

3 1/4 cups sifted
all-purpose flour

1 tablespoon
baking powder

1/2 teaspoon salt

1 cup milk
(nonfat or reduced-fat)

1 teaspoon vanilla extract

8 large egg whites

2 sticks (1 cup) unsalted
butter, softened

2 cups sugar

FOR THE FILLING:

8 large egg yolks

1 1/4 cups sugar

1 stick (1/2 cup) unsalted butter

1 1/4 cups shredded coconut

1 cup chopped pecans

3/4 cup chopped dried cherries

1/3 cup bourbon

1 teaspoon vanilla extract

1/4 teaspoon salt

3 ounces bittersweet or semisweet chocolate, finely chopped

5 to 10 tablespoons bourbon

Bourbon Mascarpone Cream Icing (233)

Bake the cakes, rotating the positions of the cakes in the oven after 15 minutes of baking, until they are golden and a toothpick inserted in the center of the layers comes out clean, 20 to 25 minutes. Let the cakes cool in the pans on a wire rack for 10 minutes. Loosen the edges of the cakes with a small sharp knife; turn them out onto a wire rack upside-down and carefully remove the parchment paper from the bottoms. Turn right-side up and let them cool completely.

To prepare the filling, combine the egg yolks and sugar in a large mixing bowl. Beat at medium speed of an electric mixer until the mixture is thick, fluffy, and pale yellow, 4 to 5 minutes. Scrape them into a double boiler or heatproof mixing bowl set in a saucepan of simmering water. Cut the butter into chunks and add. Cook on medium heat, stirring often, until the mixture is very thick and smooth, 15 to 20 minutes.

Remove from the heat and stir in the coconut, pecans, and dried cherries. Stir in the bourbon, vanilla, and salt. Cover and refrigerate until well chilled, about 2 hours. Stir in the chopped chocolate.

Using a long, sharp knife, cut each layer horizontally into 2 layers and place them, cut sides up, on a work surface; you should have 6 thin cake layers. Brush the cut sides of the layers with 1 to 2 tablespoons of bourbon, if desired. Place 1 cake layer on a cake platter; spoon one-fifth of the filling evenly on the layer. Repeat the stacking process using 4 of the remaining cake layers and the remaining filling. Place the remaining cake layer, cut side down, on top of the stack.

Spread the Bourbon Mascarpone Cream Icing on the top and sides of the cake. Refrigerate until the cake is well chilled, 6 hours or overnight.

From Bourbon: A Savor the South® Cookbook by Kathleen Purvis, University of North Carolina Press, 2013. Used with permission. For more information, visit www.uncpress.unc.edu.

Buttermilk Chocolate Cake

—**Brian Ross,** DOUGH

Chef/owner Brian Ross bakes an incredibly moist and tender chocolate cake. Here is his well-honed ratio of ingredients that go into the layer cakes you can order from Dough. We suggest frosting the cake with your favorite frosting; ours is the Dark Chocolate Caramel Icing (page 235.)

Preheat the oven to 350° F. Butter and flour 2 (8-inch) cake pans.

Combine the eggs, sugar, and oil in a large mixing bowl. Beat the mixture at low speed of an electric mixer fitted with the paddle attachment, until the mixture is lightened, about 10 minutes.

Sift the flour, cocoa, baking soda, and salt together into a bowl. Whisk together the buttermilk and sour cream. Add the flour mixture in three additions alternately with the buttermilk mixture, beginning and ending with the dry ingredients; beat the mixture at low speed after each addition, just until blended. Scrape the bowl as needed. Scrape the batter into the prepared cake pans, dividing evenly.

Scrape the batter into the prepared cake pans, dividing evenly. Bake until a toothpick inserted in the center of the cakes comes out clean, 25 to 30 minutes. Let the cakes cool in the pans for 10 minutes on wire racks. Loosen the edges of the cakes with a knife; invert onto the racks and let the layers cool completely. Frost as desired.

MAKES 2 CAKE LAYERS

2 large eggs

2 cups sugar

3/4 cup oil, such as canola

1 2/3 cups cake flour

1 cup unsweetened cocoa

1 1/2 teaspoons baking soda

1/2 teaspoon salt

1 cup whole buttermilk

1/2 cup sour cream

Asheville Wine and Food Festival

During the month of August, we celebrate our renowned culinary excellence with the Asheville Wine and Food Festival. The Grand Tasting is a showcase for area restaurants, wineries, breweries, distilleries, farmers, and artisan food producers, who line the concourse and main floor of the arena with tasting booths.

While you sample chef-prepared dishes and sweets, you can also meet the farmers, chefs, cookbook authors, and artisan food makers, as well as select nonprofits, who work to make our region a food destination. Plus, you get to taste the hundreds of wines, local Beer City brews, ciders, moonshine, and other beverages made here in Western North Carolina.

Two additional ticketed events lead up to the Grand Tasting on Saturday: Elixir and Sweet. Elixir is a craft cocktail mixology competition that happens on Thursday night, and Sweet is a decadent evening of desserts, champagne, wine, and spirits tastings. For the year's schedule, ticket information, and more about the events, visit ashevillewineandfood.com.

World's Best Tropical Carrot Cake

—Avi Sommerville, HIGHCLIFFE BAKED GOODS, LLC
— HOME OF THE WORLD'S BEST CARROT CAKE

MAKES ONE
(9-INCH, 3-LAYER) CAKE

2 1/3 cups all-purpose flour, divided

1 cup sweetened flaked coconut

1 cup dry-roasted macadamia nuts

3/4 cup chopped crystallized ginger

2 1/2 teaspoons baking powder

1/2 teaspoon baking soda

3/4 teaspoon ground cinnamon

1 teaspoon salt

2 cups sugar

1 1/4 cups vegetable oil

4 large eggs

2 teaspoons vanilla extract

2 cups finely grated carrots

2 (8-ounce) cans crushed pineapple in unsweetened juice, well drained

Coconut Cream Cheese Icing (page 233)

12 to 14 whole macadamia nuts (as garnish)

1/4 cup finely diced crystallized ginger (as garnish)

Customers who order baker Avi Sommerville's cakes say they are the best they've ever eaten. We were thrilled to have this version of her World's Best Carrot Cake.

Preheat the oven to 350° F. Butter and lightly flour 3 (9-inch) cake pans; line the bottoms with parchment paper.

Combine 1/3 cup of the flour, the coconut, macadamia nuts, and ginger in a food processor bowl; process until the nuts are finely chopped. Transfer to a large bowl; whisk in the remaining 2 cups flour, baking powder, soda, cinnamon, and salt.

Beat together the sugar and oil in a large mixing bowl at medium speed of an electric mixer. When the mixture is blended, add the eggs, one at a time, beating well after each addition. Add the flour mixture; beat at low speed, just until blended. Stir in the coconut mixture, then the carrots and pineapple.

Spoon the batter into the cake pans, dividing evenly. Bake until a toothpick comes out clean, about 30 minutes. Let the cakes cool on wire racks for 1 hour.

Meanwhile, prepare the Coconut Cream Cheese Icing. When the cakes have cooled 1 hour, loosen the edges with a small, sharp knife and turn them out onto the racks. Frost between the layers and on the outside with the icing. Space the nuts and sprinkle the ginger evenly around the top edge of the cake. Cover and refrigerate for at least 1 hour and up to 1 day.

Chocolate Beetroot Cake

—**Jennifer Thomas,** MONTFORD WALK-IN BAKERY

"Earthy beets and chocolate flavor this rich, beet-colored cake, inspired by a Russian recipe," tells pastry chef and owner Jennifer Thomas. Located in a space within her home that was renovated for her bakery, she bakes pies, cookies, granola, and breads that vary with the seasons and use produce from her extensive garden. Neighbors, friends, and customers receive a newsletter on Sundays previewing what she'll be offering and on which days so they can place orders.

Preheat the oven to 350° F. Butter and flour an 8-inch cake pan or 10 to 12 small ramekins. If you are using ramekins, place them on a rimmed baking sheet for easier handling.

Sift together the sweet ground chocolate, self-rising flour, and salt into a medium bowl. Whisk in the brown sugar.

Melt the dark chocolate and butter together in a double boiler, stirring until smooth. Alternatively, melt them in a microwave-safe bowl at medium power for 2 to 3 minutes or until the chocolate is softened; stir until smooth. Let it cool 5 to 10 minutes.

Mix together the beet purée, eggs, and vanilla in a small bowl. Stir the melted chocolate mixture and the beet mixture into the dry ingredients, blending well. Scrape the mixture into the prepared cake pan or two-thirds of the way up the sides of each ramekin.

Bake until a toothpick inserted in the center of the cakes comes out clean, about 45 to 50 minutes for the 8-inch cake or 20 to 35 minutes for the ramekins. Remove them from the oven and let them cool for 10 minutes. Loosen the edges with the tip of a small, sharp knife, and invert the cakes onto a wire rack to cool completely.

Serve at room temperature; dust each serving with confectioners' sugar and add a dollop of crème fraîche and a grating of beet, if desired.

MAKES 8 TO 12 SERVINGS

3 1/2 ounces sweet ground chocolate, such as Ghiradelli

8 ounces (2 cups) self-rising flour

Pinch of salt

7 ounces light brown sugar (not packed)

3 1/2 ounces 60% cacao dark chocolate, finely chopped

1 stick plus 1 tablespoon (4 1/2 ounces) unsalted butter

9 ounces beets, pre-cooked and puréed in a food processor

3 large eggs, whisked

1 teaspoon vanilla extract

Confectioners' sugar

1 cup crème fraîche or whipped cream

Piece of raw beet to grate (optional)

Coconut Cake

—Roz Taubman, THE BLACKBIRD

The layers of this cake from chef/owner Rox Taubman are rich but light and tender, the filling creamy and sweet, and the frosting pure cream cheese coconut decadent. It's paradise for coconut cake lovers like us.

Position the oven racks in the upper and lower thirds of the oven. Preheat the oven to 325° F. Butter and flour 3 (9-inch) cake pans; line the bottoms with parchment paper.

Combine the flour, baking powder, and salt; sift together. Combine the cream and sour cream; whisk to blend.

Combine the butter and sugar in the large mixing bowl of a stand mixer; beat with the paddle attachment at low speed until blended, about 1 minute. Add the eggs and egg yolk; beat until blended, about 1 minute, scraping the bowl as needed. Increase the speed to medium and beat until fluffy, about 2 minutes. Beat in the vanilla and coconut extracts.

Add the flour mixture alternately with the cream mixture, beginning and ending with dry ingredients; beating at low speed after each addition, just until blended. Scrape the bowl as needed. Scrape the batter into the prepared cake pans, dividing evenly.

Place the pans in the oven on upper and lower racks. Bake 25 minutes. Very carefully rearrange the cake pans, switching their positions; continue baking until a wooden pick inserted in the centers comes out clean, 5 to 8 minutes. Let the cakes cool in the pans on wire racks for 10 minutes. Loosen the edges of the cakes with a knife; invert onto the racks and let the layers cool completely.

Place one cake layer on a serving plate; spoon half of the Coconut Filling on top, spreading just to the edges. Stack another cake layer on top and spread with the remaining Coconut Filling. Spoon and spread the Coconut Cream Cheese Icing on the sides and top of the cake. Sprinkle the top with toasted coconut.

The cake may be assembled, filled, and frosted a day before serving; store it, covered, in the refrigerator.

MAKES ONE
(9-INCH, 3-LAYER) CAKE

3 1/4 cups all-purpose flour

1 tablespoon
baking powder

1 teaspoon salt

3/4 cup heavy
whipping cream

1/4 cup plus
2 tablespoons sour cream

3 sticks (1 1/2 cups)
unsalted butter, softened

2 1/4 cups sugar

4 large eggs plus 1 large
egg yolk

1 tablespoon vanilla extract

2 1/4 teaspoons
coconut extract

Coconut Filling (page 234)

Coconut Cream Cheese
Icing (page 233)

1/2 cup sweetened flaked
coconut, toasted

Sweet Cravings

Icing on the Cake

Bourbon Mascarpone Cream Icing • 233

Coconut Cream Cheese Icing • 233

Coconut Filling • 234

Strawberries in Port Reduction
Sugar Syrup • 234

Dark Chocolate Caramel Icing • 235

Bourbon Mascarpone Cream Icing

1/4 cup mascarpone or cream cheese, softened

1/2 cup confectioners' sugar, divided

2 tablespoons bourbon

1 teaspoon pure vanilla extract

1 1/3 cups cold whipping cream

Debby Maugans, AUTHOR

In her book Bourbon, *Kathleen Purvis uses a different icing: "The icing varies, but such a special cake deserves effort, so I use my mother's old-fashioned, boiled-syrup, buttercream-tinted icing with a hint of bourbon." We love that one, too, but for the sake of time, we whipped up this creamy version. We highly recommend* Bourbon *and its smart ways to use bourbon in your cooking.*

Place the mascarpone, 1/4 cup of the confectioners' sugar, the bourbon, and the vanilla in a small bowl, and stir until smooth.

Place the cream and the remaining 1/4 cup of confectioners' sugar in a large mixing bowl and beat until firm peaks form. Add the mascarpone mixture and beat just until blended.

Coconut Cream Cheese Icing

—**Avi Sommerville,** HIGHCLIFFE BAKED GOODS, LLC

— HOME OF THE WORLD'S BEST CARROT CAKE

3 (8-ounce) packages cream cheese, at room temperature

1 1/2 sticks (3/4 cup) unsalted butter, at room temperature

2 cups confectioners' sugar

3/4 cup well-stirred canned cream of coconut

1 teaspoon vanilla extract

1/2 teaspoon coconut extract

Cream of coconut sweetens the icing and makes it taste extra coconut-y. Look for it in the cocktail mixer section of your grocery. It's helpful to take the top off the can and scrape the contents into a bowl; then stir until it is well mixed. Refrigerate the leftovers in a covered container in the fridge up to 1 month.

Beat the cream cheese and butter until smooth in a large mixing bowl at medium speed of an electric mixer. Add the confectioners' sugar and beat until smooth. Beat in the cream of coconut and extracts. Let the icing chill until it's firm enough to spread, about 30 minutes.

Coconut Filling

—**Roz Taubman,** THE BLACKBIRD

The rich cake from chef/owner Roz Taubman is divinely layered with this fluffy, coconut-laden filling.

Heat the cream, sugar, and butter in a small saucepan over medium heat until the butter melts and the sugar is dissolved, stirring constantly.

Meanwhile, stir together the cornstarch and water in a small bowl until smooth. Scrape the mixture into the hot cream mixture, stirring until blended. Return to the heat and bring to a boil, stirring constantly; boil gently until thickened, 20 to 30 seconds. Remove from the heat; stir in the vanilla, salt, and coconut. Pour into a bowl; let cool, then cover and refrigerate overnight.

MAKES 2 1/2 CUPS

2 cups heavy whipping cream

1 1/4 cups sugar

1 1/3 sticks (1/2 plus 1/3 cup) unsalted butter

1 tablespoon plus 1 teaspoon cornstarch

1 tablespoon plus 1 teaspoon water

1 teaspoon vanilla extract

1/8 teaspoon salt

3 cups unsweetened flaked coconut

Strawberries *in* Port Reduction Sugar Syrup

—**Brian Canipelli,** CUCINA 24

MAKES ABOUT 3 1/2 CUPS

1/2 cup port wine

2 tablespoons sugar

1 vanilla bean, split

1 pound fresh strawberries, large ones quartered

Chef/owner Brian Canipelli glazes strawberries with this reduced port sugar syrup for a burst of flavor. They would also make a grand garnish on a rich chocolate tart.

Combine the port, sugar, and vanilla in a small saucepan; bring to a simmer over low heat, stirring constantly until the sugar melts. Simmer until the mixture is reduced to syrup, about 20 minutes. Pour through a wire mesh sieve into a medium bowl. Add the strawberries and toss gently to coat them.

Dark Chocolate Caramel Icing

—**Debby Maugans,** AUTHOR

This is my go-to chocolate icing for birthday and other special occasion cakes. It makes almost 4 cups of icing; I keep the leftovers in a covered container in the refrigerator and sneak in spoonfuls when I need a chocolate fix. You want the butter to be soft and cool — not quite at room temperature; the just-cooled-down chocolate mixture will ensure it beats to fluffy perfection without melting. For the best taste, use a dark chocolate that is at least 60% cacao. Using brewed coffee instead of water in the caramel lends a deep richness.

Bring the cream to a simmer in a small saucepan over low heat. Stir it often to make sure it doesn't burn.

Meanwhile, combine the sugar, coffee, and corn syrup in a medium saucepan. Cook, stirring very gently, over medium heat until the sugar melts. Continue cooking, without stirring, until the caramel is dark amber, 5 to 8 minutes. Watch it carefully to make sure it doesn't burn. Remove the saucepan from the heat and let it stand for 1 minute.

Add the hot cream to the hot caramel; stir slowly for 2 minutes to blend it. Pour that caramel mixture over the chocolate, and let it stand for 1 minute to soften the chocolate. Starting in the center of the bowl and working your way out, slowly stir the mixture in a circle until the chocolate is melted and the mixture is smooth. Let it cool for 15 minutes.

Scrape the chocolate mixture into a large mixing bowl; fit the mixer with the paddle attachment. Mix on low speed until the bowl feels cool to touch. Increase the speed of the mixer to medium-high and gradually add the butter pieces, beating until well blended. Scrape the bowl and beat on high speed until the icing is fluffy.

MAKES ENOUGH FOR 1 (8- OR 9-INCH) LAYER CAKE

1 1/2 cups heavy whipping cream

1 cup sugar

1/4 cup strong brewed coffee

2 tablespoons light corn syrup

1 pound dark chocolate, finely chopped

4 sticks (2 cups) unsalted butter, cut into 1/2-inch pieces, softened but still cool

Sweet Cravings

Puddin' & Pie

Peach and Rhubarb
Lattice-Top Pie • 238

Rose Water Rice Pudding • 240

Caramel Apple Bread Pudding • 240

Fried Apple Hand Pies • 241

Strawberry-Hand Pie Filling • 242

Blackberry Pie • 243

Fennel Panna Cotta with Strawberries
& Pistachio Shortbread Crumbs • 245

Lemon Verbena Custards • 246

Basic Tupelo Pie Crust • 247

Our Favorite Quiche and Tart Crust • 247

Chocolate Mousse with
Candy Roaster Cream • 248

FOR THE PIE CRUST:

2 cups unbleached
all-purpose flour

1/3 cup whole wheat
pastry flour

1/4 teaspoon
baking powder

Generous grating of
nutmeg, about
1/2 teaspoon

1/2 teaspoon salt

2 sticks (1 cup) cold
unsalted butter, cut into
1/2 inch dice and
kept chilled

1/2 cup ice water mixed
with 1 tablespoon
lemon juice

FOR THE FILLING:

5 ripe peaches (about
1 1/2 pounds), peeled,
pitted, and sliced

2 cups sliced rhubarb
(1/2-inch slices)

Leaves from several
sprigs fresh lemon thyme,
chopped

1/2 cup sugar

3 tablespoons
tapioca starch

1/2 teaspoon ground
cinnamon

1/4 teaspoon freshly
grated nutmeg

1/4 teaspoon salt

Juice and grated zest
of 1/2 lemon

FOR THE PIE:

2 tablespoons cream or
whole milk

2 tablespoons turbinado or
regular sugar

Peach *and* Rhubarb Lattice-Top Pie

—Jennifer Thomas, MONTFORD WALK-IN BAKERY

This pie is a unique mix of sweet and tart summer fruits with an herbal lemon-thyme accent. Says pastry chef Jennifer Thomas, "I use rhubarb and lemon thyme from my own garden, plus peaches from the tailgate markets around Asheville, along with NC grown and Carolina Ground milled all-purpose and whole wheat pastry flour."

To prepare the pie crust, combine the flours, baking powder, nutmeg, and salt in a food processor; pulse to blend the dry ingredients. Add the butter pieces and pulse until the mixture resembles very coarse meal with irregular pieces of no larger than the size of garden peas. Transfer to a large bowl; add the water mixture, a tablespoon at a time, tossing with a fork and pressing the flour butter mixture together until it roughly comes together.

Turn out the dough onto a work surface and form it into a large mound; divide the dough in half and press together into 2 thin discs. Wrap each in plastic wrap and refrigerate for at least 1 hour.

To prepare the filling, combine the peaches, rhubarb, lemon thyme, sugar, tapioca starch, cinnamon, nutmeg, salt, and lemon juice and zest in a large bowl; toss well. Let it stand for 15 minutes for the juices to release.

In the meantime, roll out the dough into 2 (13- to 14- inch) rounds on a lightly floured surface. Gently drape one pastry disc in a 9-inch glass or ceramic pie plate and fill with the fruit mixture.

Cut the remaining pastry disc into 10 (1-inch-wide) strips. Lay 5 strips, evenly spaced, across the pie. Weave in the other 5 strips in lattice-form, spacing them evenly; let the ends of the strips hang over the edge of the pie plate.

Trim all the edges of the pastry — the strips and bottom pie crust — together to about 1/2 inch beyond the pie plate rim. Roll the edges together with the top strips under the bottom pie crust. Crimp the edges, and refrigerate for 30 minutes.

Preheat the oven to 450° F. Brush the cream over the pie crust and sprinkle liberally with the sugar. Place the pie on a rimmed baking sheet lined with foil and place it in the oven. Reduce the oven temperature to 425° F. and bake for 20 minutes. Reduce the oven temperature to 400° F. and bake for about 30 additional minutes or until the juices bubble and the crust is golden brown. Tent the pie with foil if the pastry browns too much. Let the pie cool on a wire rack before serving.

The Montford Walk-in Bakery is a neighborhood bakeshop; every Friday, they bake selected breads and pastries to order. Customers have two options: sign up for a monthly CSB ("Community Sustained Bakery") to receive their selected products on a weekly basis, or fill out an order form for a single week. For more about this unique bakery, visit monfordwibakery.com.

Rose Water Rice Pudding

—Anthony Cerrato, STRADA

MAKES 8 TO 10 SERVINGS

1 1/2 cups uncooked long-grain white rice

2 cups plus 2 tablespoons heavy whipping cream

1/2 cup sugar

2 tablespoons rose water

1 tablespoon plus 3/4 teaspoon cornstarch

Before vanilla was available in the 1840s, rose water was the primary flavoring in European desserts and pastries, like this pudding from chef/owner Anthony Cerrato. Look for bottled rose water in health food stores and natural groceries.

Combine 3 cups water with the rice in a heavy, medium saucepan; bring to a simmer over medium heat. Cover, reduce heat, and simmer for 20 minutes. Add 2 cups of the cream and the sugar; simmer, stirring occasionally to prevent sticking, until the pudding is creamy, 40 to 45 minutes.

Stir the remaining cornstarch and the 2 tablespoons cream in a small cup. Stir mixture and rosewater into the rice pudding; simmer 1 minute, stirring constantly. Remove from the heat; cover and let stand for 5 minutes to thicken. Serve warm or chilled.

Caramel Apple Bread Pudding

—Denny Trantham, FORMERLY OF GROVE PARK INN

Chef Denny Trantham lets the bread pudding sit at least 1 hour for the bread "to soak up the love." After baking, he drizzles pure maple syrup over the bread pudding for some "Good Lovin'!"

Peel, core, and coarsely chop the apples. Toss the apples with the butter and 1/3 cup of the brown sugar.

Whisk the eggs in a large bowl until blended. Whisk in the milk, cream, sugar, the remaining 1 cup brown sugar, cinnamon, nutmeg, and salt. Stir in the rolls, apple mixture, and pecans, if using. Scrape into a buttered 13 x 9-inch baking dish. Cover the baking dish and refrigerate at least 1 hour and up to overnight.

Preheat the oven to 350° F. Let the bread pudding come to just slightly cool before baking. Spray the top of the bread pudding with butter flavor or regular cooking spray. Bake until the bread pudding is puffed and golden, about 45 minutes. Serve warm.

MAKES 12 SERVINGS

4 large apples, such as Braeburn, Gala, Fuji, or Empire

1/4 cup unsalted butter, melted

1 1/3 cups firmly packed light brown sugar, divided

6 large eggs

1 1/2 cups whole milk

1 1/2 cups heavy whipping cream

1 cup sugar

1 teaspoon ground cinnamon

1/4 teaspoon ground nutmeg

1/2 teaspoon salt

1 (12-pack) package Hawaiian rolls, cut into 1-inch pieces

1 cup chopped pecans or walnuts, toasted (optional)

FOR THE CRUST:

2 1/2 cups all-purpose flour

1/4 teaspoon
baking powder

1/2 teaspoon salt

2 sticks (1 cup) cold
unsalted butter, finely diced
and kept chilled

4 to 6 tablespoons
ice water

**FOR THE
APPLE FILLING:**

4 cups diced firm apples

3 tablespoons
unsalted butter

2/3 cup sugar

1/4 cup firmly packed light
brown sugar

1 teaspoon ground
cinnamon

1 teaspoon lemon juice

TO PREPARE THE PIES:

1 or 2 eggs, beaten with
1 or 2 tablespoons water

Additional sugar

Fried Apple Hand Pies

—**Miki Kilpatrick,** HOMEGROWN

Here's how we felt about these individual pies as we were trying them warm: "Oh my — so delish!" We fried half of them and baked the rest for comparison, and both were wonderful! Since owner and food mastermind chef/owner Miki Kilpatrick shared several seasonal variations, we tested a strawberry-basil version, too.

To prepare the dough, sift together the flour, baking powder, and salt into a large bowl. Add the butter pieces and cut into the flour mixture using a pastry blender or your fingers to pinch the butter chunks into the flour mixture until they are no larger than the size of small peas. Drizzle 4 tablespoons of the ice water over the mixture, and toss with a fork until the dough holds together. Add additional water, by tablespoons, if needed.

Turn the dough out onto a floured surface and divide into two equal pieces; form each into discs. Wrap and refrigerate at least 1 hour.

To prepare the filling, combine the apples, butter, sugars, cinnamon, and lemon juice in a medium saucepan; cook over medium-low heat, stirring constantly, until the butter melts and the sugar is dissolved. Continue cooking, stirring frequently, until the apples are just tender, 5 to 10 minutes. Let the filling cool.

241

To prepare the pies, roll out each disc dough into to 1/8 to 1/4 inch thick; cut out 6 to 7-inch To prepare the pies, roll out each disc dough into to 1/8 to 1/4 inch thick; cut out 6- to 7-inch circles. Place about 3 tablespoons of the filling on half of each circle; brush the edges with the beaten egg white mixture. Fold the circle over to enclose the filling and form a half-moon. Seal the edges by pressing them together with the tines of a fork. Brush the tops with some of the egg wash and sprinkle with a little sugar.

Fill a deep fryer or a deep saucepan halfway with oil; heat to 350° F on a candy thermometer. Working with a few at a time, slide them, one by one, into the hot oil and fry until they are golden brown, turning as needed, 5 to 8 minutes. Drain on paper towels and sprinkle with confectioners' sugar.

Pear Variation:
Prepare the apple filling as directed above, substituting 3 1/2 cups peeled, chopped firm ripe pears. Stir 1/4 cup crushed toffee and 1/4 cup chopped pecans into the prepared filling.

Strawberry-Basil Hand Pie Filling

—**Miki Kilpatrick,** HOMEGROWN

At Homegrown, when local berries are ripe and sweet, and herbs are plentiful, chef/owner Miki Kilpatrick cleverly adds a hint of basil to the filling for a fresh taste.

MAKES ENOUGH FILLING FOR
16 TO 18 PIES

1 tablespoon cornstarch

1/2 cup sugar

1/4 cup firmly packed light brown sugar

4 cups fresh strawberries, chopped

6 to 8 slivered basil leaves

3 tablespoons unsalted butter

1/2 teaspoon ground cinnamon, optional

1 teaspoon lemon juice

Combine the cornstarch with the sugar and brown sugar in a heavy, medium saucepan; mix well. Add the strawberries, basil leaves, butter, cinnamon, and lemon juice to the saucepan. Cook over medium-low heat, stirring constantly, until the butter melts and the sugar is dissolved. Continue cooking, stirring frequently, until the strawberries are just tender and the mixture is thickened, 5 to 10 minutes. Let the filling cool completely.

Blueberry-Mint Variation:
Substitute 4 cups fresh blueberries for the strawberries and 2 to 3 tablespoons slivered mint leaves for the basil.

Blackberry Pie

—Brian Sonoskus, TUPELO HONEY CAFÉ

A favorite mountain pastime in the summer is to hike along the many trails that meander off the Blue Ridge Parkway with your blackberry buckets in hand.

Toss the blackberries with the vanilla in a large bowl. Combine the 1/2 cup sugar, the flour, cinnamon, and nutmeg in a small bowl and whisk to blend well. Add to the blackberries and toss gently to coat.

Preheat the oven to 375° F. Roll out 1 disk of the pie dough on a floured surface using a floured rolling pin. Fit the dough into the pie plate and then mound the fruit mixture on top of the crust. Roll out the second disk of pie dough and fit it over the pie, turning the edges under the bottom crust and crimping the 2 crusts together.

Using the tip of a small, sharp knife, cut 5 petal-shaped vents in the center of the top crust, forming a flower design. Brush the top crust with the egg wash mixture and sprinkle lightly with the 1 teaspoon sugar.

Place the pie on a rimmed baking sheet for easier handling. Bake until the bottom crust is golden and the fruit is bubbling, 1 hour to 1 hour and 15 minutes. If necessary, cover the edges with foil if they begin to over-brown. If the center browns quickly, cover the whole pie loosely with a piece of foil. Let the pie cool before cutting. Serve warm or at room temperature.

From *Tupelo Honey Café: New Southern Flavors from the Blue Ridge Mountains* by Elizabeth Sims with chef Brian Sonoskus, Andrews McMeel Publishing, LLC, 2014. Used with permission.

MAKES 1 (9-INCH) PIE

7 cups fresh blackberries (6 pints)

1 teaspoon vanilla extract

1/2 cup plus 1 teaspoon sugar

2 tablespoons all-purpose flour

1/2 teaspoon ground cinnamon

1/2 teaspoon ground nutmeg

Basic Tupelo Pie Crust (page 247)

1 egg, beaten with 1 tablespoon water

MAKES 4 SERVINGS

1 medium-size fennel bulb, stalks removed, leaves reserved as garnish

3/4 cup heavy whipping cream

1/4 cup sugar

2 tablespoons milk

1 tablespoon honey

Pinch of salt

2 tablespoons anise-flavored liqueur

Pistachio Shortbread Cookies (page 253)

Strawberries in Port Reduction Sugar Syrup (Page 242)

Fennel Chips (recipe follows)

Fennel pollen (optional)

Fennel Panna Cotta *with* Strawberries *and* Pistachio Shortbread Crumbs

—**Brian Canipelli**, CUCINA 24

A signature dessert at Cucina 24, the chilled custard is infused with fresh fennel, with its flavor intensified by a splash of anise-flavored liqueur. Fresh local strawberries, coated with a port wine reduction sugar syrup, together with a sprinkling of buttery pistachio shortbread cookie crumbles, make up a sensational playground of tastes and textures.

Slice the fennel bulb in half vertically, through the core. Reserve one half of the bulb for making Fennel Chips. Thinly slice the remaining fennel half and place in a non-reactive, 1-quart saucepan. Add the cream, sugar, milk, honey, and salt; bring to a simmer over low heat, stirring until the sugar dissolves. Once the cream mixture barely simmers; cover, remove from the heat, and let stand for 20 minutes to allow the flavors to infuse.

Meanwhile, soak the gelatin sheet in 2 tablespoons cold water in a small bowl until it blooms, or swells as it softens, 5 to 10 minutes.

Strain the warm cream mixture through a wire mesh sieve into a medium bowl. Squeeze the gelatin to expel as much water as possible and whisk into the warm cream. Whisk in the liqueur. Pour through a clean sieve into a large measuring cup; pour into 4 (1/2-cup) ramekins, dividing evenly. Refrigerate until set, at least 4 hours or until well chilled.

To serve, gently invert custards on serving plates. Coarsely crush some of the Pistachio Shortbread cookies and arrange small rings of crumbs around the custards. Arrange the strawberries around the custards; top with several pieces of Fennel Chips and a few fronds. Sprinkle a pinch of fennel pollen on the custard, if desired. Serve chilled.

Fennel Chips
Preheat the oven to 225° F.; line a baking sheet with parchment. Slice the reserved fennel bulb paper thin, with the care attached. Toss with 1/4 cup confectioners' sugar. Lift them out, shaking off the excess sugar. Arrange on a single layer on the baking sheet. Bake until slices are dry and crisp, about one hour.

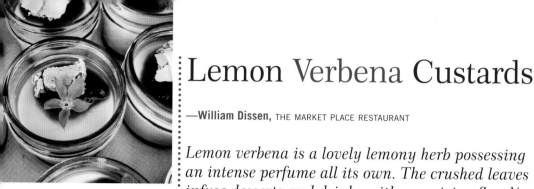

Lemon Verbena Custards

—William Dissen, THE MARKET PLACE RESTAURANT

Lemon verbena is a lovely lemony herb possessing an intense perfume all its own. The crushed leaves infuse desserts and drinks with energizing floral/ citrus flavors. These infused custards are creamy like classic pots de creme; chef/owner William Dissen pairs them tastefully with fresh blackberry preserves, basil macaroons, and borage flowers.

MAKES 4 CUSTARDS

7 (2-inch) leaves fresh
lemon verbena

5 (2 1/2-inch-long) strips
lemon peel (pith removed)

3 tablespoons sugar

3/4 cup heavy
whipping cream

3 large egg yolks

1/2 teaspoon fresh
lemon juice

Preheat the oven to 325° F. Place 4 (1/2-cup) ramekins in a square baking pan for easier handling.

Combine 1/2 cup water with the lemon verbena and lemon peel in a small saucepan. Bring to a boil over medium heat; boil until the mixture is reduced by half, about 4 minutes. Add the sugar; simmer, stirring constantly until the sugar dissolves; simmer until the mixture is reduced by one third, about 3 minutes. Stir in the cream; heat just until simmering and remove from the heat.

Whisk the egg yolks in a medium bowl. While you continue to whisk, gradually pour in about 1/4 cup of the hot cream mixture. Whisk in the remaining cream mixture and the lemon juice. Strain the custard through a wire-mesh sieve into another bowl. Pour the custard into the prepared ramekins, dividing it evenly.

Add boiling water to the square baking pan to come halfway up the sides of the ramekins. Bake the custards just until set, about 20 to 25 minutes. Allow the custards to cool to room temperature in the water bath. Transfer the ramekins to the refrigerator; cover and let chill for 4 hours or overnight.

To serve, spoon about 2 teaspoons fresh blackberry preserves on each custard and top with a basil macaroon. Decorate with a borage flower.

Basic Tupelo Pie Crust

MAKES 2 (9-INCH) CRUSTS

—Brian Sonoskus, TUPELO HONEY CAFÉ

2 1/2 cups all-purpose flour

1 teaspoon sea salt

1 teaspoon sugar

1 cup cold unsalted butter, cut into pieces

1/2 cup ice water

Combine the flour, salt, and sugar in a food processor. Add the butter and pulse until the mixture resembles coarse meal, about 15 pulses. Add the ice water in a slow stream, pulsing until the dough starts to clump together, 12 to 15 pulses. Remove the dough from the processor and gather into a mass. Divide the dough in half and flatten each half into a disk. Wrap each disk in plastic wrap and refrigerate for at least 1 hour.

From *Tupelo Honey Café: New Southern Flavors from the Blue Ridge Mountains* by Elizabeth Sims with chef Brian Sonoskus, Andrews McMeel Publishing, LLC, 2014. Used with permission.

Our Favorite Quiche *and* Tart Crust

—Emily Flynn McIntosh, A BED OF ROSES VICTORIAN BED & BREAKFAST

This recipe is the Inn's go-to crust for all sorts of pie. The secret is a mix of shortening and butter and then cutting them — while very cold — into the flour mixture as quickly as you can so the pieces don't soften.

Combine the flour, sugar, and salt in a large bowl; whisk the dry ingredients to blend.

Sprinkle the shortening and butter pieces over the flour mixture; use a pastry cutter to cut in the pieces until the mixture resembles coarse crumbs. Pour in the cold water all at once; stir with a fork until the dough starts to hold together.

Turn the dough out onto a large, lightly floured surface; divide into 2 equal parts, form each into a ball, and flatten each into a disk. Wrap them individually with plastic wrap and refrigerate for at least 30 minutes and up to 1 day. The dough can be put into a zip-top bag and frozen up to 1 month.

MAKES 1 (9 1/2-INCH) QUICHE OR TART CRUST

1 1/2 cups all-purpose flour

2 teaspoons sugar

1/4 teaspoon salt

1/2 cup cold vegetable shortening, cut into 1/2-inch pieces

1 tablespoon cold unsalted butter, cut into 1/4-inch pieces

1/4 cup ice water

Chocolate Mousse *with* Candy Roaster Cream

—**Jael and Dan Rattigan,** FRENCH BROAD CHOCOLATE LOUNGE

"The best time of year to enjoy this dessert is when local squash is in season. While pumpkin is traditional, this recipe is excellent with other sweet winter squash varieties. Our favorite is Candy Roaster squash," tells chef/owner Jael Rattigan. "Choose ingredients with the same care and attention you would use to pick a babysitter for your kid. Dessert is serious business! We use all organic dairy, free-range local eggs, organic sugar, and locally grown squash."

To prepare the Candy Roaster cream, place 1/4 cup cold water in a small saucepan. Sprinkle the gelatin evenly over the water and let stand for 5 minutes. Place the saucepan of softened gelatin over low heat and swirl gently to melt. Scrape the gelatin into a large bowl. Whisk the sugar, egg yolks, and spices together in a medium bowl.

Bring the cream and squash purée just to a boil in a medium saucepan. Temper the egg yolks by whisking a little of the hot pumpkin cream mixture into the egg mixture. Repeat a few times until all of the winter squash cream is incorporated. Return the mixture to the saucepan.

Cook over medium heat, stirring constantly, until a candy thermometer registers 180° F. Strain over the gelatin mixture in the large bowl; whisk until blended. Cover and refrigerate while preparing the chocolate mousse.

To prepare the chocolate mousse, place the chocolate in a large, microwave-safe bowl; microwave at medium power until the chocolate appears glossy and soft, 3 to 4 minutes, stirring once. Let it stand for 1 minute; stir until the chocolate is melted and smooth. Let it cool.

Combine the sugar and 2 tablespoons water in a small saucepan; bring to a boil over medium heat, stirring constantly until the sugar melts. Boil, without stirring, until a candy thermometer registers 249° F.

MAKES 6 TO 8 SERVINGS

FOR THE WINTER SQUASH CREAM:

1 envelope gelatin

1/4 cup plus 3 tablespoons sugar

6 large egg yolks

1/2 teaspoon ground cinnamon

1/4 teaspoon ground ginger

1/4 teaspoon ground nutmeg

Pinch of ground cloves

1 cup heavy whipping cream

1 cup winter squash purée

FOR THE CHOCOLATE MOUSSE:

11 ounces (2 cups) chopped dark bittersweet chocolate

1/2 cup plus 1 tablespoon sugar

2 cups heavy whipping cream

6 large egg yolks

4 large eggs

Meanwhile, beat the cream in a large mixing bowl with a stand mixer or hand-held mixer until it's soft and firm peaks form. Beat the egg yolks and eggs in a medium mixing bowl until pale and thick, about 5 minutes.

With the mixer running, gradually add the sugar syrup to the beaten eggs, beating until the bowl feels warm to the touch. Fold half of the whipped cream into the cooled melted chocolate. Whisk in the egg mixture. Fold in the remaining whipped cream.

To assemble, pipe or carefully spoon a layer of the mousse into a parfait glass, wine glass, or small jar. Pipe or carefully spoon a layer of winter squash mousse on top. Finish with another layer of chocolate mousse. Cover and refrigerate until well chilled, at least 2 hours. Serve with a kiss of whipped cream, if desired.

COOK'S NOTE:

Cook the Candy Roaster Squash as you would a pumpkin and purée it for this dessert.

Fair Food
—Maggie Cramer

We're not talking funnel cakes; two Asheville eateries source fairer than fair trade coffee and cacao.

We Ashevillians are staunch local foodies, supporting our neighboring farmers at every turn. We also seriously love coffee and chocolate, the plants of which simply don't grow in our climate. So, we seek out cups and confections from local vendors who support organic growers and fair trade whenever possible.

Enter Green Sage Café and French Broad Chocolate Lounge. Through sourcing, both eateries support the fair trade movement, which aims to ensure that farmers are fairly compensated. In fact, they go above and beyond, looking for standard fair trade certification and work to pay their farmers not just fairly but handsomely.

Green Sage implements a fair trade-like model called "farmer direct." It yields farmers the highest potential profit by giving them the lion's share of the sale,

and it allows the restaurant's owners to have a direct connection with their growers in other countries.

The folks behind French Broad Chocolates also value the relationships with their suppliers to guarantee truly fair compensation. They own a cacao farm in Costa Rica that will eventually supply beans for their chocolate, and they visit it often. They've also traveled to their farm partners in Peru and Nicaragua to see the operations firsthand.

In the end, these eateries strive to do right by their customers, staff, and suppliers — operating businesses that are good for people as well as for the planet.

Visit Green Sage's website (thegreen-sage.net/our-green-philosophy/) to learn more about their green mission. And head online to read about French Broad's farm (frenchbroadchocolates.com/cacao-farm/) and cacao partners (frenchbroadchocolates.com/cacao-farm/our-cacao-farm-partners/).

Sweet Cravings

Cookies

Citrus Ginger Mint Sugar Cookies • 251

Chocolate Cayenne Cookies • 252

Pistachio Shortbread • 253

Carrot Cake Sandwich Cookies • 254

Vegan Double Chocolate Chip Cookies • 255

Gluten-Free Chocolate Chip Cookies • 256

Citrus Ginger Mint Sugar Cookies

—Aimee Mostwill, SWEETHEART BAKERY

These refreshing cookies from bakery owner Aimee Mostwill are perfect to bake in summer when your mint is prolific; serve them with a tall glass of cold milk or iced tea for a snack.

Preheat the oven to 350° F. Line baking sheets with parchment paper.

Combine the flour and baking soda in a medium bowl; whisk to blend. Add the mint and ginger and toss well.

Combine the butter and sugars in a large mixing bowl; beat on medium speed with an electric mixer until they are blended and fluffy. Add the egg yolks, citrus fruit zest, and vanilla; beat at medium speed until fluffy, scraping the sides of the bowl as needed. With the mixer on low, gradually beat in the flour mixture until just combined.

Spoon rounded tablespoons of dough on the prepared baking sheets, spacing them 2 inches apart. Bake until the edges are lightly brown, about 14 minutes, rotating the baking sheets halfway through. Lift the cookies from the baking sheets and place on wire racks to cool.

MAKES 3 TO 4 DOZEN

2 cups all-purpose flour

1/2 teaspoon baking soda

1/4 cup packed fresh mint leaves, finely chopped

1/4 cup finely chopped crystallized ginger

1 cup unsalted butter, softened

1/2 cup granulated sugar

1/4 cup powdered sugar

1/4 cup packed light brown sugar

2 egg yolks, at room temperature

Finely grated zest from 1 lemon, 1 lime, and 1 orange

1 teaspoon vanilla extract

1/4 cup coarse sugar, for sprinkling

Chocolate Cayenne Cookies

—Aimee Mostwill, SWEETHEART BAKERY

MAKES 4 TO 5 DOZEN

2 1/2 cups all purpose flour

3/4 cup unsweetened cocoa

2 teaspoons ground red pepper

1 1/2 teaspoons baking soda

3/4 teaspoon salt

1 cup firmly packed brown sugar

1 cup sugar

1/2 cup unsalted butter, softened

1/2 cup sunflower oil

1 large egg

1/4 cup whole milk

1 teaspoon vanilla extract

2 cups (12 ounces) bitter-sweet chocolate chips

Owner Aimee Mostwill's Sweetheart Bakery booth at tailgate markets is always a treat. Her scones, pies, vegetable and fruit tarts and pies, and cookies have the dreamiest flavor combinations. And you can count on them to spotlight what's fresh at the markets.

Preheat the oven to 350° F. Line baking sheets with parchment paper.

Sift the flour, cocoa, ground red pepper, baking soda, and salt together into a medium bowl. Combine the sugars, butter, and oil in a large mixing bowl; beat at high speed of an electric mixer until well blended. Beat in the egg, milk, and vanilla at low speed. Add the dry ingredients, mix until combined. Stir in the chocolate chips by hand.

Drop the dough by well-rounded spoonfuls (depending on your preferred cookie size) onto the prepared baking sheets. Bake until the cookies are dry on the top and appear set, about 12 to 15 minutes. If you are baking more than one baking sheet of cookies at a time, rotate and reverse the baking sheets from the upper rack to the lower midway through baking for even browning. Let the cookies cool 1 minute on the baking sheets; lift them with a flat spatula and place on wire racks to cool completely.

Pistachio Shortbread

—Debby Maugans, AUTHOR

These tasty cookies are perfect to crumble on the Fennel Panna Cotta with Strawberries and Pistachio Shortbread Crumbs (page 244). You can freeze the unsliced rolls of dough for up to 2 months; thaw, slice, and bake the cookies when you get a craving.

Place the pistachios in a food processor; pulse until they are coarsely chopped. Add the flour, sugar, and salt; pulse until the pistachios are finely chopped. Add the butter, egg yolk, and vanilla; pulse just until the dough comes together in moist clumps.

Turn the dough out onto a work surface and divide it into 2 balls. Form each half into a 1 1/2-inch-diameter log; if the dough is too soft to work with, refrigerate it for about 30 minutes. Wrap the logs in plastic wrap and refrigerate until firm, 3 to 4 hours or overnight; roll them occasionally as they chill to keep the logs from squaring off at the bottom.

Preheat the oven to 325° F. Line a baking sheet with parchment paper. Slice the dough into 1/4-inch-thick rounds, rolling the logs every 2 or 3 slices to keep the logs from squaring off at the bottom. Place the rounds on the parchment, spacing them 1 inch apart. Bake until they are just beginning to brown, 15 to 18 minutes. Let the cookies cool on the baking sheet on a wire rack.

MAKES ABOUT 5 DOZEN COOKIES

3/4 cup shelled natural unsalted pistachios

1 1/4 cups all-purpose flour

1/2 cup plus 2 tablespoons confectioners' sugar

1/2 teaspoon salt

1 1/2 sticks (3/4 cup) cold unsalted butter, cut into 1/2-inch cubes

1 large egg yolk

1 teaspoon vanilla extract

Carrot Cake Sandwich Cookies

—Avi Sommerville, HIGHCLIFFE BAKED GOODS, LLC
— HOME OF THE WORLD'S BEST CARROT CAKE

COOK'S NOTE:
We like the cookies with ice cream sandwiched between them, too; wrap individually and freeze.

MAKES 12 SANDWICH COOKIES

1 cup plus 2 tablespoons all-purpose flour

1 teaspoon ground cinnamon

1/2 teaspoon baking soda

1/2 teaspoon salt

1 stick (1/2 cup) unsalted butter, softened

1/3 cup plus 2 tablespoons firmly packed brown sugar

1/3 cup plus 2 tablespoons sugar

1 large egg

1/2 teaspoon vanilla extract

1 cup coarsely grated carrots

1 cup finely chopped walnuts

1/2 cup raisins

3/4 cup honey

6 ounces cream cheese, softened

These cookies from baker/owner Avi Sommerville have the flavors of her famous carrot cake in a cookie with slightly chewy texture. When they are filled with honey-sweetened cream cheese, they taste even more like carrot cake!

Preheat the oven to 325° F. Line 1 or 2 baking sheets with parchment paper.

Combine the flour, cinnamon, baking soda, and salt in a medium bowl; whisk to blend. Combine the butter and sugars in a large mixing bowl; beat at medium speed of an electric mixer until the mixture is fluffy. Beat in the egg and vanilla. Fold in the carrots, walnuts, and raisins.

Scoop the dough onto the parchment using a small ice cream scoop. Make 24 mounds, spacing 1 inch apart. Bake until they are a lightly browned but still a little soft in the centers. Let them cool slightly on the parchment; place on wire racks to cool completely.

While the cookies cool, beat the cream cheese and honey in a small mixing bowl until it is smooth and creamy, about 2 minutes. When the cookies are cool to the touch, spread 1 tablespoon of the cream cheese mixture on the flat sides of 12 cookies; sandwich together with the remaining cookies.

Vegan Double Chocolate Chip Cookies

—Cathy Cleary, WEST END BAKERY

"These are the easiest cookies in the world to make, and we've baked them since the bakery opened," tells chef/owner Cathy Cleary. "I've never met a chocoholic who could resist them. The variations are endless. Try some that we've baked or make up your own. They make great sandwich cookies, too." West End Bakery, uses organic evaporated cane sugar and soy milk in the cookies.

Preheat the oven to 350° F. Line baking sheets with parchment paper.

Sift the flour, cocoa, baking dry ingredients together into a large bowl. Whisk in the sugar. Combine the oil and soy milk; add to the dry ingredients and stir until just blended. Stir in the chocolate chips.

Using an ice cream scoop or spoon, scoop out golf ball-size pieces of dough and roll into balls. Space evenly, 2 inches apart, on the parchment. Flatten the tops slightly and bake until the edges of the cookies are darker in color and the tops of the cookies appear dry, 10 to 12 minutes. Let the cookies cool on the parchment for 5 minutes; remove them from the parchment and let them cool completely on a wire rack.

Variations:
Chocolate Cinnamon Hazelnut Cookies: Add 1 teaspoon ground cinnamon to the dry ingredients and stir in 1/2 cup chopped toasted hazelnuts.

Mexican Chocolate Cookies: Add 1 teaspoon ground cinnamon, 1 teaspoon vanilla extract, and 1/4 teaspoon almond extract to the liquid ingredients before adding to the flour mixture.

MAKES ABOUT 4 DOZEN

1 1/2 cups all-purpose flour

1/2 cup unsweetened cocoa

1/2 teaspoon baking powder

1/2 teaspoon baking soda

1/2 teaspoon salt

3/4 cup sugar

3/4 cup canola oil

1/4 cup soy milk

3/4 cup (4 ounces) dairy-free chocolate chips, such as Whole Foods brand or Trader Joe's

Gluten-Free
Chocolate Chip Cookies

—**Rebekah Abrams,** EAT MORE BAKERY

MAKES 3 DOZEN

1 1/2 cups white rice flour

1/2 cup potato starch

1/4 cup tapioca starch

1/2 teaspoon guar gum

1 teaspoon baking powder, sifted

1 teaspoon baking soda, sifted

1/2 teaspoon salt

1 1/2 sticks (3/4 cup) unsalted butter, softened

3/4 cup firmly packed light brown sugar

1/2 cup sugar

2 large eggs

2 teaspoons vanilla extract

2 cups (12 ounces) chocolate chips

1 cup chopped nuts, optional

You won't know the difference between this gluten-free variation from bakery owner Rebekah Abrams and the classic version.

Preheat the oven to 375° F. Line baking sheets with parchment paper.

Combine the flour, potato starch, tapioca starch, guar gum, baking powder, baking soda, and salt in a medium bowl; whisk to blend.

Combine the butter and sugars in the large bowl of a stand mixer fitted with the whisk attachment. Beat at medium speed until light and fluffy, scraping the bowl as needed. Add the eggs, one at a time, beating at low until just blended. Beat in the vanilla. Gradually add the flour mixture, beating at low speed until combined. Stir in the chocolate chips and optional nuts.

Spoon the dough by rounded teaspoons onto the parchment, spacing 2 inches apart. Bake until the cookies are lightly browned, 10 to 12 minutes.

Grove Park Inn Hosts the National
Gingerbread House Competition

In 1992, the Grove Park Inn hosted a small competition of
gingerbread house designs between community members as a way
to celebrate the holiday. With no plans to continue the next year,
they had no way of knowing that more than two decades later,
The Omni Grove Park Inn National Gingerbread House
Competition would become one of the nation's most celebrated
and competitive destination holiday events.

As this event grew, so did the caliber of judges and competitors.
The panel of judges represents nationally renowned food, arts,
and media professionals, and the level of competition has attract-
ed the highest quality of design, artistry, and pastry expertise.
The competition has merited media coverage by the likes of ABC's
Good Morning America, the Travel Channel, and the Food Network.
As importantly, it has become a true family holiday tradition for
both the community and visitors from all over the world. From the
very young to the very young at heart, the reaction to this magical
experience is one of wonder and delight.

For more information, see groveparkinn.com.

Sweet Cravings

Spectacular Scoops

Ring of Fire Ice Cream • 259

Ring of Fire Sauce • 260

World's Best Carrot Cake Ice Cream • 261

Birch Ice Cream • 261

Strawberry & Pisachio Trifle • 262

Strawberry Ice Cream • 263

Ring of Fire Ice Cream

—**Ashley Garrison,** THE HOP ICE CREAM CAFÉ

Who'd have thought? This ice cream from owner Ashley Garrison features pieces of local homemade doughnuts from Vortex and a swirl of Vortex's homemade fiery apricot Ring of Fire Sauce.

To prepare the custard base, whisk the egg yolks and 1/4 cup of the sugar in a medium bowl until it is pale in color.

Cook the cream, milk, and 1/2 cup remaining sugar in a heavy medium saucepan over medium heat, stirring constantly, until the sugar is dissolved, 3 to 4 minutes. Slowly pour 1/2 cup of the cream mixture into egg yolks while whisking constantly. Whisk the egg mixture into the cream.

Cook over medium-low heat, stirring constantly, until the custard thickens and coats the back of a spoon, 10 to 15 minutes. Strain through a fine-mesh sieve into a medium bowl. Let the custard cool, then refrigerate overnight.

Before freezing, whisk in the cinnamon, red pepper, and vanilla. Freeze in an ice cream machine according to the manufacturer's instructions. Transfer to a freezer-safe container and gently swirl in the doughnut chunks and the Ring of Fire sauce. Freeze and serve with extra sauce drizzled over top, if desired.

MAKES 1 QUART

FOR THE CUSTARD BASE

5 large egg yolks

3/4 cup sugar, divided

2 cups heavy whipping cream

3/4 cup whole milk

1/2 teaspoon ground cinnamon

Pinch of ground red pepper

1 teaspoon vanilla extract

FOR THE ICE CREAM

3/4 cup torn cinnamon sugar doughnut pieces (from 1 doughnut, rough 1-inch pieces)

1/4 cup Ring of Fire Sauce (page 260)

Valerie and Ron Patton, Vortex Doughnuts

Both professionals from Seattle, these two food enthusiasts moved to Asheville and, long story short, won the Blue Ridge Food Venture's Big Tasty contest. Their Vortex Doughnuts are made with truly indigenous ingredients. In Valerie Patton's words: "I created [the Ring of Fire Sauce] as a glaze for our doughnuts, which won an award at the NC Bacon Fest: we poured it over our bacon sugar-crusted doughnut holes for the winning Hole Hog on a Stick with Squeal Sauce."

Ring of Fire Sauce

—Valerie and Ron Patton, VORTEX DOUGHNUTS

MAKES 4 CUPS

1 cup plus 3 1/2 tablespoons
fresh squeezed tart orange
juice, divided

3 1/2 tablespoons Aleppo
pepper flakes

4 small plump dried
apricots

2 cups plus
1 1/2 tablespoons sugar

9 tablespoons plus
2 teaspoons water

1 1/4 sticks (1/2 cup plus
2 tablespoons) organic
cultured butter

1 teaspoon fine sea salt

COOK'S NOTE:
"Cook the caramel in a
heavy, deep, non-reactive
saucepan scrubbed very
clean. Any microscopic
residue can make the
sugar crystallize," explains
Patton. Aleppo pepper
flakes are available at
spice stores or online; you
can substitute crushed
red pepper, but the seeds
change the texture and
flavor of the sauce.

The night before, mix 3 1/2 tablespoons of the orange juice and the pepper flakes in a small bowl; cover and let it stand overnight.

To make chunky sauce, finely chop the apricots and add them to a deep bowl; cover with the remaining 1 cup orange juice. Cover and refrigerate overnight.

To make a smoother sauce, puree the apricots and remaining 1 cup orange juice in a food processor. Cover and refrigerate overnight.

Add the water to a heavy, deep, non-reactive saucepan. Add the sugar, distributing it over the bottom. Cook over medium-low heat, stirring very gently until the sugar dissolves. Do not agitate. If a sugar scum forms on the top, it means the sugar didn't dissolve completely. Add 2 tablespoons more water, reduce heat to low, and cook to dissolve the sugar. Then bring the syrup back up to a boil.

Boil until the syrup is light golden and measures 340° F. on a candy thermometer. Do not stir; the sugar may crystallize with stirring or slow heating. Gently swirl the pan and remove from the heat. If the caramel continues to brown, place the bottom of the pan in cool water a few minutes. Allow to cool to about 250° F. Whisk in the butter by tablespoons, a few at a time.

Strain the pepper flakes; add to the apricot mixture, and salt. Do not stir or the peppers will lose color. If some of the sugar hardens, cook over low heat, without stirring, until the sauce is uniform. It should be soft, even when refrigerated. If it is too thick, thin with orange juice, adding a tablespoon at a time. Refrigerate or freeze until serving time; serve warm.

World's Best
Carrot Cake Ice Cream

—Ashley Garrison, THE HOP ICE CREAM CAFÉ

MAKES 1 QUART

Custard base (page 259)

1 teaspoon ground cinnamon

1 teaspoon vanilla extract

1/2 cup crumbled "World's Best Carrot Cake", about one cupcake's worth

At the Hop, you can try a world of creative, homemade ice cream flavor combinations. When owner Ashley Garrison, the chief ice cream guru, sees an idea for a smart ice cream pairing with another local food product, she goes for it. For this one, she adds cake from the "World's Best Carrot Cake" to the creamy base, and we think it's one of the world's best ice creams!

Prepare the ice cream base as directed on page 259. Before freezing, whisk in the cinnamon and vanilla. Freeze in an ice cream machine according to the manufacturer's instructions. Transfer to a freezer-safe container and gently swirl in the cake pieces. Freeze.

Birch Ice Cream

—Steven Goff, KING JAMES PUBLIC HOUSE

Birch twigs give a slightly minty, wintergreen scent to the ice cream. You can substitute fresh rosemary for a more familiar herbal flavor.

Beat the eggs and 2 1/2 cups of the sugar in a large bowl at medium speed of an electric mixer until lightened in color and blended. Combine the cream, milk, and the remaining sugar in a heavy medium saucepan. Cook over medium heat, stirring constantly, until the sugar is dissolved, about 5 minutes. Add the birch twigs; simmer 1 minute. Remove from the heat and let stand 30 to 45 minutes. Strain and discard the twigs.

Slowly whisk 1/2 cup of the cream mixture into the egg yolks. Whisk the egg mixture into the cream. Cook over medium-low heat, stirring constantly, until the custard thickens and coats the back of a spoon, 10 to 15 minutes. Strain into a medium bowl. Let the custard cool, then refrigerate until cold.

MAKES ABOUT 2 QUARTS

9 large eggs

4 large egg yolks

5 cups firmly packed light brown sugar, divided

1 quart heavy whipping cream

1 quart whole milk

1 tablespoon kosher salt

Handful of cleaned birch twigs, 4 to 5 inches long

Strawberry &
Pistachio Trifle

MAKES 6 TO 8 SERVINGS

—Jael Rattigan, FRENCH BROAD CHOCOLATE LOUNGE

FOR THE
PISTACHIO CAKE:

2 sticks (1 cup) unsalted
butter, softened

5 ounces (1 1/4 cups)
pistachio flour

3 3/4 ounces (3/4 cup)
all-purpose flour

10 ounces (2 1/2 cups)
confectioners' sugar

8 large egg whites, at
room temperature

FOR THE
MASCARPONE CREAM:

8 ounces mascarpone,
at room temperature

3 large egg yolks

4 ounces (1/2 cup) sugar

1 cup heavy whipping
cream, divided

1/2 vanilla bean pod, seeds
scraped and reserved, or
1 teaspoon vanilla extract

FOR THE DESSERT:

Strawberry Ice Cream
(recipe follows)

Chocolate Wafer Cookie

"Inspired by the luscious strawberries showing up at the markets this spring, we created this pretty pink and green trifle," says owner Jael Rattigan. "You'll probably have extra cake and ice cream. Keep 'em in the freezer for a dessert emergency!"

To prepare the pistachio cake, melt the butter in a medium saucepan over low heat heat. Cook until dark golden, taking care not to let it burn, 7 to 10 minutes. Let it cool to room temperature.

Preheat oven to 350° F. Line a 13 x 9-inch baking pan with parchment paper.

Combine the flours and confectioners' sugar in the bowl of a standing mixer; whisk to blend. Add the egg whites all at once and mix, using the paddle attachment, on medium speed for 3 minutes. Add the butter and mix on medium speed until the batter is thickened, about 3 minutes. Pour the batter into the prepared pan.

Bake for 15 minutes, rotate the pan, and bake until a toothpick inserted in the center comes out clean, 10 to 15 minutes more. Let the cake cool in the pan on a wire rack.

To prepare the mascarpone cream, place the mascarpone in a medium bowl. Beat the egg yolks in a medium mixing bowl at medium speed of an electric mixer, using the whisk attachment, until they are thick and pale, 3 to 5 minutes.

Bring the sugar and 2 tablespoons water to a boil in a small saucepan, stirring until the sugar melts. Boil, without stirring, until the syrup registers 250° F. on a candy thermometer. With the stand mixer running, gradually pour the hot sugar syrup into the yolks; continue to beat the mixture until the bowl is cool to touch.

Clean the whisk attachment. Pour the cream into a large mixing

bowl and beat until soft, firm peaks form. Add half of the whipped cream to the softened mascarpone and fold to combine. Add the cooled yolk mixture and whisk to combine. Fold in the remaining whipped cream and vanilla bean seeds or vanilla extract.

To assemble the dessert, use a biscuit cutter or circle pastry cutter to cut cakes to fit the dessert glasses you're using. Place a circle of cake in the bottom of each. Spoon or pipe in a layer of mascarpone to come halfway to two-thirds up the sides of each glass. Top with another cake circle; add a scoop of Strawberry Ice Cream and a cookie, if using.

Strawberry Ice Cream

MAKES ABOUT 2 CUPS

Combine the strawberries, 1/4 cup plus 1 tablespoon of the sugar, and lemon juice in a bowl; let stand for 1 hour. Purée the strawberry mixture in a blender until smooth.

Beat the eggs until they are light and fluffy in a medium mixing bowl with a hand-held electric mixer, about 4 minutes. Gradually add the remaining 3/4 cup sugar, about 3 tablespoons at a time, mixing after each addition. Beat in the cream, milk, and strawberries in three additions at low speed.

Freeze in an ice cream maker according to the manufacturer's directions.

1 pint fresh strawberries, caps removed

1 cup plus 1 tablespoon sugar, divided

1 tablespoon lemon juice

2 large eggs

1 cup heavy whipping cream

1 cup whole milk

Resource Guide

Many of the recipes in this book call for ingredients that are only found in this area. And while we've tried to identify substitutions in those cases, we know that the products have everything to do with the integrity of the recipes. Many of them can be purchased online and in markets outside North Carolina, while some are only available at local markets. This listing gives buying information on some of the products specified in the recipes, as well as give information on local businesses that have contributed to this book.

ASAP's Local Food Guide is an excellent resource and free directory to family farms, farmers tailgate markets, wineries, grocers, restaurants, caterers and bakers, farm stores and stands, farms to visit, B&Bs and farm lodging, apple farms, u-pick farms, CSAs, and distributors in the Southern Appalachians. asapconnections.org/find-local-food/local-food-guide/.

Asheville Independent Restaurants: They are a group of independent restaurant owners who are devoted to local people, food, brews, businesses, and philanthropies. For a complete list and information on the good work they do in Asheville, go to www.airasheville.org.

Dry Ridge Farm: The Brugh's raise all their animals on pasture, without the use of antibiotics, hormones, or steroids. The sell eggs, rabbit, chicken, pork, and lamb at local farmers markets and to many area restaurants. Sign up for their CSA and read the blog at: www.dryridgefarm.org.

East Fork Farm: Look for their poultry, eggs, lamb, and rabbit at Asheville farmers markets. Read more about them: eastforkfarm.net/

French Broad Chocolate Lounge and Factory: Chocohollics can't come to this city without a sip and taste of the homemade chocolate drinks, desserts, and confections at this bean-to-bar lounge. The story behind the company is sweet, too; see www.french-broadchocolates.com to read about their award-winning chocolates and order chocolate for eating, baking, and drinking online. For a complete list of stores that sell the chocolate throughout the US, click the "where to buy" link on their website.

Hickory Nut Gap Farm: This century-old farm raises grass-fed beef and pastured pork and poultry, selling locally and to the surrounding area. Visit their farm store at 57 Sugar Hollow Rd., Fairview, NC 38730. Order online at http://www.hickorynutgap-farm.com/categories.php. And look for them in other Southeastern markets.

Flying Cloud Farm: Members of the same family operate a 14-acre Flying Cloud Farm, an organic vegetable and fruit farm that markets produce through local farmers markets, a CSA, and a roadside stand at 1860 Charlotte Hwy., just down the road from the farm.

Imladris Farm: To purchase jams for the Pop Tarts recipe on page 37, look for them for sale in local markets and online: imladrisfarm.fatcow.com/store/index.

Looking Glass Creamery: An artisanal producer of exceptional, handmade cheese, and traditional goat's milk caramel, they craft a spectrum of cheeses, from fresh chèvre and Cheddar curds to soft-ripened pasteurized varieties to hard, aged raw milk cheeses. Visit ashevillecheese.com to order online; a selection of their cheeses are also featured on the Williams-Sonoma website.

Lusty Monk is a family-owned company that crafts condiments in small batches. The robust flavored mustards are staples in Asheville area restaurants, and you'll find them in the refrigerator case of select retailers in the U.S. Check the stores listings or order it directly from the Monk: lustymonk.com.

Rio Bertolini's fresh cut pasta sells the pastas, ravioli, and gnocchi at Asheville City Market on Saturdays from April through December. Be sure to get there early; the pasta company has quite a following.

Seasonal School of Culinary Arts: for more information, email ssca@schoolofculinaryarts.org or go to schoolofculinaryarts.org.

Sunburst Trout Farms: If you've ordered trout at a restaurant in this area, most likely it was a Sunburst. Their many products are widely distributed throughout the Southeast, and are available in many stores and coops. Look through their online store for home delivery: sunbursttrout.com

The Mushroom Man: Alan Muskat To sign up for a foraging tour and read more about Muskat, visit notastelikehome.org.

Wake Robin Farm Breads: Look for the breads at Asheville Tailgate Markets.

Wild Salmon Company: Owner Heidi Dunlap's summer catch arrives in Asheville by October, selling at local tailgate markets through December. Sign up for the Buying Club to receive deliveries November through January, or find out more: thewildsalmonco.com

World's Best Carrot Cake: The bakery ships carrot cakes and cupcakes all over the country, including gluten-free and vegan. For ordering information, go to worldsbestcarrotcake.com.

Index by Subject

Aioli
Aioli and Smoked Paprika
Aioli, 203
Chickweed Pesto Aioli, 208
Jalapeno Aioli, 203

Appetizers
SMALL PLATES
Chicken Liver Pate, 66
Cold Smoked Trout Wrap with
Goat Cheese and Hudson's
Smoked Tomato Jam, 81
Deviled Eggs with Smoked
Paprika Aioli, Bacon Jam,
and Fried Sage, 64
Fried Green Tomato
Napoleon, 69
Gravlax, 64
Jumbo Lump Crab
Cakes, 65
Venison Pate, 67

PICK UP SNACKS
Chocolate Covered Bacon, 77
Asiago Truffle Popcorn, 77
Candied Marcona Almonds, 81

DIPS & SPREADS
Baked Pack Square with
Peach Chutney, 79
Bruschetta with Fresh
Ricotta & Minted Lima &
Green Pea Mash, 70
Crostini with Goat Cheese and
Lemon Chutney, 73
Pimiento Cheese, 78
White Tire Dip & Pretzel
Bites, 78

Beef
Beef Bacon, 150
Bourbon Honey Marinated
Hangar Steak with
Blackberry BBQ Sauce, 146
Corned Beef, 150
Rolled Flank Steak, 147

B&B Specials
Blackberries in Sweet
Basil Syrup with
Mascarpone Cream, 14
Blueberry Buckle, 27
Breakfast Pizza, 23
Egg Flowers, 24
Fried Sage, 21
Lemon Chess
Morning Cake, 17

Mountain Quiche, 19
Pineapple Sticky Buns with
Sweet Cream, 26
Peach Vanilla Breakfast
Soufflé, 16
Provencal Starter, 22
Pumpkin Pudding with Spiced
Apple & Pear Compote with
Fried Sage, 20
Ratatouille Goat Cheese
Tart, 26
Roasted Organic Vegetable
Frittata, 18
Spiced Apple & Pear
Compote, 21

Breads
QUICK BREADS
Apple Pecan Streusel
Muffin, 39
Cornbread, 42
Fresh Fig and Walnut
Muffins, 38
Gluten-Free Banana Nut
Muffins, 41
Gluten-Free Buttermilk
Biscuits, 43
Pineapple Sticky Buns with
Sweet Cream, 26

YEAST BREADS
No-Knead Bread, 44
Spent Grain Bread, 47

Cakes
CAKES AND ICINGS
Blueberry Buckle, 27
Buttermilk Chocolate
Cake, 227
Chocolate Beetroot Cake, 229
Coconut Cake, 230
Lane Cake, 225
Lemon Chess Morning
Cake, 17
Olive Oil Apple Cake, 224
World's Best Tropical Carrot
Cake, 228

ICINGS & FILLINGS
Bourbon Mascarpone
Cream Icing, 233
Coconut Cream Cheese
Icing, 233
Coconut Filling, 234
Dark Chocolate Caramel
Icing, 235

Chicken
Chicken, Black Bean, and
Chèvre Enchiladas with
Salsa Verde, 166
Chicken Liver Pate, 66
Coronation Chicken Salad, 165
Fried Chicken, 168
Grilled Romaine Salad
with Grilled Chicken, Curry
Vinaigrette, & Lemon
Chutney, 100
Malabar Chicken Curry, 167
Paprika Chicken with Krimzon
Lee Peppers, 164
Roast Chicken, 163

Cocktails
Aardvark Gin Sing, 54
End of the Tunnel, 53
Erato, 55
Hopped Scotchem, 56
Knickerbocker, 58
Nebulous, 55
Pocket Square for
a Nehru Jacket, 59
Spiced Sorghum Syrup, 57
Sorghum Old Fashioned, 58

Cookies
Carrot Cake Sandwich
Cookies, 254
Chocolate Cayenne
Cookies, 252
Citrus Ginger Mint Sugar
Cookies, 251
Gluten-Free Chocolate Chip
Cookies, 256
Pistachio Shortbread, 253
Vegan Double Chocolate
Chip Cookies, 255
Vegan Chocolate Cinnamon
Hazelnut Cookies, 255
Vegan Mexiacn Mexican
Chocolate Cookies, 255

Condiments
Apple Butter, 206
Bacon Jam, 207
Candied Apricots, 209
Lemon Chutney, 205
Peach Chutney, 207
Pepper Jelly, 206

Drinks
Aztec-Inspired
Hot Chocolate, 187
Rosemary Lemonade with
Sage Honey, 88
Strawberry Basil Smoothie, 93

Duck
Duck Confit & Crepinettes, 151

Eggs
Breakfast Pizza, 23
Breakfast Veggie Strata, 32
Deviled Eggs with Smoked
Paprika Aioli, Bacon Jam,
and Fried Sage, 64
Egg Flowers, 24
Mountain Quiche, 19
Roasted Organic Vegetable
Frittata, 18
Roasted Tomato, Smoked
Mozzarella & Basil Frittata,
21
Sausage & Sweet Potato
Scramble, 33
Scrambled Eggs with Ramps &
Asparagus, 30

Fish & Shellfish
Bahn Xeo (Vietnamese
Coconut Crepe), 156
Blackened Salmon with
Candied Apricots & Grand
Marnier-Bacon Vinaigrette,
172
Gravlax, 64
Jumbo Lump Crab Cakes, 65
Lime Basil Grilled Trout, 171
NC Flounder with Rock Shrimp
in Coconut Carrot
Lemongrass Broth, 175
Nuoc Cham, 157
PBR Mussels, 124
Quick, Easy, & Lusty Trout, 171
Roasted Cod, Cabbage,&
Shiitakes with Wasabi
Sauce, 173
Seared Trout on Wilted
Greens Salad with Smoked
Tomato Vinaigrette, 174

Grains
Tabouleh, 105
Farro Risotto, 132
Granola, 49
Toasted Apricot Kernel
Granola, 92

Desserts
FROZEN
Birch Ice Cream, 261
Ring of Fire Ice Cream, 259
Strawberry & Pistachio
    Trifle, 261
Strawberry Ice Cream, 262
World's Best Carrot Cake Ice
    Cream, 261

Sauces
Strawberries in Port Reduction
    Sugar Syrup, 234
Ring of Fire Sauce, 260

Lamb
Fresh Gnocchi with Spicy Lamb
    Sausage, Tomato
    & Coconut, 143
Lamb Kebabs with Pesto Mint
    Sauce, 142
Lamb Merguez with Jalapeño
    Aioli and Pickled
    Ramps, 185
Lamb Tacos, 178
Roasted Tomatoes Stuffed with
    Ground Lamb, 144
Sloppy Jai, 145

Pasta
Fresh Gnocchi with Spicy
    Lamb Sausage, Tomato &
    Coconut, 143
Mac 'N Cheese, 169
Pasta with Mushrooms &
    Saffron Cream Sauce, 131
Penne a la Vodka, 130
Ricotta Gnudi with Porcini
    Ragout, 134
Smoky Mac 'n Cheese, 133
Vegan Pesto, 136

Pesto
Vegan Pesto, 136
Mint Pesto, 209

Pickled
Asian-Style Pickled
    Cucumbers, 213
Chow Chow, 214
Quick Fennel Pickles, 213
Natural Pickles, 211
Pickled Ramps, 185, 212
Refrigerator Garlic Pickles, 215

Pies, Pastries, & Tarts
SAVORY
Ratatouille Goat
    Cheese Tart, 25

Tomato & Gruyere Quiche 116
SWEET
Basic Tupelo Pie Crust, 247
Blueberry Mint Hand Pie
    Filling, 242
Blackberry Pie, 243
Fried Apple Hand Pies, 241
Fried Pear Hand Pies, 242
Jammin' Pop Tarts, 37
Our Favorite Quiche and Tart
    Crust, 247
Peach and Rhubarb
    Lattice-Top Pie, 238
Strawberry Basil Hand Pie
    Filling, 242

Pizza
Breakfast Pizza, 23
Fig & Pig Pizza, 76
Grilled Fresh Pear and
    Mozzarella Pizza, 182
Poblano Coulis, 160

Pork
Bahn Xeo (Vietnamese Coconut
    Crepe), 156
BBQ Carnitas Tacos, 158
Chorizo-StuffedPork
    Chops, 161
Ginger Coconut Meatballs, 193
Grilled Pork and Pineapple
    with Poblano Coulis, 160
Pork Butt Rub, 154
Pork Tenderloin with Orange
    Blossom Honey
    Mustard, 155
Roast Pork Shoulder, 154

Puddings
Pumpkin Pudding with
    Spiced Apple & Pear
    Compote with
    Fried Sage, 20
Rosewater Rice Pudding, 240
Caramel Apple Bread
    Pudding, 240
Fennel Panna Cotta
    with Strawberries and
    Pistachio Shortbread
    Crumbs, 245
Lemon Verbena Custards, 246
Chocolate Mousse with Candy
    Roaster Cream, 248

Salads
Black-Eyed Pea Relish with
    Heirloom Tomatoes, 96
Celery & Gorgonzola Salad, 98
Fried Green Tomato Salad
    with Watercress, Pepper
    Jelly, & Blue Cheese

Dressing, 103
Grilled Romaine Salad
    with Grilled Chicken,
    Curry Vinaigrette, & Lemon
    Chutney, 100
Grilled Stuffed Avocado, 104
Hendersonville County Mutsu
    Apple Salad with Candied
    Marcona Almonds, 99
Kale Salad with Manchego,
    Pumpkin Seeds,
    & Currants, 191
Marinated Tomato Salad with
    Kalamata Olives & Cheese, 97
Pantry Salad, 107
Spring Pea & Mushroom
    Salad with Beef Bacon, 97
Raw Citrus Kale Salad, 102
Tabouleh, 105

**Salad Dressings
& Vinegar**
Bacon-Dijon Vinaigrette, 99
Balsamic Vinaigrette, 201
Blue Cheese Dressing, 210
Cider Vinegar, 199
Citrus Dressing, 199
Chipotle-Citrus
    Vinaigrette, 200
Curry Dijon Vinaigrette, 202
Dried Cherry Vinaigrette, 200
Grand Marnier-Bacon
    Vinaigrette, 173
Maple Sherry Vinaigrette, 200

Salsas
Salsa Verde, 80
Simple Salsa 80

**Sandwiches, Wraps,
& Tacos**
BBQ Carnitas Tacos, 158
Sloppy Jai, 145
Cold Smoked Trout Wrap with
    Goat Cheese and Hudson's
    Smoked Tomato Jam, 81
Lamb Tacos, 178
Sloppy Jai, 145

Sauces & Gravy
GRAVY
Carlie's Giblet & Egg Gravy, 169

BBQ
Blackberry BBQ Sauce, 217
Carnitas BBQ Sauce, 218
Catawba Stout BBQ Sauce, 180
Down East BBQ Sauce, 218
East Carolina BBQ Sauce, 219
Vinegar-Based BBQ Sauce, 219

Poblano Coulis, 202
Remoulade, 208

Soups
CHILLED
Chilled Peach Gazpacho with
    Crispy Country Ham &
    Toasted Apricot
    Kernel Granola, 91
Bloody Mary Gazpacho, 93

HOT
Cream of Mussels Soup, 125
Spinach & Split Pea Soup, 126
Celeriac Bisque, 127
Oyster Chowder Purse in
    Lobster Broth, 195

Turkey
Coconut Turkey with Quinoa, 165

**Vegetables, Vegetarian
Mains, & Vegan**
Candied Yams, 115
Collard Greens in Coconut
    Milk, 112
Fennel Hushpuppies, 114
Fried Green Tomato
    Napoleon, 69
Pop Pop's Potato Pancakes, 114
Ratatouille, 111
Rattlesnake Beans with
    Mushrooms & Thyme-
    Infused Honey Drizzle, 120
Roasted Brussels Sprouts, 118
Roasted Corn on the Cob, 110
Sesame Kale, 119
Shiitake Mushroom Chips, 113
Steamed Broccolini with
    Dried Cherry Vinaigrette &
    Walnuts, 119
Summer Corn Skillet Cakes, 110
Tater Tots, 31
Tomato & Gruyere Quiche, 116
Vegan Pesto, 136
Veggie Burgers, 137

Index by Restaurant

*Find your favorite Asheville eatery here and
check out the recipes they shared in this book.*

Ambrozia: 64, 203, 207

Avenue M: 107

Blackbird: 230, 234

Cedric's Tavern: 78, 132, 165

Chai Pani: 45, 167

Cucina 24: 234, 245

DOUGH: 125, 134, 227

Early Girl Eatery: 69, 115, 201

Edison Craft Ales + Kitchen: 81, 91, 92, 99, 99, 103, 201, 206, 206

Fig: 98, 100, 119, 137, 175, 200, 202, 205, 214

Foothills Deli & Cafe: 97, 150, 150

French Broad Chocolate Lounge: 187, 193, 248, 261, 262

Green Sage Coffeehouse and Cafe: 93, 102, 199

Homegrown: 119, 133, 241, 242, 242

Isa's: 127

King Daddy's: 58, 58, 180, 199, 211, 213, 219, 261

Laurey's: 88, 155

Lexington Avenue Brewery: 160, 172, 173, 200, 202

Lioncrest at Biltmore Estate: 195

Luella's: 96, 218

Nine Mile: 136, 136

Pizza Pura: 76

Posana Café: 191

Red Stag Grill: 67

Rhubarb: 56, 57

Seven Sows Bourbon & Larder: 169, 169, 169

Social Lounge: 55, 77, 77

Strada: 41, 240

The Admiral: 31, 124, 156, 157, 200

The Cantina: 104, 200

The Hop: 256, 261

The Junction: 53, 114

The Market Place Restaurant: 14, 42, 154, 185, 185, 203, 246

Thirsty Monk: 59, 78

Tupelo Honey: 80, 110, 110, 114, 243, 247

Vinnie's: 130

Vortex Doughnuts: 260

West End Bakery: 32, 38, 39, 126, 255

White Duck Taco Shop: 158, 218

Wicked Weed: 118

Yuzu Patisserie: 116, 224

Acknowledgments

The 100+ extraordinary chefs and farmers, bakers and artisans, restaurant owners and food enthusiasts, fellow writers and editors, and the people of this community have been astounding in their generosity and encouragement. They've made this book what it is: a beautiful representation of Asheville's food scene. To all whose names appear in this book, a humble thank you from us both.

To the writers who penned essays for the book, we are honored to call you friends and colleagues. To our "Farmer & Chef South" bloggers and contributors, your insight and passion give meaning to the project. Many of the contributing writers are authors in their own right; seek out their other fantastic works and add them to your collection.

For this book we worked with some of the best photographers in the business. Beau Gustafson created images even more gorgeous than we could have imagined. For your visual genius — and for the warmth, professionalism, and experience you brought — thank you.

Thank you, Erin Adams, for your ability to capture food and people in motion, with no particular direction from us but your own instinctual eye. You got it, and the beauty of your images makes this book complete.

To Mark Bloom, we offer deep appreciation and heartfelt thanks for your skills at knowing your authors, understanding the audience, and combining the two with your wisdom of technical cookbook editing. Thank you for your eyes on this project.

Susan McBride is the mastermind behind the book design. Thank you for giving it a timeless yet tasteful and clever design we loved immediately. You embraced this project, and it shows. We are grateful for your natural sense of style, vision, and cheerful optimism.

Shane Lidell, thank you for your willingness to be a part of this project from the very beginning. Your guidance on the things that made us scratch our heads was crucial at numerous points along the way.

Sherida Buchanan, your efforts, knowledge, and exuberance for working with us made all the difference when the crunch was on.

Tremendous thanks to our Farmer and Chef South Strategic Partners, who grasped the vision and jumped in to help tell the story. To the Asheville Convention and Visitors Bureau, whose Foodtopia® promotion of our food culture is ongoing, we value your support to us and to other projects that benefit our farmers and chefs.

And to Fielding Lowe, our designated off-the-clock "CFO." You kept us on track and cleared the path to move us forward.

From Debby Maugans

With love and appreciation to "our tribe,"
the friends who have supported me through the
thick and thin of book deadlines, kept me sane
with our "porch sitting", and watch each other's
backs no matter what: Betsey Russell, Traci
Sherer, Cassie Whitesides, Cate Scales, Teesha
Johnson, and Peggy Gardner. Special thanks to
Cate — without your idea, this book might never
have happened.

Betsey, thank you for your ear, your balance,
and for being a willing and constructive critic.
Your inspiration and wit always unlocked a
writer's block.

Patty Moosbrugger, thank you for championing my
books, especially for encouraging me with your
vision of what this one could be and for your
expert guidance through the process of writing,
printing, and publishing it.

Thank you, Mary Collins-Shepard, for your
friend-ship and constant stream of culinary
inspiration. I wouldn't be writing this page without
your cheerful willingness to help make this book
a success, including testing and editing recipes
when the crunch was on. I trusted you completely
with anything you offered to do.

Thanks to Ken Shepard for making me laugh as
you ate and commented your way through the
recipes — and for your voluntary garden treks
for photos.

Lynne Caldwell, you've committed to helping
with this project from the very beginning, and I'll
always be grateful for your friendship and trust.

Eleni Nakos, my "happy tornado," you've
brightened the spots that needed tending. Thank
you for your hugs and empathy when my head
was buried in edits. JK, your drive for success
inspires me to keep on keeping on, as Papoo
taught us.

From Christine Sykes Lowe

I am humbled by this project and the support bestowed upon us. Food and the memories associated with it can stir up powerful emotions. The sights, smells, and sounds in the kitchen stay with you forever. To my grandmothers, Carolyn Detrick Kearney (Grandma K) and Lena Alteri Sykes, and to my mother Ann Kearney Gordon: I lovingly thank you for instilling a deep appreciation in me for the process of nourishing the family with wholesome food.

To my friends and colleagues, thank you for your support and unwavering optimism. If you've ever given me that look of sincere elation when you asked about the book, asked how you could help, or offered a much-needed word of encouragement, then you know who you are. I thank you from the bottom of my heart.

To the respected culinary family within our community and beyond, many of whom I have worked with personally and consider friends, thank you for the wonderful words: "Sign me up!" Believe me, I know how busy you are; your willingness to contribute is immeasurable on so many levels.

While I have to acknowledge the enthusiastic support from my whole family, none was more vital than that from my husband Fielding Lowe. You have been my biggest cheerleader for all of the 20+ years we have been together. Not once did you ever doubt me, and your calm realism provided a grounding stability to my constantly churning mind. I love you and thank you.

To Jacob and Austin Lowe, our teen and pre-teen, incessantly hungry and growing forces of nature — when you were much younger, you proclaimed in the sweetest, child-like fashion: "Mommy was the best cooker in all the world!" Whether true or not, your excitement toward this book (and recipe taste-testing) made this a true family project, bringing us closer with smiles, hugs, and kisses on the cheek. Beyond all else, to me, that made it all worth it.